The American History Series

SERIES EDITORS
John Hope Franklin, *Duke University*
A. S. Eisenstadt, *Brooklyn College*

Michael Schaller
UNIVERSITY OF ARIZONA

George Rising

The Republican Ascendancy

American Politics, 1968–2001

HARLAN DAVIDSON, INC.
WHEELING, ILLINOIS 60090-6000

Library of Congress Cataloging-in-Publication Data

Schaller, Michael, 1947–
    The Republican ascendancy : American politics, 1968–2001 / by Michael
Schaller and George Rising
        p. cm. — (The American history series)
Includes bibliographical references (p.) and index.
    ISBN 0-88295-970-0
  1. United States—Politics and government—1945–1989. 2. United States—
Politics and government—1989–1993. 3. United States—Politics and govern-
ment—1993–2001. 4. Republican Party (U.S. : 1854–)—History—20th century.
5. Conservatism—United States—History—20th century. I. Rising, George.
II. Title. III. American history series (Wheeling, Ill.)
  E839.5 .S27 2002
      324.2734'09'45—dc21

                                                    2001008359

Cover photo: President Reagan speaking at a rally for Senator Durenberger in
Minneapolis, February 8, 1982. *Courtesy Ronald Reagan Library.*

Manufactured in the United States of America
04 03 02 01 1 2 3 4 5 VP

We dedicate this book, with appreciation, to our sisters,
Karen Schaller and Susan Rising

FOREWORD

Every generation writes its own history for the reason that it sees the past in the foreshortened perspective of its own experience. This has surely been true of the writing of American history. The practical aim of our historiography is to give us a more informed sense of where we are going by helping us understand the road we took in getting where we are. As the nature and dimensions of American life are changing, so too are the themes of our historical writing. Today's scholars are hard at work reconsidering every major aspect of the nation's past: its politics, diplomacy, economy, society, recreation, mores and values, as well as status, ethnic, race, sexual, and family relations. The lists of series titles that appear on the inside covers of this book will show at once that our historians are ever broadening the range of their studies.

The aim of this series is to offer our readers a survey of what today's historians are saying about the central themes and aspects of the American past. To do this, we have invited to write for the series only scholars who have made notable contributions to the respective fields in which they are working. Drawing on primary and secondary materials, each volume presents a factual and narrative account of its particular subject, one that affords readers a basis for perceiving its larger dimensions and importance. Conscious that readers respond to the closeness and immediacy of a subject, each of our authors seeks to restore the past as an actual present, to revive it as a living reality.

The individuals and groups who figure in the pages of our books appear as real people who once were looking for survival and fulfillment. Aware that historical subjects are often matters of controversy, our authors present their own findings and conclusions. Each volume closes with an extensive critical essay on the writings of the major authorities on its particular theme.

The books in this series are primarily designed for use in both basic and advanced courses in American history, on the undergraduate and graduate levels. Such a series has a particular value these days, when the format of American history courses is being altered to accommodate a greater diversity of reading materials. The series offers a number of distinct advantages. It extends the dimensions of regular course work. It makes clear that the study of our past is, more than the student might otherwise understand, at once complex, profound, and absorbing. It presents that past as a subject of continuing interest and fresh investigation.

For these reasons the series strongly invites an interest that far exceeds the walls of academe. The work of experts in their respective fields, it puts at the disposal of all readers the rich findings of historical inquiry, an invitation to join, in major fields of research, those who are pondering anew the central themes and aspects of our past.

And, going beyond the confines of the classroom, it reminds the general reader no less than the university student that in each successive generation of the ever-changing American adventure, from its very start until our own day, men and women and children were facing their daily problems and attempting, as we are now, to live their lives and to make their way.

John Hope Franklin
A. S. Eisenstadt

CONTENTS

Photos follow page 118

PREFACE

During the second half of the twentieth century, three dramatic processes dominated American politics: the expansion of a large, active federal government at home and abroad; the extension of civil and voting rights to African Americans and other minorities; and the emergence of a strong conservative political movement behind the Republican party. In many ways, this third development resulted from the first two. The perceived failure of "big government" liberalism at home and abroad and a conservative backlash, especially among white Southerners, to legislation promoting racial equality and other liberal policies fractured the Democratic party and escalated Republican influence after 1968.

At first glance, recent Republican presidential candidates—Barry Goldwater, Richard Nixon, Gerald Ford, Ronald Reagan, George H. W. Bush, Bob Dole, and George W. Bush—appeared to have little in common beyond their party label. Yet each profited from the disaffection of Democratic voters from the old New Deal coalition forged during the Great Depression of the 1930s. Even Goldwater, who lost by a national landslide in 1964, secured vital ground for the GOP by cracking the Democrats' century-long hold on the once "solid South." From Nixon in 1968 to George W. Bush in 2000, each recent Republican president achieved victory by splitting off from the Democrats key groups that had grown disillusioned with liberal ideas and policies.

This book examines the economic, political, social, and cultural forces that pushed significant groups of Democrats to disaffiliate from their party, and it analyzes the process that made Republican candidates and ideas attractive to them. The focus is on national events, but we also discuss the emerging GOP control of state governments and the tensions among the factions that make up the modern Republican party.

Chapter One surveys the GOP before 1968, when it was a minority party in opposition to the Democrats' dominant coalition. Republicans could make little political headway until the 1960s, when new issues arose to disrupt the New Deal system that had begun in 1932. Still, the GOP learned many lessons during its "time in the wilderness" that would help the party achieve political ascendancy after 1968. By the 1950s, the Republicans under President Dwight Eisenhower had jettisoned their isolationist tendencies and embraced Cold War internationalism. During the 1968–2001 period, this often enabled them to play the "patriotism" card against Democrats, who from the late 1960s were split over the issue of global anticommunist intervention because of the disastrous Vietnam War. Also under Eisenhower, the GOP realized that directly attacking such popular government programs as Social Security constituted political suicide. After the 1950s, therefore, most Republicans focused on criticizing soaring government spending and rising taxes. This tactic proved especially effective for the GOP during the economic recessions of the 1970s and early 1980s. Finally, Republicans learned during the tumultuous 1960s that they could gain political advantage by adopting a conservative position on racial and cultural questions, issues that came to dominate political discourse after 1968.

Chapters Two through Six examine the Republican ascendancy, showing how it proceeded in fits and starts, with four distinct stages from 1968 to 2001. Chapter Two investigates the first stage of the GOP ascendancy, which began with Richard Nixon's election in 1968. Nixon won the presidency—and ended the Democratic age that had begun in 1932—by pursuing a "Southern Strategy." This strategy was based on taking conservative positions on race and other cultural issues, and it was meant to pry social conservatives, including southern whites and northern Catholics, away from the Democrats. Nixon's foreign policy reinforced his conservative domestic strategy by embracing assertive U.S. nationalism, at least rhetorically. As president, however, Nixon watered down the GOP's conservative message by following a moderate economic program and by lessening tensions with Communist powers. Throughout the 1970s, moreover, American voters still supported Democrats by large margins at all levels below the presidency—including Congress, governorships, and state legislatures.

Most important, as Chapter Three shows, the legacy of Nixon's corrupt administration, highlighted by the Watergate scandal, set back Republican fortunes during the 1974–80 period, the second stage of the post-1968 GOP ascendancy. Yet the party managed to regroup during the late 1970s by mobilizing the growing conservative movement and by criticizing Democrats for economic stagnation, inflation, liberal cultural policies, and international setbacks. In 1980, Ronald Reagan initiated the third stage of the Republican ascendancy by winning the presidency and bringing with him a GOP majority in the Senate.

Chapter Four argues that Reagan and his successor, George H. W. Bush, reaffirmed Nixon's Southern Strategy but stressed stronger commitments to economic conservatism and anticommunist nationalism. During this third stage of the GOP ascendancy, however, the conservative Reagan and Bush administrations proved able to push American government rightward only at the margins. Still, conservative rhetoric gained the upper hand, and conservative ideas set the national agenda. At the same time, Republicans became truly competitive in the Senate and in governorships for the first time since the 1920s, though they continued to lag behind in the House and in state legislatures.

Chapter Five examines the fourth phase of the Republican ascendancy, which began with the 1994 midterm elections. In that year, the "Republican Revolution" of House Speaker Newt Gingrich culminated the transformation of politics that had begun in the 1960s, enabling the GOP to capture control of both houses of Congress for the first time in four decades. The elections marked a breakthrough for the GOP at all levels of government. The process of Republican ascendancy was also evidenced by long-term shifts in party identification toward the GOP, with the trend most pronounced among conservatives, white men, and white southerners. But the "Republican Revolution" of the late 1990s failed in its goal of transforming American government into a right-wing bastion, and its strident conservatism provoked a strong public backlash.

Finally, in the conclusion, we argue that this backlash against conservative Republicanism spurred GOP candidate George W. Bush to distance himself from his party's right-wing image in the 2000 presidential campaign. But postelection polls showed that Bush, like all winning Republican presidential candidates of the 1968–2001 period, owed his electoral-college victory to the conservative strategies first successfully employed by Richard Nixon in 1968. Whether the GOP can maintain the upward trajectory of the 1968–2001 period is a question left to future historians.

Several of our friends and colleagues read and challenged the ideas we present here. We especially thank John Shaw, Robert Schulzinger, and Leonard Dinnerstein for their assistance.

CHAPTER ONE

Republicans in a Democratic Age, 1932–1968

One of Republican Ronald Reagan's first acts upon entering the White House in 1981 was to display a portrait of Calvin Coolidge. Reagan's act of devotion to a relatively obscure Republican president of the 1920s puzzled many observers. Most perplexing was the fact that Reagan, the amiable former Hollywood actor known as the "Great Communicator," seemed to share little with "Silent Cal," the taciturn, puritanical New Englander. But President Reagan's act of devotion was fraught with symbolism. It revealed his longing to return to Calvin Coolidge's conservative America—a nation characterized by Republican-controlled politics, nativist-dominated society, traditionalist cultural values, limited federal government, and an economy governed by corporate executives and financiers. "The business of America *is* business," Coolidge had proclaimed.

As Reagan lamented, the Coolidge era had marked the end of several decades of Republican ascendancy. In October 1929, a few months after Coolidge's successor Herbert Hoover took office, the onset of the Great Depression ended Republican preeminence. In 1932, Franklin D. Roosevelt's election as president launched a lengthy age of Democratic dominance and activist federal policies. A half century after Roosevelt's election, however, President Reagan expressed his wish to resurrect Coolidge's America, explaining: "You hear a lot of jokes about Silent Cal Coolidge, but . . . if he did nothing, maybe that's the answer [for] federal government."

Reagan's professed reverence for the conservative Republicanism of Presidents Coolidge and Hoover belied a significant truth. As a young man, "Dutch" Reagan had voted *against* Hoover and *for* Roosevelt. In fact, he backed FDR in four consecutive elections from 1932 through 1944 and supported Roosevelt's successor, Harry S Truman, in 1948. Yet Reagan was hardly alone in his support for liberal Democrats; he voted for the winning presidential candidate five straight times. During the 1950s, however, he began his turn to the political right, and by 1968, Governor Ronald Reagan of California was one of the nation's leading conservative Republicans.

Reagan's political journey through the 1932–68 period offers insight into the Republican party's status during that age of Democratic dominance. During the 1930s, President Roosevelt's New Deal administration confronted the Great Depression, transformed the federal government, and enacted several fundamental social programs. Republicans charged that these New Deal reforms threatened liberty, but Reagan and most other Americans rejected this claim. Consequently, Democrats built a potent electoral coalition that dominated politics until 1968. As World War II approached in the late 1930s, Republicans joined with conservative Democrats to slow liberal reform. During the years 1941–45, however, World War II transformed American society and the economy far more than the New Deal had.

From 1945 through 1952, Republicans battled Roosevelt's Democratic successor, President Harry Truman, though they endorsed Truman's anticommunist Cold War policies. Frustrated in the minority, Senator Joseph McCarthy and other Republicans exploited a widespread "Red Scare" by accusing Democrats of harboring Communist sympathies. In 1952, McCarthyism, the stalemated Korean War, and the popular Republican presidential nominee Dwight D. Eisenhower captured the votes of many Democrats, including Ronald Reagan. As a result, Republicans regained control of the presidency and Congress for the first time since the Great Depression two decades earlier.

Yet the Eisenhower era of 1953–61 represented only an interlude within the larger Democratic age. In the 1954 midterm elections, Republicans again lost control of both houses of Congress. Eisenhower won reelection in 1956 by embracing a nonpartisan "middle-way" consensus, which preserved but did not expand his Democratic predecessors' social programs and international policies.

During the 1950s, conservative Republicans, who disdained Eisenhower's centrism, gained strength from a revitalized right-wing intellectual movement. In the two decades following World War II, both socially conservative "traditionalists" and fiscally conservative "libertarians" refashioned their ideologies. By the early 1960s, moreover, conservative intellectuals had "fused" traditionalism and libertarianism through anticommunism. During this time, conservative Republicans also profited from a white backlash against the civil rights movement, population shifts toward the South and West, and postwar prosperity.

The 1960s saw both the zenith of Democratic liberalism and the launching of modern Republican conservatism. In 1964, the right united behind Senator Barry M. Goldwater, enabling him to win the Republican presidential nomination. Goldwater's campaign, which also marked the start of Reagan's own political career, began the transformation of the Republicans into a nationwide conservative party. But Goldwater lost by a landslide margin to Lyndon B. Johnson, and Congress's passage of Johnson's Great Society social legislation in 1965–66 seemed to confirm liberal Democratic hegemony. Soon, however, a conservative backlash emerged against liberal policies and radical groups, while the Vietnam War widened political and cultural divisions in America. In 1966, this backlash helped Reagan win the California governorship. Two years later, it brought Richard M. Nixon into the White House, thereby inaugurating a new era of Republican ascendancy.

Republican Party Dominance before the New Deal, 1860–1932

Who are Republicans, and why are they Republicans? Many factors can motivate an individual to identify with a particular party as a voter, party member, or candidate for office. But most scholars agree that, since the Civil War, three main factors have shaped party loyalty: geographic residence, ethnic-religious identity, and socioeconomic class. These three factors favored the Republican party from the Civil War in the 1860s until the New Deal realignment of 1932.

The North-South division determined many individuals' political preference for more than a century after the Civil War. In 1854, Republicans formed as the northern antislavery party. Six years later, the election of Republican Abraham Lincoln as president precipitated the Civil War. In the ensuing decades, Lincoln's party—which became known as the Grand Old Party (GOP)—dominated the North by depicting Democrats as the party of Civil War rebellion. Meanwhile, the GOP barely existed in the "solid South," so called because of the region's devotion to the Democratic party, which had "redeemed" the area for white supremacy after Reconstruction ended in 1877. This regional division tended to favor Republicans, because two-thirds of Americans lived outside of the South. Settlement patterns spread political sectionalism throughout the nation. Northeasterners tended to move directly west, leaving Republican settlements throughout the Midwest and Far West. Similarly, those who migrated from the Southeast spread Democratic loyalties through the South and Southwest. The GOP dominated the North and West until the Great Depression, while the white South remained solidly Democratic until the 1960s.

Ethnic and religious identity constituted a second source of party allegiance. Outside of the South, native-born "old-stock" Protestants of British, German, and Scandinavian descent generally supported Republicans. African Americans also backed the GOP as the "party of Lincoln." But voting restrictions in the South, where 75 percent of blacks lived before World War II, curbed their influence. Democrats formed a more diverse ethnic-religious mix. Native-born old-stock Protestants in the mostly rural South supported Democrats. But the party also appealed to Catholic and Jewish "new immigrants," who had arrived in large numbers beginning in the 1880s and who grouped themselves around urban political machines in the North. (However, some new immigrants, particularly Italians, backed Republicans out of resentment of Irish command of Democratic machines.) This intraparty cultural clash weakened Democratic unity.

The final ingredient shaping party loyalty was socioeconomic class, based on wealth, income, social status, and education. The GOP tended to be the party of the rich, business executives, professionals, and other higher-income groups. The Great Depression amplified the importance of class as a determinant of party preference, as many lower-income Americans shifted into the Democratic coalition. Even today, the higher a person's economic status, the more likely it is that he or she will support the Republican party.

During the 1860–1932 period, the GOP's ideological tendencies derived from its coalition's sectional, ethnic-religious, and class identities. Republicans were pro-business nationalists who championed federal promotion of economic development, protective tariffs for industry, and restriction of immigration. They also endorsed law and order and "good government," while denouncing the mass politics of ethnic Democratic machines, which they considered corrupt. Finally, the GOP reflected old-stock Protestantism by urging government regulation of morality through the prohibition of alcohol and other vices. In 1884, a Republican speaker infamously contrasted his party's agenda with Democrats' "rum, Romanism, and rebellion," mocking Democrats' strength among anti-Prohibitionist urbanites, Roman Catholics, and ex-Confederate Southerners. From the Civil War until the Great Depression, the Republican party's coalition usually constituted a national majority. This was especially true during 1896–1928, when the GOP won seven of nine presidential elections, usually by landslide margins.

After 1896, the Republican party divided into two main blocs: Eastern conservatives, who supported the status quo, and Western progressives, who promoted reform. The conservatives, known as the Old Guard, controlled the party. Strongest in the Northeast, the Old Guard consisted mainly of a native-born elite of British descent. By contrast, GOP progressives were often German or Scandinavian in ancestry and lived primarily in the rural areas of the Midwest and Far West. (Progressive Democrats tended to reside in northern urban areas.) Progressive Republicans attacked monopoly and corruption by advocating antitrust, consumer-rights, and good-government legislation. As a result, these "Main Street" Westerners often opposed the conservative "Wall Street" easterners of their own party. During the

Depression, most progressive Republicans endorsed Democratic legislation, and many of them left the GOP.

It seemed fitting that President Herbert Hoover presided over the decline and fall of Republican dominance, because he personified the pre-Depression GOP. Hoover boasted progressive roots as a Midwesterner who had gained fame for his work in government. But he also identified with conservatives by championing corporate control of the economy. Unfortunately for Hoover, the Great Depression demolished the credibility of conservative Republicans' laissez-faire policy (the doctrine of government noninterference in the economy). In October 1929, the Great Crash burst the stock-market bubble. Within three years, unemployment reached 25 percent, prices and industrial output declined by two-thirds, thousands of banks failed, farm income dropped by 60 percent, and one-third of farmers lost their land. Severe drought conditions worsened the agrarian misery. In many cities, crowds descended on garbage dumps to pick through the rotten food for supper.

Despite the catastrophe, conservative Republicans advised President Hoover to follow laissez-faire theory and allow the economy to correct itself. But Democrats gained ground in the 1930 midterm elections. In response, Hoover instituted a series of limited policies to counteract the Depression, including providing direct aid to ailing businesses. Yet he denied federal aid to unemployed individuals. This reinforced Republicans' image as heartless politicians whose policies had caused the economic disaster but who refused to alleviate human suffering. This image, though unfair, haunted the GOP for decades.

In 1932, most Americans repudiated Hoover by voting for his Democratic opponent, Governor Franklin D. Roosevelt of New York. Roosevelt, who had promised a "new deal for the American people," won in a landslide. Democrats also captured huge majorities in both houses of Congress. The 1932 results represented the greatest one-election transformation in history, realigned American politics, and marked the start of the Democratic age of 1932–68.

Republicans against Roosevelt, 1933–1945

Republicans faced a formidable foe in Franklin Roosevelt, judged the greatest president of his century by most historians. During the Great

Depression and World War II, Roosevelt's administration confronted economic misery, transformed the presidency and the federal government, turned back global fascism, established a new international order, reduced Republicans to a minority party, and captured the enduring veneration of millions of Americans, including the young Ronald Reagan.

In 1933, Roosevelt's New Deal administration won congressional passage of momentous legislation. These laws created several new federal agencies that stabilized prices and wages, subsidized farm income, regulated banking and the stock market, and provided welfare relief to the poor and unemployed. Though many of the reforms failed, others became an essential part of American life. Roosevelt's administration also created a new, modern system of government. The New Deal centralized power in the national government, away from states and localities, and it concentrated federal authority in the executive branch at the expense of Congress and the Supreme Court. These changes represented a transformation of American government. But New Deal policies altered society and the economy less dramatically. FDR's liberal administration, unlike communist or fascist governments in other countries, reformed rather than revolutionized the existing system of free-market capitalism.

Republicans could do little to stop New Deal reforms, and most GOP progressives endorsed Roosevelt's agenda. Conversely, conservatives condemned the New Deal for several reasons. Business executives and the wealthy were angered because they had lost their tight grip on government and because Roosevelt blamed them for the Depression. Nativists despised the administration's inclusion of Catholic and Jewish Americans; "the Jew Deal," antisemites called it. Many Republicans viewed relief programs as a vast political machine to funnel "bribes" to Democratic voters. They also derided the personal style of FDR and his wife, Eleanor, an outspoken progressive. Most important, conservatives loathed the New Deal's expansion of federal power into areas of life previously dominated by business or by state and local governments.

Conservative Republicans reacted by harshly condemning New Deal programs. Senator Arthur H. Vandenberg of Michigan denounced the Agricultural Administration Act as the "most revolutionary proposal in American history." Congressman Joseph W. Martin of

Massachusetts imagined that the Tennessee Valley Authority was "patterned closely after one of the Soviet dreams." And Herbert Hoover claimed that Roosevelt's policies represented a "new philosophy which marks the end of liberty." But most Americans welcomed FDR's reforms, and they overwhelmingly supported Democrats in the 1934 congressional elections.

Inspired by election victories and by popular demands to "share our wealth," Roosevelt in 1935 initiated the "Second New Deal." These economically liberal laws included protections for labor unions, government jobs for the unemployed, taxation of large fortunes, and the Social Security Act. The Second New Deal left a momentous legacy. It put conservatives on the defensive, undercut support for left- and right-wing radicals, cemented organized labor and the unemployed into the Democratic coalition, and established the modern American welfare system. Historian Carl Degler later wrote that the New Deal marked "the crossing of a divide [from] which, it would seem, there could be no turning back."

The 1936 elections vindicated the New Deal. Roosevelt crushed his Republican opponent in the biggest landslide ever, and Democrats won the largest congressional majorities in history. These results confirmed the New Deal's realignment of politics, which lasted until 1968. The new "Democratic political order" established an intertwined, symbiotic relationship between the "regular" Democratic party (centering around urban political machines in the North and "courthouse rings" in the South), the federal government, and various interest-group activists: progressives (now called liberals), urbanites, organized labor, Catholics, Jews, and African Americans. In addition, many multinational corporations acquiesced to labor laws in return for federal promotion of foreign trade. The New Deal assisted each of its interest groups through the power of the federal government, generating a loyal Democratic coalition that dominated national politics for three decades.

Meanwhile, the Republican coalition shrank during the Great Depression. Many working-class Protestants and northern African Americans left the party. GOP strength remained concentrated in the rural areas and small towns of the Midwest and Northeast and among business executives, professionals, and the wealthy. As the "regular"

Republican party machinery crumbled, the GOP became an organizationally amorphous, activist-based party. The only organized interest within the party was the small-business faction centered around local Chambers of Commerce. For the next three decades, the GOP could only capture control of the presidency or Congress if Democrats faltered.

Despite the New Deal's realignment of politics, Republicans capitalized on a short but sharp economic recession and several tactical blunders by Roosevelt and other Democrats to make a comeback in the 1938 midterm elections, especially in the rural districts of the Midwest and Northeast. The elections fortified an informal conservative coalition of Republicans and Southern Democrats. The coalition was never firm, and it proved unable to advance its own conservative agenda. But it stalled ambitious liberal initiatives until President Lyndon Johnson's Great Society legislation of the mid-1960s.

As the GOP revived after 1938, intraparty tensions also returned between moderate internationalists in the East and conservative Western isolationists. Out of political expediency, Eastern and urban Republicans promised to maintain popular New Deal programs. In addition, many large corporations and banks with headquarters in the East accepted federal intervention in the economy and endorsed Roosevelt's internationalism. This moderate faction of the GOP was often viewed as the "Republican establishment." It was led by Governor Thomas Dewey of New York in the 1940s, President Dwight Eisenhower in the 1950s, and Governor Nelson Rockefeller of New York in the 1960s and 1970s.

Meanwhile, the GOP in the Midwest and Far West became more conservative after 1938. Many liberals abandoned the party during the Depression. Beginning in World War II, moreover, a growing class of newly wealthy businessmen, entrepreneurs, and professionals revitalized Western conservatism. Unlike Eastern "country-club" Republicans, these populist conservatives viewed themselves as plain people who had prospered through hard work. And unlike "Wall Street" Easterners, "Main Street" entrepreneurs typically ran local businesses, so they had little need for federal promotion of national and international commerce. Consequently, most Midwestern Republicans professed "isolationism" before World War II, criticizing

U.S. military and political involvement overseas. The conservative Republicans were led by Senator Robert Taft of Ohio in the 1940s and early 1950s, Senator Barry Goldwater of Arizona in the late 1950s and 1960s, and President Ronald Reagan in the 1970s and 1980s.

World War II, like the Great Depression and the New Deal realignment, reconfigured American life and the Republican party. On December 7, 1941, Japan's attack on Pearl Harbor ended the popular appeal of isolationism. But the split between Eastern moderates and Western conservatives continued to shape internal GOP debates for the next several decades. World War II also marked the end of Roosevelt's New Deal reforms. Ironically, however, the war itself revolutionized American society far more than the New Deal had. Sixteen million Americans served in the armed forces, and the G.I. Bill of 1944 helped recast postwar society by enabling veterans to attend college and trade schools and to finance home mortgages. Another 20 million Americans, including two million southern blacks, migrated within the United States, and six million women joined the workforce.

World War II also permanently transformed the U.S. economy. Massive war expenditures showed that federal spending could stimulate extraordinary economic growth. The war also generated several long-term consequences. Business power was consolidated into fewer, larger firms, and the close relationship between the military and defense contractors continued during the postwar era. The war helped the working class, too, as union membership doubled and industrial wages rose. Wartime deficits also compelled the federal government to establish the modern income-tax structure. Finally, huge federal expenditures on industry and research laid the foundation for the lengthy economic boom that lasted until the 1970s.

World War II also reoriented U.S. foreign policy toward internationalist engagement. After Pearl Harbor, most Americans, including many former isolationists, embraced internationalism. With GOP support, Roosevelt's administration in 1944 established a new international economic structure designed to avoid future depressions— the Bretton Woods system—which included the World Bank and the International Monetary Fund. A year later, the United States entered the newly created United Nations.

conclusion, the 1944 elections reaffirmed ιinance. Roosevelt won an unprecedented ts increased their congressional majorities. DR died, thrusting his relatively unknown vice president, Harry Truman, into the presidency.

The Cold War, the Red Scare, and Republican Resurgence, 1946–1952

Republicans battled Harry Truman throughout his nearly eight years as president. Truman vowed to continue Roosevelt's policies of domestic reform and international engagement. But he lacked his predecessor's charisma and skill, and he soon angered a wide array of interests. During his first eighteen months as president, his public approval rating plummeted from 82 to 32 percent. "To err is Truman" went the joke. A short-term recession and the president's unpopularity cost the Democrats in the 1946 midterm elections, as the party lost control of both houses of Congress for the first time since 1932.

In 1947–48, however, Truman managed to win the Republican Congress's approval for his internationalist policies, which committed the nation to permanent, large-scale global involvement. The emerging Cold War with the Soviet Union, which shaped U.S. policy for the next four decades, constituted the most important issue. From 1945 to 1947, the relationship between the two superpowers shifted from that of uneasy wartime allies to adversaries. Ideologically, the Soviet rhetoric of a world communist revolution disturbed capitalist democracies in America and Western Europe. Geopolitically, the Soviet desire for a security sphere led to its control and isolation of Eastern Europe. Meanwhile, U.S. leaders concluded that world peace and American success required global capitalist prosperity, which necessitated the rebuilding of the country's former enemies Germany and Japan—policies that outraged the Soviets.

In 1947, the Truman administration institutionalized the Cold War by pledging to "contain" Soviet and Communist power. In March of that year, the president's Truman Doctrine speech established the containment of communism as the foundation of U.S. foreign policy. Three months later, Secretary of State George C. Marshall proposed the European Recovery Program, or Marshall Plan, intended to contain communism by dispensing $12 billion in economic aid to anticommunist governments in Western Europe and Japan. In July 1947, Truman's National Security Act established the Defense Department, the Central Intelligence Agency, and the National Security Council. Two years later, the Senate ratified the North Atlantic Treaty Organization (NATO), an anti-Soviet military alliance. For the next two decades, until the Vietnam War, a bipartisan consensus endorsed anticommunist Cold War globalism.

In the 1948 campaign, Truman revitalized the Democratic coalition by reaffirming his faith in federal social programs begun during the New Deal. Helped by Republican blunders, Truman won the presidency in a famous upset, and Democrats regained control of Congress. But Truman's campaign marked the end of Democrats' populist rhetoric aimed at business and wealthy elites. After 1948, most liberals abandoned their ambitious Depression-era plans to restructure American capitalism and to create a more egalitarian society. Instead, they championed the theories of British economist John Maynard Keynes. These Keynesians advocated promoting growth and full employment through federal management of fiscal (taxing and spending) policy and controlling the money supply. Hence, the government would stimulate the entire economy rather than micromanage individual sectors. Additionally, economic growth would raise all levels of income, making unnecessary government attempts to redistribute wealth downward. The economic boom and wealth redistribution toward the middle and working classes during World War II seemed to confirm Keynesian theory.

Despite Democratic majorities, Truman's second administration of 1949–53 was characterized by partisan stalemate. Southern Democrats resented Truman's modest initiatives for racial equality, so they united with Republicans to block passage of his liberal "Fair Deal" social legislation. Meanwhile, Republicans, frustrated by their electoral defeats since 1932, harshly attacked liberal Democrats. Exploiting a widespread "Red Scare," they used exaggerated claims of Communist menace inside America to detach voters, particularly Catholics, from the Democratic coalition. They also alleged that Truman "coddled" Communists in government.

GOP red-baiting intensified in 1948 when ex-Communist Whittaker Chambers accused Democrat Alger Hiss, a former State Department official, of spying for the Soviets. These charges took on added gravity in October 1949 with the Communist takeover of China. Republicans claimed that Communist subversion within the Truman administration explained both this "loss" of China and the Soviets' recent development of atomic-bomb technology. In February 1950, Senator Joseph R. McCarthy of Wisconsin emerged to lead the anticommunist inquisition, soon called McCarthyism. During four years of investigations, McCarthy failed to uncover any real Communist spies. But his character assassinations poisoned the political atmosphere by smearing Democrats as disloyal Americans.

The outbreak of the Korean War escalated both the Cold War and the GOP's support for McCarthyism. In June 1950, Soviet-backed North Korean Communists invaded South Korea. President Truman sent U.S. troops to Korea without congressional consent, thereby setting a precedent for the executive using military means to contain communism anywhere in the world. The Korean War also entrenched the defense establishment within American society and economy. Truman's intervention in Korea drew widespread public approval until November 1950, when Chinese Communist troops entered the conflict and brought U.S. forces to a standstill.

The 1952 elections, which took place during the height of the McCarthy era and the Korean War, were bitterly partisan. Truman withdrew his candidacy, and Governor Adlai E. Stevenson of Illinois won the Democratic nomination. Retired general Dwight D. Eisenhower, with the backing of moderate Eastern internationalists, captured the Republican nomination. The likeable "Ike" appealed to a broad constituency as a Midwestern farm boy who had become a World War II hero. Eisenhower's vague promise to end the Korean War helped him win a landslide victory, and his coattails aided other GOP candidates. As a result, Republicans regained control of the presidency and Congress for the first time since 1932.

President Eisenhower's Republican Interlude, 1953–1960

The Eisenhower era of the 1950s displayed a curiously mixed character. The United States remained haunted by Cold War anxieties. Those years also witnessed growing prosperity, suburban expansion, a continuing baby boom, the birth of rock'n'roll, and a flourishing consumer culture centered around home ownership, automobiles, and television. Finally, the 1950s symbolized conformity, complacency, and consensus. The death of Soviet dictator Joseph Stalin in March 1953 reduced international tensions, as did an armistice ending the Korean conflict in July. At home, Senator Robert Taft's death that same month and Joseph McCarthy's political demise in 1954 fostered consensus by eliminating the GOP's two most polarizing partisan figures.

President Eisenhower personified the consensus politics of the 1953–60 period. Eisenhower had described New Deal programs as "creeping socialism," but he privately noted that, "Should any political party attempt to abolish Social Security, unemployment insurance, and eliminate labor laws and farm programs, you would not hear of that party again." Consequently, he embraced a "middle way" that preserved but did not expand the domestic social programs and international policies initiated under Democrats Roosevelt and Truman. Yet the president's pragmatic concessions outraged conservative Republicans, who had hoped to slash federal programs.

In foreign policy, Eisenhower's anticommunist internationalism also reflected the era's bipartisan consensus. In the 1952 campaign, he had promised to discard Truman's "negative, futile, and immoral" containment policy. As president, however, he retained that strategy, though he reduced military spending. His foreign-policy moderation frustrated right-wing Republicans, who wanted to engage Communists militarily. In sum, "Eisenhower Republicanism" came to mean pragmatic centrism, despite the president's personal conservatism.

Eisenhower's middle-way policies and affable public personality made him one of the most popular presidents ever. But other Republicans benefited little from this adulation. In the 1954 congressional elections, following an economic recession, the GOP lost control of Congress. The party did not regain a Senate majority until 1980 or a House majority until 1994. In 1956, voters affirmed the status quo, as Eisenhower routed Adlai Stevenson in a rematch while Democrats retained their congressional majorities. Thus, the Eisenhower administration represented only a fleeting Republican interlude within the Democratic age.

The president usually worked well with congressional Democrats. They, too, became less partisan during the mid-1950s. Most important, they discarded the class-based populist rhetoric of the New Deal era. This move toward the political center, especially on economic matters, occurred because organized labor, the Democratic party's mainstay since the Depression, lost political clout beginning in the 1950s. Moreover, rank-and-file workers showed less militancy than during the Great Depression, because they enjoyed rising wages and benefits in the postwar boom. Finally, Democrats moved toward the center by embracing Keynesian economic strategy, which stressed economic growth at home and abroad rather than the redistribution of wealth from richer to poorer Americans.

In the late 1950s, however, the bipartisan consensus began to erode somewhat. The most dramatic challenge to consensus came on the issue of race relations. In 1954, the Supreme Court, under Chief Justice Earl Warren, outlawed racial segregation in public schools in *Brown* v. *Board of Education*. This landmark ruling infuriated conservative southerners. They promised "massive resistance," and more than a hundred congressmen from the region signed a "Southern Manifesto" opposing *Brown*. The decision also energized the civil rights movement, which was soon led by the Rev. Martin Luther King, Jr. In September 1957, President Eisenhower reluctantly sent troops to Little Rock, Arkansas, to enforce a federal-court desegregation order, further enraging southern conservatives. Bipartisanship broke down on other issues, too. In October 1957, the Soviets launched *Sputnik*, the first artificial satellite, and Democrats charged that Eisenhower's reductions in defense spending had allowed the development of a "missile gap" supposedly favoring the Soviets. Democrats also criticized Eisenhower's economic management after a sharp recession began in 1957.

Democrats capitalized on these issues in the 1958 midterm elections, capturing their largest congressional majorities since the New Deal era. Most alarming for Republicans were their losses throughout the Midwest and New England, traditional GOP areas. The 1958 elections transformed the political atmosphere. Led by Senate liberals, northern Democrats spurned bipartisan cooperation and demanded federal activism in economic growth, civil rights, and defense. In foreign policy, Democrats chided Eisenhower for allowing Fidel Castro's anti-U.S. revolution in Cuba in 1959, and they criticized him for failing to compete effectively with energetic Soviet leader Nikita Khrushchev.

In 1960, the Democratic presidential candidate, Senator John F. Kennedy of Massachusetts, differed from his Republican opponent, Richard M. Nixon, more in style than in substance. Nixon, Eisenhower's vice president, had won the nomination because Republicans appreciated his party loyalty and because his anticommunism, internationalism, and pragmatism made him a good compromise candidate. Nixon was endorsed by the GOP's leading moderate, Governor Nelson Rockefeller of New York, as well as by the party's leading conservative, Senator Barry Goldwater of Arizona, although Goldwater urged conservatives to "take this party back" after the 1960 election. Kennedy edged out Nixon for the presidency, but Republicans made inroads into the Democrats' large congressional majorities.

Revitalizing Conservative Thought in the Postwar Era, 1945–1964

For nearly two decades after World War II, disheartened conservatives perceived themselves as fighting a desperate, uphill struggle against the surging ideologies of domestic liberalism and international communism. Even within the Republican party, the home of American conservatism, the moderate Dewey-Eisenhower-Rockefeller wing seemed ascendant. It was no wonder that author Albert Jay Nock viewed himself and his fellow conservative intellectuals as a scattered "remnant." After World War II, however, right-wing scholars and journalists responded to their plight by refashioning and popularizing their ideas. By 1964, the revitalized conservative movement had created a cohesive orthodoxy by "fusing" traditionalism and libertarianism through anticommunism, and had recaptured the GOP behind presidential nominee Barry Goldwater.

A main weakness of the conservative intellectual movement was that it split between traditionalists and libertarians. Traditionalists— also known as "social," "cultural," or "religious" conservatives—espoused an authoritarian ideology focusing on social and cultural issues. They rejected the essential goodness of human nature and insisted that individuals required moral instruction and supervision. This philosophy led them to promote an authoritarian social and political system based on a natural hierarchy and led by a virtuous elite. Consequently, social conservatives dismissed the idea that equality was natural and beneficial, and they rejected the "corrupting idea that [government] can legislate prosperity, legislate equality, legislate opportunity," as Senator Robert Taft put it.

Since the American Revolution, socially conservative thought had fought an uphill battle within the United States because American ideology had typically championed such antitraditionalist values as modernity, progress, optimism, freedom, equality, and democracy. Only in the antebellum Old South did authoritarian politics dominate. After the Civil War, socially conservative traditionalism remained most influential among Southerners, rural residents, and religious groups, and it found its political expression in such policies as racial segregation, restriction of immigration, prohibition of alcohol, and laws against teaching the theory of human evolution. In sum, traditionalists had been "routed" since the eighteenth century, as conservative historian Russell Kirk wrote in 1953, "but they have never surrendered."

After World War II, several conservative intellectuals worked to revitalize traditionalist thought. Kirk, Richard M. Weaver, Peter Viereck, Leo Strauss, and others claimed that the decadence, materialism, and moral relativism of mass society had caused modernity's violence and oppression. Most traditionalists called for restructuring modern society and politics on the absolutist, universal moral values of an ancient "Great Tradition" centered on Christianity. The "first canon" of traditionalism, Kirk argued, was the belief that "a divine intent rules society. . . . Political problems, at bottom, are religious and moral problems."

Traditionalism coexisted throughout U.S. history alongside a very different strain of conservative thought: libertarianism, also called "fiscal," "economic," "free-market," or "laissez-faire" conservatism. Libertarians drew on the Enlightenment philosophies of John Locke and Thomas Jefferson to argue that government power threatened individual liberty and economic opportunity. "That government is best which governs least," they maintained. During the nineteenth century, such extreme individualists as Henry David Thoreau and Lysander Spooner further developed libertarian thought. Libertarians cherished entrepreneurship and competitive laissez-faire capitalism. By the late nineteenth century, however, fiscal conservatives had begun to use libertarian ideas to justify the economic inequality and social hierarchy produced by industrial corporate capitalism. After 1929, libertarians' laissez-faire policy was discredited by the Great Depression and repudiated by Franklin Roosevelt's coalition. In response, libertarians criticized the New Deal's attempt to centralize power, redistribute wealth through taxation, help the poor, regulate business, and defend workers' rights. But World War II only intensified America's "big-government" tendencies.

Like traditionalist conservatives, libertarian intellectuals revitalized their ideology in the two decades after World War II. These "individualists" believed they were fighting a great battle against "collectivists," a wide-ranging group that included fascists, communists, socialists, and liberals. Extreme libertarians such as Frank Chodorov, John Chamberlain, Murray Rothbard, and Ayn Rand interpreted freedom in an almost anarchist manner, and Rand's best-selling novels— including *The Fountainhead* (1943) and *Atlas Shrugged* (1957)— helped popularize libertarian thought.

Also helping to revitalize postwar libertarianism was an influential group of fiscally conservative economists centered around the University of Chicago. Friedrich A. Hayek, Ludwig von Mises, Milton Friedman, and other libertarian economists drew on the thought of eighteenth-century philosopher Adam Smith and other classical economists. Libertarians argued that political freedom rested upon economic freedom and criticized liberal Keynesian policies encouraging government intervention in the market. As the Depression receded in memory, the social base for libertarians' economic ideas increased. The postwar boom greatly expanded higher education, managerial occupations, home ownership, and suburban lifestyles, which enlarged the numbers of middle-class and upper-class Americans drawn to libertarian criticism of big government and high taxes.

Obviously, socially conservative traditionalism and fiscally conservative libertarianism embodied somewhat conflicting legacies. Traditionalists emphasized religious faith, moral virtue, community, and social order, whereas libertarians stressed scientific reason, material satisfaction, individualism, and freedom. Regional tensions between the traditionalist South and the libertarian West intensified these differences. In practice, though, the two strains of conservatism often overlapped—symbolized by the pious businessman. During the Cold War, moreover, conservatives de-emphasized their disagreements to unite against the common threats of communism abroad and liberalism at home.

As right-wing ideas and movements accelerated during the 1950s, conservative intellectuals worked to construct a more cohesive ideology. The effort was led by Frank Meyer, an editor at William F. Buckley, Jr.'s journal, the *National Review*. Meyer recommended that conservatives downplay sectarian differences by employing libertarian means for traditional ends, thereby achieving individual freedom within an orderly, virtuous society. He "fused" the new ideology by stressing conservatives' common hostility toward communism. Both traditionalists and libertarians, Meyer observed, "see Communism as an armed and messianic threat to the very existence of Western Civilization and the United States."

By the early 1960s, Meyer, Buckley, and other *National Review* intellectuals had successfully established a new conservative orthodoxy. In the process, these "fusionists" excluded isolationists, egotistical and atheistic libertarians like Ayn Rand, the John Birch Society and other extreme anticommunists, militant racists, and blatant anti-Semites. In reality, however, the new conservatism drew much of its energy and passion from these grassroots movements.

Revitalized by fusionism, conservatives sought to recapture the Republican party. They disparaged Eisenhower's bland, centrist policies as a "dime-store New Deal," in Senator Barry Goldwater's words. In contrast to the Eisenhower administration, conservative Republicans accentuated their differences with liberal Democrats with an agenda emphasizing limited federal government (except in defense), diminished welfare spending, confrontational anti-communism, a conservative judiciary, and traditionalist religious values.

Conservatives also capitalized on a regional power shift within the GOP from the less conservative Northeast to the more conservative West and South. Beginning in World War II, population and economic power moved from the Northeast's older industries, Wall Street, and small-town bankers toward the newer industries, car dealerships, and real-estate tycoons in the "Sunbelt" of the South, Southwest, and West. Conservative Republicans also gained converts from the Democratic party among white Southerners angered by civil rights reforms. Consequently, political power with the GOP shifted from Northeastern centrists toward Sunbelt conservatives. And the defeat of Eisenhower's vice president, the relatively moderate Richard Nixon, in the 1960 presidential election opened the way for the conservative takeover of the GOP led by Senator Barry Goldwater.

Goldwater, a Sunbelt conservative from Arizona, personified the new fusionist orthodoxy. "Conservatism, we are told, is out of date," Goldwater wrote in *The Conscience of a Conservative* (1960). "The charge is preposterous. The laws of God, and of nature have no date-line." Goldwater's best-selling book became a manifesto for such conservative groups as the Young Americans for Freedom, founded in 1960, and for segregationists who shared his opposition to civil rights legislation. These grassroots conservatives proved to be skillful organizers and fundraisers, and they helped Goldwater win the GOP presidential nomination in 1964. Though humiliated by a liberal Democrat landslide that year, the revitalized conservative movement helped build the foundation for the Republican ascendancy of the post-1968 era.

Liberalism, Backlash, and Republican Revival, 1961–1968

After Goldwater's crushing defeat by Democrat Lyndon Johnson in 1964, conservative Republicanism seemed routed. Just four years later, however, social turmoil and the backlash it provoked had ended the Democratic age of 1932–68. The turbulent 1960s shocked Americans accustomed to the bland Eisenhower era. In fact, however, the sixties culminated several long-term trends. The civil rights movement continued to evolve, but it split and became identified with the Democratic party, Black Power, and ghetto rioting. Meanwhile, a huge middle-class generation, born during the post–World War II baby boom and shaped by postwar abundance, entered college. Many baby boomers challenged both political authority, often through the New Left, and cultural conformity through the counterculture and feminism. Finally, the Vietnam War, a product of two decades of Cold War containment, spawned a strident peace movement that intensified social and cultural conflicts. By 1968, these pressures had incited a conservative backlash, weakened the New Deal coalition, and ended the Democratic age that had begun in 1932.

President John F. Kennedy set the activist tone for the 1960s. His New Frontier domestic agenda promoted economic growth through Keynesian tax cuts and called for civil rights and antipoverty legislation. Despite his vigorous and idealistic rhetoric, Kennedy moved hesitantly on such controversial questions as race relations. In foreign policy, JFK, like Truman and Eisenhower, pursued anticommunist containment through his "Flexible Response" strategy, most notably in Cuba, Berlin, and Vietnam. But an assassin's bullet in November 1963 ended the president's life.

As the nation mourned the loss of its charismatic young leader, the new president, Lyndon B. Johnson, vowed to expand JFK's liberal agenda. Johnson ushered through Congress the Civil Rights Act of 1964, which prohibited racial discrimination at work and in public places. The momentous law was a turning point because it identified the national Democratic party with the advancement of African Americans. The GOP intensified racial partisanship by selecting Barry Goldwater, who opposed the Civil Rights Act, as their 1964 presidential candidate.

A conservative ideologue, Goldwater rejected the consensus politics of Democrats and moderate Republicans. He denounced the power of the federal government, called for escalating the still-limited Vietnam War, appeared willing to risk nuclear war to "defeat communism," and criticized popular programs such as Social Security. "Extremism in the defense of liberty is no vice," he proclaimed. Not surprisingly, 46 percent of Americans considered him an "extremist" or "radical." The only bright spot in the Goldwater campaign came when actor Ronald Reagan gave a stirring television speech on behalf of the GOP nominee, which launched Reagan's own political career.

The 1964 elections produced the largest Democratic victories in three decades. Johnson captured the biggest popular majority in history, and Democrats won their largest congressional majorities since the New Deal. But Goldwater's breakthrough in the Deep South, where he won five states, heralded major changes in national politics by identifying Republicans with racial conservatism. In the short term, however, the 1964 landslide enabled Johnson and congressional Democrats to build their Great Society, the most significant reform legislation since the New Deal. Johnson's timing proved impeccable; polls showed that Americans professed unprecedented faith in government action. The Great Society legislation revised immigration restrictions and expanded federal responsibility for economic opportunity, health, education, public housing, and urban renewal. Additionally, the Voting Rights Act of 1965 allowed federal officials to register minority voters, which reshaped southern politics. Though criticized by conservatives, these Great Society programs achieved real, though limited, successes.

Meanwhile, the Supreme Court under Chief Justice Earl Warren continued to promote federal activism. During the 1960s, the liberal Warren Court ruled that criminal defendants had to be informed of their constitutional rights, ordered reapportionment in state legislatures and Congress under the principle of "one person, one vote," banned compulsory prayer in public schools, overturned state laws prohibiting birth control devices, and broadened protections for free speech and privacy. These liberal decisions reflected a "rights revolution," which sought expanded legal protection for marginalized groups. Conservatives, especially traditionalists, reacted in anger. "Impeach Earl Warren" read a popular bumper sticker.

The liberal tide of the mid-1960s soon ebbed, however, for several reasons. The gap between Johnson's promises for his Great Society programs and their more modest results disillusioned many Americans. In addition, a white backlash grew against liberal support for African American advancement and against the growing assertiveness of blacks themselves. Many African Americans, still facing informal racism and economic inequality, grew increasingly frustrated. Some youths united behind Black Power, a militant, separatist philosophy, and ghetto rioting began in 1965 and recommenced each summer for several years. Growing numbers of whites blamed rioting and street crime on Black Power and on liberal "permissiveness" toward African Americans (especially by the Warren Court).

To make matters worse, many working-class whites, the group that felt most threatened by black advancement, turned against 1960s liberalism. Previously, poorer whites typically had viewed New Deal liberalism as promoting their values and ambitions. But now they often expressed populist resentment against Great Society programs and Warren Court decisions, which they viewed as commitments to the nontraditional, abstract values of middle-class "limousine liberals."

Finally, the Vietnam War helped cut short the liberal era. In 1965, Johnson sent to Vietnam the first of more than half a million U.S. combat troops who would eventually fight there. The president's growing obsession with Vietnam diminished his interest in domestic reform and diverted funds from social programs. In the 1966 congressional elections, Republicans capitalized on the growing backlash against the Great Society, the Warren Court, rioting, and Vietnam to cut Democrats' large majorities and end liberal control of Congress. The GOP also made gains at the state level. The most significant Republican victory was that of political newcomer Ronald Reagan, who became governor of California.

In 1967–68, controversy over the Vietnam War mounted. The brutality of the combat, brought home by television, unsettled many Americans. In January 1968, Viet Cong forces inside South Vietnam staged the massive Tet Offensive. Although beaten back by U.S. troops, the Communist guerrillas had exposed the harsh, no-win nature of the war. After that time, a U.S. victory seemed increasingly remote, and public approval of Johnson's management of the war plunged to 26 percent. The antiwar movement grew in intensity, and many Democrats became disillusioned with the direction of their party. By 1968, domestic conflict over the Vietnam War had shattered the bipartisan consensus supporting America's role as the policeman of the world.

Disillusionment with U.S. foreign policy in the late 1960s fed a more comprehensive critique of America. The New Left, led by student radicals, criticized the liberal establishment and called for "participatory democracy" to make America measure up to its ideals. In the late 1960s, however, the frustrated New Left movement degenerated into promoting violence and burning American flags, which sparked an angry "patriotic" backlash. Similarly, the counterculture's highly publicized rejection of conventional middle-class lifestyles provoked conservative outrage and widened the cultural "generation gap" between young and old. The counterculture's questioning of traditional values also helped to reinvigorate feminism. And because "women's liberation" literally hit so close to home, it, too, drew sharp criticism from traditionalists.

Vietnam, racial turmoil, radical politics, and cultural upheaval were the backdrop to the turbulent 1968 presidential campaign. In the Democratic contest, Johnson was challenged for renomination by two liberal antiwar senators, Eugene J. McCarthy of Minnesota and the better-known Robert F. Kennedy of New York, JFK's brother. After the Tet Offensive, Johnson dramatically withdrew his candidacy, throwing his support behind Vice President Hubert H. Humphrey, a pro-war liberal. Robert Kennedy's shocking assassination in June, just two months after the murder of Martin Luther King, Jr., allowed Humphrey to win the nomination. Outside the Democratic national convention in August, Chicago police beat antiwar protestors in plain view of reporters and television news cameras, further fracturing the party and escalating a public condemnation of Democrats and liberals.

Meanwhile, presidential candidate George C. Wallace courted the white vote by manipulating such emotional "wedge" issues as race, rioting, crime, patriotism, and religion. Wallace, the former governor of Alabama, had symbolized white resistance to integration since 1963, when he promised "Segregation forever!" In 1968, he left the Democratic party and ran for president as an independent. A right-wing populist, Wallace exploited hostility toward militant blacks, welfare mothers, middle-class radicals, intellectuals, hippies, feminists, antiwar protesters, draft dodgers, Great Society programs, and Warren Court decisions. He stressed his militant patriotism by choosing as his running mate a retired Air Force general, Curtis LeMay, who recommended ending the Vietnam War by "bombing North Vietnam back to the Stone Age."

Unlike the Democrats, the GOP remained relatively united over U.S. policy in Vietnam. Few Republicans, either moderate or conservative, openly opposed the prosecution of the war. In 1968, Richard Nixon achieved a remarkable comeback by winning the GOP presidential nomination with support from conservatives and southerners. On Vietnam, the hawkish Nixon promised to achieve "peace with honor" but provided few details. He followed Wallace's lead by emphasizing a "Southern Strategy," attacking liberalism, and exploiting wedge issues to attract southern whites.

In November, Nixon won a close victory and the GOP recaptured a gubernatorial majority, while Democrats retained congressional control. While these results ended the long age of Democratic dominance, they "dealigned" rather than realigned politics. In dealignment, the electorate exhibits less party loyalty, more concern for individual issues or candidates, and a higher proportion of independents.

Dealignment resulted primarily from the breakdown of the Democratic coalition. White southerners began leaving the party, mainly because of Democrats' promotion of the advancement of blacks. As a result, Democratic presidential candidates averaged only 33 percent of the southern white vote from 1968 through 2000. Additionally, postwar suburbanization weakened urban political machines, which had commanded a solid base of Democratic votes, both black and white. Meanwhile, three decades of affluence and social-welfare programs had eased the economic insecurity that had first unified the coalition during the Depression. Finally, many influential Democrats now embraced racial equality, the antiwar movement, and the counterculture. Support for these liberal social values angered traditionalist Democrats, especially those from working-class and Catholic backgrounds. By the late 1960s, consequently, most voters associated the national Democratic party and its leadership with liberal values on economic, social, and foreign-policy issues.

Republican ascendancy remained insecure in the dealignment era, however. Nixon had won only 43 percent of the popular vote in 1968, and the GOP's electoral base in rural areas and small cities was shrinking. To win over conservative Democrats and Wallace's independents, Nixon realized the need to exploit his conservative stances on such wedge issues as race, crime, patriotism, drug use, and sexual behavior. Consequently, voters increasingly associated Republicans with conservative stances on economic, social, and foreign-policy issues, a situation that the incoming Nixon administration believed would prove to be a boon for the party. "This country's going so far right, you won't believe it," predicted John Mitchell, Nixon's attorney general.

CHAPTER TWO

Richard Nixon and the Paradox of the "New Republican Majority," 1969–1974

At the end of the 1980s, Republican Senator Bob Dole of Kansas spoke at a press corps Gridiron roast of former presidents. He summed up the legacies of Presidents Jimmy Carter, Gerald Ford, and Richard Nixon by labeling them, respectively, "See No Evil, Hear No Evil, and Evil." Dole's acerbic characterization of Nixon seemed all too accurate to many Americans who had followed the long and controversial political career of "Tricky Dick," as a congressman and senator from California (1947–52), vice-president (1953–61), and president (1969–74).

Admired by some and reviled by others for his partisan attacks and gutter-style politics during the 1950s, Nixon was regarded—even by many of his harshest critics—as among the most important post-1945 presidents. Journalist Robert Herhold insisted that Nixon intrigued Americans "not because he is so different from us, but because he is so much like us." Filmmaker Oliver Stone captured this notion in his movie *Nixon*. In one scene, a restless Nixon walks the White House corridors at midnight, gazing at presidential portraits on the walls. Speaking to the image of a forever young and handsome

John F. Kennedy, he says: "When people look at you, they see who they wish they were. But when they look at me," he continued, "they see who they really are."

A fascination by historians, journalists, and the public with Nixon's dark and complex psyche, and especially with the Watergate scandal, has overshadowed two important paradoxes of his legacy. First, his administration represented both a continuation and a repudiation of Great Society liberalism. Second, although his presidency ended in disgrace and almost destroyed the Republican party, it also cleared a path for the ascendancy of a far more conservative GOP after 1980.

The election of Republican Richard Nixon in November 1968 was celebrated by the victor and heralded by the media as a repudiation of the Democrats' "big-government liberalism" born during the New Deal. In truth, Nixon's political coattails were so short that Democrats retained control of both houses of Congress, by wide margins. In addition, Nixon received barely 43 percent of the popular vote in the three-way race—hardly a ringing endorsement. But many Republicans hoped that regaining the White House represented the first step toward restoring their ascendancy.

Nixon's presidency, however, confounded friend and foe alike. He displayed a masterful command of the "politics of resentment"— the ability to direct racial, cultural, religious, and class grievances against his political enemies. Nixon spoke contemptuously of liberals and big government but backed what was arguably the most liberal legislation proposed between 1968 and 2000. In spite of his lifelong criticism of communism, moreover, he pursued a policy of détente (reduction of tension) toward the Soviet Union and initiated ties to the Communist regime in China. Despite his many successes, Nixon's lack of interest in electing Republicans to Congress and the lawbreaking he sanctioned against his political rivals in the Watergate scandal nearly sank the GOP.

Many liberal northern Democrats in Congress disliked Nixon personally but had grudging respect for some of his domestic and foreign policies. By contrast, conservative Southern Democrats felt a bond with Nixon on racial issues, and he established warm ties with several of them. Meanwhile, moderate Republicans endorsed most of Nixon's policies but disliked his coarse manner. The Republican president's harshest policy critics came from the GOP's emerging "New Right," such as California Governor Ronald Reagan, who considered Nixon's pragmatic approach a distortion of the party's true conservative vision. Presidential speechwriter William Safire observed that while Nixon's "heart was on the right, his head was, with FDR, slightly left of center." The president himself told a friend that the only thing "as bad as a far left liberal" was a "damn right wing conservative." He called himself a pragmatist—"I'm a non-extremist." Thus, Reagan and other conservative Republicans were not entirely upset by Nixon's disgrace, because it opened the way for them to become the dominant GOP faction.

Nixon had a secret taping system installed in the White House, so we know far more about his personal views than those held by most other presidents. The hundreds of hours of taped conversations with administration officials between 1971 and 1973 reveal much not only about the Watergate scandal—in which the tapes played a critical part—but also about Nixon's opinion of almost every issue and person that came before him. While usually reserved in public speech, the president was unusually vulgar in private, appending four-letter words and ethnic slurs to almost everyone he disliked. He reserved his rudest observations for racial and ethnic minorities, especially African Americans and Jews.

Some of this was merely "blowing off steam" and a crude effort by the president to impress his staff with his "toughness." But it also revealed his many grievances against the world and his inability to distinguish between honest differences among people and politicians and alleged enemies out to get him. The president's us-versus-them sentiments led him to create an "enemies list" of politicians and their campaign contributors whom he intended to punish.

Yet it would be a mistake to say that Nixon was fundamentally motivated by prejudice. He was, strangely enough, an equal-opportunity hater who disliked people in general, questioned everyone's motives but his own, and took little satisfaction in his real accomplishments. He craved victories and adulation but never found pleasure in them.

Soon after the 1968 election, Nixon's campaign manager and incoming attorney general, John Mitchell, admitted that the new president had no concrete plans to demolish the liberal policies of the New

Deal and Great Society. "Watch what we do, not what we say," Mitchell told reporters privately. Nixon had campaigned on traditional conservative promises to "get tough" on crime, quiet antiwar protesters, clean up the "welfare mess," and halt "forced" busing to achieve racial balance in schools. Yet his interest in these issues was political, not ideological. They were examples of the "wedge" issues he used to pry voters away from the Democratic party and build a majority for himself.

A political realist, Nixon recognized that to pass legislation, he needed support from the heavily Democratic Congress and from federal agencies that were often run by career officials sympathetic to liberal goals. At the same time, some of those who criticized Nixon most harshly, especially on his approach to the Soviet Union and China, were conservative Republicans. Consequently, Nixon campaigned (in 1968, 1970, and 1972) as a conservative, but he governed as a moderate.

Although a lifelong Republican who frequently questioned Democrats' loyalty to their country, Nixon was never a strict "party man." He campaigned enthusiastically for Republican candidates, but he was more interested in creating a reserve of political obligations to his own candidacy than in building a congressional majority. He also seemed indifferent to the nitty-gritty work of passing legislation; he compared domestic policy to "building outhouses in Peoria." Instead, he hoped to focus his presidency on bold, dramatic ventures in foreign policy.

Members of both parties recognized that Nixon had a low regard for Congress as a whole. Robert Hartmann, an aide to then-Representative Gerald Ford, recalled that "Nixon could not hide his disdain for the Congress and he treated some individual [members] very badly." The president seldom met with politicians of either party. He had especially bad relations with moderate Republican senators who favored most of his policies (including Charles Mathias of Maryland, Clifford Case of New Jersey, Charles Goodell of New York, and Charles Percy of Illinois). Their mild criticisms enraged him. Nixon vowed revenge for imagined slights by congressional and other critics, telling his aide Charles Colson, "One day we'll get them. We'll get them on the ground where we want them. And we'll stick our heels in, step on them hard and twist."

The Republican party during the Nixon era was in transition. The Northeastern wing consisting of Rockefeller Republicans still favored active, if better-managed, government. These moderates outnumbered the Goldwater wing of the GOP, which rejected many tenets of the New Deal. But these conservatives were increasing their ranks in the South and West. Aiming to unite the party, Nixon employed conservative rhetoric but consistently pushed a moderate legislative program.

Continuity of Liberal Domestic Policy

Nixon attacked the methods of the Great Society reforms more than their goals. A favorite target was the allegedly bloated federal bureaucracy that misspent funds and mismanaged programs. He privately claimed that "We've checked and found that 96 percent of the bureaucracy are against us. They're bastards who are here to screw us." To bypass federal agencies, Nixon advocated shifting responsibility for social programs to state and local governments, arguing that they could do a more cost-effective job than the "incompetent bureaucrats" in Washington. The administration also hoped that locally managed programs would have a more conservative slant.

To promote this "New Federalism," Nixon got Congress to approve a system of revenue sharing and block grants to states. Instead of, say, the Department of Health, Education, and Welfare (HEW) overseeing a school program in Mississippi, Congress allocated to the state a sum of money for education. Total funding might remain the same, but it came with fewer strings attached and less federal oversight. States and localities could therefore use the funds to pay for buildings and equipment rather than for direct services to the poor.

Nixon campaigned in 1968 on a promise to clean up the "welfare mess." He shared the view of 84 percent of the public who told pollsters, "There are too many people receiving welfare money who should be working." During the 1960s, the number of Americans on

Aid to Families with Dependent Children (AFDC), the basic federal welfare program begun in the 1930s, increased from 3 million to 8.4 million despite general prosperity. The federal government paid part of the welfare costs, while states picked up the remainder. This led to inequities among recipients. For example, New York gave a family on AFDC $200 per month, while Mississippi provided only $33.

In 1969, Nixon endorsed a welfare-reform proposal formulated by presidential adviser Daniel Patrick Moynihan, a former Harvard social scientist. Moynihan recommended replacing AFDC with a Family Assistance Program, or FAP. Designed to break the "cycle of dependence," FAP would have given each head of household about $1,600 per year—with the provision that the person hold a paying job. This payment, a sort of negative income tax, was meant as an incentive to help poor families escape what Moynihan called a "culture of poverty." The president was also intrigued by his adviser's prediction that FAP would "wipe out social workers," a profession Nixon detested.

Despite the help that FAP could have provided poor families, members of both parties opposed the initiative. Liberal Democrats objected to the small amount of money and the mandatory-work provision of the bill, while conservative Republicans complained about giving too big a handout to the poor. Nixon's own commitment to FAP was questionable. The president told his chief of staff, H. R. Haldeman, that he wanted to be "sure it is killed by Democrats. We make a big play for it, but don't let it pass." As a result, the proposal died.

Congress, with Nixon's approval, did augment the Social Security system. Among other reforms, payments to retirees were indexed to the rate of inflation, thereby increasing benefits to retirees by 55 percent during Nixon's presidency. As some critics noted, Social Security expanded while welfare payments stagnated because politicians in both parties recognized that the elderly voted in large numbers, but children and the poor did not.

Confounding conservatives, Nixon signed legislation promoting the environment, health, and safety. These laws created the Environmental Protection Agency (EPA), the Consumer Product Safety

Commission (CPSC), and the Occupational Health and Safety Administration (OSHA). He also signed the Clean Air Act, the Water Pollution Control Act, and measures to protect endangered species. Recognizing public anxiety about rising rates of cancer, in 1971 he proclaimed a federally funded "war on cancer" with great fanfare. He also signed the Voting Rights Act of 1972, which included lowering the voting age to eighteen. He had hesitated to support the lower voting age until polling data showed him that younger voters were no more likely to vote Democratic than those over twenty-one.

High levels of public support for these health, environmental, and workplace-safety bills made Congress eager to pass this legislation and the administration reluctant to oppose it. Although he approved the new federal oversight agencies, Nixon continually tried to reduce funding for the EPA and OSHA. By 1972, moreover, he was speaking out bitterly against environmentalists, whom he added to his growing "enemies list."

Gender issues entered mainstream political debate during Nixon's presidency. In 1969, he established the Task Force on Women's Rights and Responsibilities, which issued a report calling for the creation of a permanent office on women's issues, stronger federal antidiscrimination measures, and passage of the Equal Rights Amendment (ERA) to the Constitution. Except for endorsing the ERA (as had every president since 1940) Nixon ignored the recommendations. Congress approved the ERA in 1972 and sent it to the states for ratification—which it never received.

Nixon appointed no women (or minorities) to his cabinet and few women to other federal posts. Representative Bella Abzug, a Democrat from New York, exaggerated only slightly when she called Nixon "the nation's chief resident male chauvinist." The president felt extremely uncomfortable with nontraditional gender roles and unconventional notions of sexuality. Describing women as by nature "erratic" and overly "emotional," he told aides he was "not for women in any job." "Thank God," he added, "we don't have any in the cabinet."

Nevertheless, in hope, as he put it, of "picking up a half percentage point" of the vote in 1972, he considered nominating a woman to the Supreme Court. For a time, he showed interest in New York Republican lawyer Rita Hauser. But when she expressed the view that the Constitution did not forbid same-sex marriage, an astounded Nixon yelled, "There goes a Supreme Court Justice! I can't go that far. Negroes and Whites okay. But that's too far."

In spite of his conservative image, Nixon deeply upset fiscal conservatives by utilizing liberal Keynesian economic tools. The American economy, which had boomed in the 1960s, confounded economic models during the Nixon years. For the first time, stagnant economic growth and relatively high inflation occurred simultaneously—so-called stagflation. As a candidate, Nixon had criticized liberal economic theory. But when confronted with the problems of paying for the Vietnam War, importing increasingly expensive foreign oil, and managing the growing trade deficit with Europe and Japan, the Republican president embraced liberal ideas that he claimed to despise.

In 1969, Nixon promoted a tax-reform bill that raised rates on the wealthy. Early in 1971 he told an interviewer, "I am now a Keynesian in economics." One startled economist likened this to a "Christian Crusader saying 'all things considered, I think Mohammed was right.'" That August, in response to the declining value of the dollar, Nixon imposed wage and price controls on business and labor, levied special fees on imports, and "closed the gold window."

With the world awash in dollars, the Treasury could no longer redeem greenbacks at the rate of $35 for one ounce of gold. Since the Bretton Woods agreement of 1944, America's willingness to convert dollars freely into gold at a fixed rate had anchored the global trading system. By ending convertibility, Nixon hoped to force up the value of foreign currencies and decrease that of the dollar, making foreign imports more expensive and U.S. exports cheaper.

Nixon dubbed his moves to restrict imports, control wages and prices, and stop the outflow of gold the "New Economic Policy." His actions temporarily eased pressure on the dollar and slowed inflation. They shocked Republicans who favored a hands-off economic policy, but reassured nervous voters that Nixon was doing something. Yet by 1973, America's trade deficit had resumed its sharp increase. Rising oil prices and imports from Japan proved especially costly to the economy during the 1970s.

In sum, Nixon implemented a more active, hands-on federal government, despite advocating a smaller, less active public sector. But his skillful use of conservative rhetoric—especially his pursuit of the "Southern Strategy"—masked his liberal policies.

The Southern Strategy: Building a Conservative Bloc

Despite Nixon's continuation of many liberal policies, he cultivated a conservative image. This approach, often called the "Southern Strategy," was designed to attract white southerners, northern Catholics, right-wing labor leaders, and other socially conservative Democrats alienated by the social upheavals associated with the civil rights movement and the 1960s counterculture. Nixon frequently relied on symbols and code words in making his pitch to these groups. He condemned "forced busing" to desegregate public schools, denounced "activist" federal judges, promoted "law and order," declared a "war on drugs," opposed abortion rights, and accused liberal Democrats of being "socialists." This strategy, the president and other Republicans hoped, would drive a wedge between a socially conservative "silent majority" and the Democratic party controlled by middle- and upper-class liberals.

Two authors of popular political tracts, Kevin Phillips and Ben Wattenberg, articulated Nixon's gut feeling and influenced his strategy. Phillips' *The Emerging Republican Majority* (1969) and Wattenberg's *The Real Majority* (1970) were often cited by Nixon's advisers as guides to winning elections. Republicans, Wattenberg argued, could coast to success by playing to a majority that was "unyoung, unpoor, and unblack."

Phillips outlined how the GOP could build a powerful voting bloc in the once solidly Democratic South. He noted that many white southerners (and working-class whites in northern cities) who supported George Wallace's 1968 candidacy had previously been life-long Democrats. Having broken their links of party loyalty, they were "in motion between a Democratic past and a Republican future." In a remarkably cynical tone, Phillips urged Nixon to promote African American voting rights in the South. This would drive growing numbers of blacks into the Democratic party and drive white conservatives out of it—and into the GOP. By following this strategy, Phillips argued, the Republican party could capture control of the fast-growing Sunbelt states of the South and Southwest. This would leave Democrats with a shrinking base of voters concentrated in the Northeast, the industrial Midwest, and decaying major cities.

Nixon seemed of two minds on racial matters. In private, he derided African Americans as "genetically inferior" and "just down out of the trees." In an unguarded moment caught on videotape during the 1968 campaign, Nixon explained why he thought many white Democrats would turn to him: "It's all about law and order and the damn Negro–Puerto Rican groups out there." Publicly, however, he shunned outright appeals to white racism and endorsed racial equality under the law.

Nixon realized that most white voters no longer backed segregation by law and that they paid at least lip service to the principle of racial equality. But he also knew that they still resented government programs that they believed unfairly promoted the interests of "ungrateful" minorities or that represented "reverse discrimination." In 1968, Nixon told southern delegates to the Republican convention that he supported the principle of racial equality, but he denounced "activist" liberal federal judges who interfered with local arrangements. He promised that if elected he would appoint "strict constitutionalists" to the Supreme Court who would interpret, not make, law.

Two years into his first term, Nixon ceased meeting with representatives from most Jewish and African American groups that he considered unfriendly. Instead, he sought contact with ethnic-European organizations whose members he hoped to attract to the GOP. In his effort to split the Democrats and troll for newly Republican voters, Nixon told aides early in 1971 that he would no longer "play" to issues such as "consumers, environment, youth, press, business elites, intellectuals, volunteers, etc."

Nixon's choice of Maryland governor Spiro Agnew as his running mate in 1968 also reflected his Southern Strategy and his attempts to appeal to ethnic Democrats. A relatively unknown politician, Agnew made national headlines in April 1968 when violence flared in Baltimore following the assassination of Martin Luther King, Jr. He brazenly blamed a group of African American community leaders for being partly responsible for the rioting because they had not distanced themselves from black radicals. Nixon also believed that Agnew, a Greek American, would attract voters of Eastern European ancestry who had traditionally voted Democratic but resented their party's recent support for racial minorities.

Liberals cringed at Agnew's campaign rhetoric, such as calling an Asian journalist a "fat Jap." Nixon could not stand his running mate personally, but Agnew proved popular among southern and northern conservatives and Republicans in general. Nixon campaigned in 1968 on a promise to "bring Americans together," but he assigned less pleasant duties to his vice president. In 1971, Agnew boasted that "dividing the American people has been my main contribution to the national political scene. I not only plead guilty to this charge, but I am somewhat flattered by it."

Nixon aides such as Attorney General John Mitchell and presidential adviser Harry Dent believed that the administration could build a new Republican power base in the formerly solid Democratic South by drawing disgruntled whites into the GOP. Unlike George Wallace and even more extreme race-baiters, Nixon and Mitchell used code words to target white southerners without being explicitly racist. They talked of "law and order," a new "war" on illegal drugs, a crusade against obscenity, and opposition to what they called "forced" busing of schoolchildren for racial integration.

Nixon exploited the combined fear of crime and drugs as a wedge issue to gain support from conservative Democrats. The president spoke of a massive heroin-driven crime wave that endangered the lives and property of law-abiding citizens. Weak judges and laws, he charged, perpetuated the problem. Nixon cited largely imaginary statistics and called for a stepped-up war on drugs to be led by federal agencies such as the newly created Drug Enforcement Administration (DEA). Congress agreed to appropriate more federal funds for local police and expanded the number of crimes covered by federal law. The crusade nabbed many small-time drug dealers but had little impact on national patterns of drug use. In contrast to his public rhetoric, Nixon quietly endorsed funding for methadone maintenance clinics, which were more effective in helping heroin users than was throwing them in jail.

Harry Dent, Nixon's chief Southern strategist, told his boss that the "miracle of the age" would be to "push desegregation on the South in such a way that made sure the courts and the Democrats," rather than the Republicans, "received the blame." In other words, the GOP could benefit from a white backlash against court-ordered desegregation. Following Dent's advice, Nixon instructed executive agencies to turn most desegregation efforts over to federal courts. The president could then cynically blame "activist judges," over whom he had no control, for desegregating schools.

Nixon spoke out frequently against "forced busing." In 1972, he urged Congress to pass legislation imposing a moratorium on judicial busing orders, knowing that it would not do so. When Congress ignored him, he endorsed an antibusing amendment to the Constitution. Privately, he said of the amendment: "I know it's not a good idea, but it will make those bastards [in the Democratic party] take a stand and it is a political plus for us."

As part of his appeal to southern whites, Nixon promised to reverse the direction of the Supreme Court by appointing conservative judges. He implied that they would halt government efforts to assist minorities in achieving equality. Nixon made four appointments to the Supreme Court—Chief Justice Warren Burger, who replaced Earl Warren in 1969, and Associate Justices Harry Blackmun, Lewis Powell, and William Rehnquist.

After selecting Burger, Nixon tried to fulfill his promise to name southern conservatives to the high court. In August 1969, he nominated Clement F. Haynsworth, a federal appeals court judge from South Carolina, to replace Abe Fortas. But questions about Haynsworth's ethics and racial views led thirty-eight Democrats and seventeen Republicans in the Senate to reject his nomination. Nixon called Haynsworth a "martyr" but cynically remarked in private that "We may gain enormously [in the South] from this incident." He told his aides to "go out this time and find a good federal judge further south and further to the right."

The president then nominated G. Harold Carswell, a federal appeals court judge in Florida. Carswell had a long history of defending what he called "segregation of the races" and the "principles of white supremacy." Nixon aide Bryce Harlow explained the near-unanimous opposition to Carswell among law professors by telling Nixon, "They think he's a boob, a dummy. And what counter is there to that? He is."

In April 1970, the Senate rejected Carswell's nomination. Nixon accused Democratic senators of harboring anti-southern prejudice. He then nominated Minnesotan Harry Blackmun, and the Senate unanimously confirmed him. In 1971, Nixon nominated two more justices, the moderately conservative Lewis F. Powell, Jr., of Virginia and William Rehnquist of Arizona to replace retiring justices Hugo Black and John Marshall Harlan. While Powell was a respected jurist, Rehnquist was a little-known, right-wing functionary in the Justice Department associated with the Goldwater wing of the GOP. As one Nixon aide quipped, Rehnquist (whom Nixon called "Renchburg," complaining that he "dressed like a clown" and "looked Jewish") made Goldwater "seem liberal." For example, as a young lawyer, Rehnquist had outspokenly defended the rights of states to segregate schools and had opposed the 1964 Civil Rights Act, which he believed was unconstitutional. When Nixon's advisers lamented that the nominee was not a woman, a southerner, or a Catholic, the president joked that maybe "Renchburg" could "get a sex-change operation." In any case, the Democratic-controlled Senate easily confirmed both Powell and Rehnquist.

Despite Nixon's efforts, the Burger Supreme Court did not reverse the pro–civil rights stance of the Warren Court (1953–69). Justices Powell and especially Blackmun proved more moderate than expected, and rulings by the Court affirmed most desegregation efforts. Equally telling was the Court's 1973 *Roe* v. *Wade* decision, upholding a woman's constitutional right to have an abortion. Although the Catholic Church and some Protestant denominations denounced the ruling, abortion rights did not fundamentally divide Democrats and Republicans on a national level until the 1980s. In several states, such as Ohio, Iowa, Michigan, and Missouri, anti-abortion Republicans defeated moderate Democrats in state and congressional races in the late 1970s.

Nixon's anti-abortion views and criticism of the *Roe* decision seemed motivated in part by his desire to split Catholic voters off from the Democratic party. In 1971, for example, he issued an order barring women married to military personnel from having abortions in military hospitals. He also urged Congress to increase aid to parochial schools. The president's appeal for law and order, call for tougher judges, and denunciations of obscenity, like his stand on abortion, were at least partially aimed at attracting support from white southerners and northern working-class Democrats, especially Catholics.

During his first term, Nixon worried that if George Wallace ran for president as an independent again in 1972, he might tip the balance in favor of a Democratic candidate. To counter this possibility, Nixon created a special task force to focus on increasing the number of Republican voters. The group, led by William Safire, explored ways to gain the support of what they called the "silent center" or "silent majority."

Nixon and his advisers targeted labor unions and their members to encourage defections from the Democratic party. The White House spread rumors that liberal labor leaders such as Walter Reuther, head of the United Automobile Workers, were socialists. At the same time, Nixon heaped praise on George Meany, the aging conservative leader of the AFL-CIO. The president went even further by soliciting support from the powerful and notoriously corrupt Teamster's Union. In 1971, he pardoned Jimmy Hoffa, the imprisoned former head of the union. Nixon's efforts paid off in 1972 when the AFL-CIO declined, for the first time in decades, to endorse a Democrat for president, and the Teamsters actively supported Nixon's reelection. In 1972, large numbers of working-class voters cast their presidential ballots for the Republican candidate.

Nixon implemented another scheme to fracture labor support for the Democrats. To nearly everyone's surprise, he embraced a policy by the federal Equal Employment Opportunity Commission (EEOC) to initiate "preferential treatment for minorities" in employment. He also backed the so-called Philadelphia Plan, an affirmative-action proposal to increase minority employment in the building trades. In truth, Nixon's interest in affirmative action had less to do with economic justice than with promoting friction between African Americans and white members of building-trades unions—two pillars of the Democratic party. Nixon made this point during his 1972 campaign. He denounced the Philadelphia Plan that he had supported three years earlier, declaring: "When young people apply for jobs and find the door closed because they don't fit into some numerical quota, despite their ability, and they object, I don't think it is right to condemn those young people as insensitive or even racist." Nixon's appeal to working-class whites hit home in 1972 partly because they were the first to feel the effects of a slowing economy. They also worried that any redistribution of wealth to poor minorities would come at their expense.

Nixon's War: Vietnam and Foreign Affairs

Part of Nixon's political insecurity stemmed from his difficulty in ending the Vietnam War. He had been a vigorous hawk on Vietnam since his days as Eisenhower's vice president, but by 1968 he had "come to the conclusion that there is no way to win the war." Of course, he added, "We can't say that." They would "have to say the opposite just to keep some degree of bargaining leverage."

The president's ability to maneuver was also hampered by a powerful antiwar movement. When he took office, 30,000 Americans had already died in Vietnam, almost half of them in the previous year. In reaction, a broad-based movement against the war had mobilized hundreds of thousands of demonstrators to march in Washington and other cities. Students, many politicians in both parties, and influential business leaders had come to oppose the war as a waste of lives and resources. Senator George Aiken, a Republican from Vermont, typified this view when he proclaimed that the United States should "declare victory" and get out of Vietnam. The war still had defenders in both parties, but even they saw no point in continuing the slaughter if the United States was not prepared to "win." But winning was nearly as hard to define as to achieve. The new president told his staff, "I am not going to end up like LBJ, holed up in the White House, afraid to show my face on the street. I'm going to end that war. Fast."

Nixon believed that centralizing the foreign-policy apparatus in the White House would allow him to cut a deal with North Vietnam as well as effectively handle the Soviet Union and even China. He did not want foreign policy run by, as he put it, "the striped pants faggots in the State Department." Instead, his powerful national security adviser, Henry Kissinger, would act for him.

Nixon's top foreign-policy adviser shared both his world outlook and his contempt for bureaucrats. Kissinger, who had fled Nazi Germany as a child, made his mark as a foreign-policy intellectual at

Harvard during the 1950s and 1960s. He shared Nixon's view that the Vietnam War had to be ended without the appearance of defeat, as a prelude to establishing new relationships with the Soviet Union and China. Under Nixon's supervision, Kissinger transformed the National Security Council from a bureaucratic backwater into a powerful presidential agency, mostly at the expense of the State Department.

Nixon respected Kissinger's intellect, and the professor recognized that he needed the president's power to implement his diplomatic designs. In private, however, they expressed contempt for each other. Kissinger referred to Nixon as a "meatball president" and a drunk. Nixon called his aide "my Jew Boy." Yet they agreed on larger policy goals and worked together well.

When Nixon entered the White House in 1969, he and Kissinger hoped to clinch a deal in Vietnam within six months. They proposed to Hanoi that it withdraw North Vietnamese troops from the South and promise not to resume fighting for what they informally called a "decent interval"—meaning, in effect, not until after Nixon was safely reelected in 1972. In return, U.S. forces would leave South Vietnam, though aid to the Saigon regime would continue. "Peace with honor," as Nixon called it, rather than a policy of "cut and run," would confirm U.S. power and the president's reputation. But he showed little interest in South Vietnam's long-term survival.

To Nixon's surprise, neither his threat to expand the war nor his promise of financial assistance following peace persuaded North Vietnam. Instead, Hanoi continued to demand the unconditional withdrawal of American forces and the cessation of all U.S. aid to South Vietnam. The Communist regime's determination to unify Vietnam as quickly as possible, rather than on Nixon's timetable, led to four more years of American military involvement in Southeast Asia.

Nixon recognized that he must reduce casualties and get the war out of the headlines even if he could not quickly end it. He adopted a strategy conceived at the end of the Johnson administration called "Vietnamization." This involved building up the strength of the army of South Vietnam, gradually withdrawing U.S. ground combat troops, and escalating the air war against North Vietnam. Nixon believed that once the North Vietnamese realized that they could not outlast American resolve or count on the antiwar movement to force his hand, they would accept his terms. In addition, the president undermined antiwar sentiment by substituting a fairer lottery system for the unpopular military draft, while simultaneously condemning war protesters as virtual traitors in league with the enemy.

Nixon and Kissinger also worked to improve relations with the Soviet Union and, more surprisingly, with the People's Republic of China (PRC). The American leaders believed that an improvement in relations with Moscow and Beijing, Hanoi's key allies, might increase Soviet and Chinese pressure on North Vietnam to compromise. But this policy of détente had importance beyond Vietnam. For the first time since the Cold War had begun, a U.S. president sought to manage competition with the Soviet Union and China through arms control rather than an arms race, and through expanded trade in place of an export ban.

The decision by Nixon and Kissinger to pursue détente reflected the fact that by the late 1960s, the Soviet Union had achieved something close to nuclear-weapons parity with the United States. Rather than plunging into another round of an expensive and dangerous race to regain nuclear superiority, the new administration favored a pact with Moscow to limit the number of long-range missiles on both sides and to refrain from developing or deploying an anti–ballistic missile (ABM) system capable of shooting down offensive nuclear-tipped missiles. They also hoped that expanded trade with the Soviet bloc would give Moscow an incentive to help preserve world stability.

The administration's opening to China was a bigger gamble. Nixon had always demonized Mao Zedong and his Communist revolutionaries. Indeed, American leaders had initially justified the Vietnam War as a way of containing China. But in August 1969, the Soviet Union and China, who had once been allies, had fallen out with each other and fought the first of several bloody skirmishes along their long, ill-defined border. Nixon and Kissinger saw an opportunity to "play the China card," as they put it, improving U.S. relations with Beijing as a lever to compel the Soviets to act more responsibly. Also, a China fearful of the Soviets (like a Soviet Union fearful of China) would have added reason to cooperate with the United States. A friendly China would be especially important in stabilizing Asia after U.S. forces exited Vietnam.

Nixon's secret approach to China began in 1969 and culminated with a dramatic presidential visit to the PRC in February 1972. The American public learned of the new policy in July 1971 when Nixon announced that Kissinger had met secretly with Chinese leaders in Beijing to discuss a presidential visit. Leading Democrats applauded the openings to the Soviet Union and China, but the Republican right was furious. Senator Barry Goldwater and Representative John Ashbrook of Ohio denounced Nixon for dealing with communist leaders and "selling out" Taiwan, the island held by the anticommunist Nationalist Chinese since 1949 and previously recognized by Washington as the legal government of China. Governor Reagan of California shared this view. Nixon managed to calm Reagan by explaining that the opening of relations with Communist China was justified as a way to undermine the Soviet Union, which was the greater Communist threat. But Reagan remained skeptical of dealing with any Communists. Suspicion of Nixon's pet policy of détente energized the Republican right in the later 1970s.

The Soviets, who feared U.S. cooperation with China, responded to Nixon's February 1972 visit to Beijing by hosting the president in Moscow three months later. Nixon and Soviet leader Leonid Brezhnev signed the Strategic Arms Limitation Treaty (SALT), and they soon agreed to bar missile defense (the ABM treaty) and expand trade. Neither China nor the Soviet Union abandoned North Vietnam, but both countries made it clear to Hanoi that they favored a compromise deal to end the war.

Between 1969 and 1972, Nixon steadily withdrew U.S. ground troops from Vietnam, reducing casualties and taking the steam out of the American antiwar movement. South Vietnam's army, helped by expanded U.S. aid and air support, improved its performance. After a North Vietnamese offensive failed in the spring of 1972, and as Nixon's reelection seemed a sure thing, the Vietnamese Communists began serious talks with Kissinger.

On October 26, 1972, two weeks before the U.S. presidential election, Hanoi and Washington reached a tentative agreement. It provided for a ceasefire in place, the return of prisoners, and the departure of U.S. troops. North Vietnamese forces retained control of large parts of South Vietnam, virtually assuring a resumption of the war following the U.S. withdrawal. Hanoi's main concession was agreeing that the United States could continue to aid the Saigon regime after its own forces left.

Following Nixon's reelection, negotiations again broke down, largely because of South Vietnam's opposition to the agreement. Partly to appease Saigon, Nixon unleashed yet another wave of B-52 bombers against Hanoi during Christmas 1972. When a formal treaty was signed in Paris in January 1973, Nixon proclaimed that he had achieved "peace with honor." But in spite of having extended the war for four more years, with hundreds of thousands of casualties on both sides, he had done little more than buy a few years' survival for the government of South Vietnam. Now that China, Asia's largest nation, had become what Kissinger called a "tacit ally," few Americans cared any longer about the fate of South Vietnam. The disputed "lessons" of Vietnam continued to divide Americans long after the last U.S. soldier departed that war-torn nation.

Nixon and other Republicans later blamed the Democratic Congress and the Watergate scandal for the U.S. failure to defend South Vietnam against a resumed North Vietnamese offensive in 1975. But by then, with American troops long gone and China a friendly state, the public had no interest in reentering the war. In any case, by the time North Vietnam swept to victory at the end of April 1975, Nixon had already been forced from office.

The Road to Watergate and Ruin

Shortly after Nixon resigned as president in August 1974, Kansas Senator Bob Dole, whom Nixon had earlier appointed and then removed as chairman of the Republican National Committee, quipped that "the Republican Party was not only *not* involved in Watergate, but it wasn't involved in the nomination, the convention, the campaign, the election, or the inauguration" of Richard Nixon to a second term. Dole's comment reflected the disillusionment with Nixon that he and millions of other Americans felt by 1974. The president had employed dirty tricks, burglaries, and intimidation to undermine his rivals and manipulate free elections.

Nixon viewed the 1970 congressional election as a rehearsal for his 1972 reelection campaign. In 1970, he frequently spoke of and to the "silent majority" that he claimed to represent. When Democratic candidates criticized his handling of the economy and failure to end the war in Vietnam, Nixon told his aides to "emphasize anti-crime, anti-demonstrations, anti-drug, anti-obscenity—get in touch with the mood of the country which is fed up with the liberals." This "stuff," he argued, was "dynamite politically."

Nixon assigned the task of attacking Democrats primarily to Vice President Spiro Agnew. In his angry, alliterative style, Agnew denounced student antiwar activists, journalists, and Democrats as "nattering nabobs of negativism," as well as "effete snobs and eunuchs" and "Radiclibs" out of touch with real Americans. Despite these attacks, Republican candidates fared poorly in the 1970 election. Democrats gained 9 House seats and lost a Senate seat in Tennessee, so that they now held a 255-180 majority in the House and an edge of 55-45 in the Senate. More ominous, the Democrats raised their total vote margin over the GOP from 1.1 million in the 1968 congressional election to 4.5 million in 1970. In state elections, Democrats stunned the GOP by ousting thirteen sitting Republican governors and losing only two of their own, a net gain of eleven. Even worse, an early presidential preference poll taken in May 1971 showed Senator Edmund Muskie, a Democrat from Maine, beating Nixon 47 percent to 39 percent.

These disappointing results and gloomy prospects aroused Nixon's worst tendencies. As he began campaigning for reelection, he changed his strategy from merely attacking and splitting the Democrats to manipulating events to weaken the election prospects of any opponent.

Nixon was especially worried about the impact of another presidential run by George Wallace. To weaken the Alabama populist, Nixon had secretly funded an unsuccessful gubernatorial bid against Wallace in 1970. Then fate intervened. On May 15, 1972, gunman Arthur Bremer shot and seriously wounded Wallace, forcing him to drop out of the upcoming presidential race. When he learned of the attack, Nixon ordered his aide Charles Colson (whom he praised for having the "balls of a brass monkey") to make it seem that the gunman was working for the Democrats. Colson sent E. Howard Hunt, a retired CIA operative then working for the president, to secretly break into Bremer's apartment to plant pro-Democratic materials. Presumably, this would turn Wallace's supporters against the Democrats and toward Nixon. But the FBI had already sealed the apartment. Colson and Hunt then planted false rumors with journalists that Bremer was a left-wing Democrat, rather than the mentally unbalanced young man that he actually was.

Nixon was also obsessed with Edward Kennedy, the Massachusetts Democratic senator and heir to the JFK legacy. Kennedy's car accident on Chappaquidick Island in July 1969, in which a female campaign worker died, had eclipsed his presidential prospects. But Nixon took no chances, assigning private investigators to snoop on Kennedy. Two years later, the surveillance became full-time. John Ehrlichman, Nixon's chief domestic adviser, explained that the president's operatives sought "evidence that will become part of our growing file of ammunition for use [against Kennedy] when and if it becomes necessary." Nixon hoped "We might just get lucky and catch this son of a bitch"; the goal was "ruining him for 1976" and perhaps permanently. Getting Kennedy was "going to be fun," he chortled.

Rattled by the weak GOP showing in the 1970 elections, Nixon created a separate presidential reelection organization in March 1971, headed by former attorney general John Mitchell. Called the Committee to Re-elect the President, the group became known by its unfortunate acronym, CREEP. Former commerce secretary Maurice Stans, the president's chief fundraiser, amassed a record-breaking $40 million campaign chest. Most of the money came from large corporations that had contracts with the federal government and feared retaliation if they did not contribute. In addition, to pay for "dirty tricks," Nixon also raised $2 million in secret contributions from wealthy personal friends. In contrast, the Republican National Committee collected barely $4 million for all GOP candidates in 1972.

Democrats, on the other hand, faced special fundraising problems. Nixon passed his growing "enemies list" on to the Internal Revenue Service in order for the agency to audit rich individuals who supported Democrats. Liberal Hollywood celebrities such as Barbra Streisand and Robert Redford, as well as pro-Democratic business leaders, were subjected to special audits and told that their problems would go away if they changed their donation habits.

Ironically, Nixon and CREEP put much of their energy and funds into helping Senator George McGovern of South Dakota win the Democratic presidential nomination. When the senator, far to the left of most Democrats, declared his candidacy in 1971, he seemed a long shot. But, as White House aide Pat Buchanan told Nixon, "McGovern is our candidate, the Goldwater of the Democratic Party." Buchanan and others in the White House worked to implement the secret plan to assure "McGovern's rise."

After the 1968 election, Democrats had implemented new rules for choosing a presidential candidate. These reforms reduced the influence of congressional Democrats and party "bosses," such as Chicago Mayor Richard J. Daley, in selecting convention delegates and increased the number of women and minority delegates. Most of the women, liberals, and antiwar and civil rights activists who were chosen in primaries or grassroots meetings favored McGovern over his rivals Edmund Muskie and former vice president Hubert Humphrey.

To assist McGovern's drive for the nomination, CREEP mounted numerous "dirty-tricks" operations to sow discord among Democrats. Among the sleazy actions were burglaries to steal sensitive information. The most notorious of these occurred on June 17, 1972, when five burglars were arrested inside the Democratic party headquarters in the Watergate office building in Washington, D.C. These five—along with two men on the outside, E. Howard Hunt and G. Gordon Liddy—composed a CREEP dirty-tricks team attempting to install listening devices on the telephones of Democratic officials.

Nixon denied any knowledge of what he instructed presidential spokesman Ron Ziegler to call a "third rate burglary." The president also stressed that those arrested were employed by CREEP, not the White House. Yet the team leaders, Hunt and Liddy, had previously worked directly for Nixon as part of his "plumbers" unit, which had engaged in break-ins and other illegal acts aimed at "enemies." It remains uncertain whether Nixon knew in advance that John Mitchell, the head of CREEP, had approved the Watergate break-in. However, the president had authorized previous criminal actions by the same group—and this, rather than the Watergate operation itself, made it important to hide his ties to them.

During the following nine months, through March 1973, Nixon and his close aides John Ehrlichman, H. R. Haldeman, and Charles Colson orchestrated an effective cover-up of presidential knowledge of the Watergate burglary and other crimes. They destroyed evidence and paid "hush money" to the burglars in exchange for their guilty pleas and their silence on Nixon's link to past criminal misconduct. And the brazen tactics worked, as Watergate stayed out of the headlines until Nixon had been safely reelected in November 1972.

As Nixon hoped, George McGovern had defeated his rivals and gained the Democratic presidential nomination. In contrast to the atmosphere at the 1968 party convention, McGovern's backers relished the opportunity to reject the credentials of an Illinois delegation selected by Chicago's Mayor Daley because it had not been chosen by the new procedures. The convention seated a rival delegation composed of large numbers of African Americans, Hispanics, and women. This led *Chicago Sun-Times* writer Mike Royko to complain in his nationally syndicated column that few Poles, Italians, or Slavs were included among the new delegates. Royko charged that the party's reforms "have disenfranchised Chicago's white ethnic Democrats which is a strange reform." Anyone hoping to revitalize the Democratic party by alienating ethnic white voters, he asserted, "would probably begin a diet by shooting himself in the stomach."

After some delegates took to mocking the entire process by proposing to nominate Mao Zedong as vice president, the convention heeded McGovern's plea to accept Senator Thomas Eagleton of Missouri as his running mate. But McGovern dropped him from the ticket a few weeks later after Eagleton confirmed that he had earlier received electric-shock therapy following a nervous breakdown. This carnival atmosphere gave some credence to the outrageous but evocative charge by Republican Senator Hugh Scott of Pennsylvania that McGovern and the Democrats were the party of the "Three A's— Acid, Abortion and Amnesty" (for draft resisters).

During the 1972 campaign, nearly everything went well for Nixon and poorly for McGovern. The news media largely ignored Watergate (52 percent of the public said in September that they had not heard of the break-in), and 90 percent of the nation's newspapers endorsed Nixon. Many Democratic officeholders deserted their party's nominee. Two weeks before the election, moreover, the hapless McGovern lost his only campaign issue, the Vietnam War. On October 26, 1972, Kissinger revealed that he had reached a tentative peace accord with North Vietnam, announcing: "Peace is at hand."

On November 7, Nixon won reelection in a 61 to 38 percent landslide. He received almost 18 million votes more than McGovern, losing only in Massachusetts and the District of Columbia. Despite the scale of Nixon's triumph, congressional Republicans actually lost two Senate seats and gained only twelve House seats. This gave the Democrats a majority of 243 to 192 in the House and 57 to 43 in the senate. In state races, the Democrats achieved a net gain of one governorship. This disappointing result for Republicans showed that many Democrats who had voted for Nixon had still voted for their own party in congressional and state contests. In fact, 30 percent of voters split their tickets, the highest proportion in history. The size of the remaining Democratic congressional majority would prove disastrous for Nixon, for throughout the course of 1973, the ugly details of the Watergate scandal began to unfold.

Right after the election, Nixon took the unusual step of asking his senior staff and cabinet for their resignations. The president promised to retain most of them, but he wanted a free hand to launch what he called a "New American Revolution" through a mass firing of bureaucrats. He complained privately that even many of his close associates were tainted by having worked with career officials who had been "screwing us for years." The time had come, he said, to "clean those bastards out." Nixon's wrath even fell on Henry Kissinger, whom he resented for surpassing him in favorable publicity. After reading an interview in which the national security adviser described himself as a "cowboy, leading the caravan alone astride his horse," Nixon snapped: "He's going back to Harvard; that's where he belongs."

The president backed off from his threatened purge and named Kissinger secretary of state. Nixon did remove the volatile Bob Dole as head of the Republican National Committee, giving the job to former Texas congressman and U.S. ambassador to the United Nations, George H. W. Bush. Colson, the White House aide, told Nixon that Bush "takes our line beautifully" and would be a useful mouthpiece for the president.

But Nixon had no opportunity to launch his New American Revolution. In March 1973, the Watergate cover-up began to unravel when one of the burglars, James McCord, told Judge John Sirica that "political pressure" had been applied to the defendants to have them plead guilty and "remain silent" about the involvement of high GOP officials. Sirica then sentenced Hunt, Liddy, and the other uncooperative defendants to lengthy prison terms in an attempt to pressure them to talk to government prosecutors and a recently formed Senate investigatory committee chaired by Democrat Sam Ervin of South Carolina. The formerly dormant press now took an increasing interest in the Watergate story. Bob Woodward and Carl Bernstein, two young *Washington Post* reporters, led the way in investigating Nixon's involvement.

Under this scrutiny, two presidential aides, Counsel John Dean and CREEP deputy Jeb Magruder, concluded that Nixon had set them up to take the blame for the Watergate burglary and cover-up. To protect themselves, Dean and Magruder cooperated with federal prosecutors and the Ervin committee, providing detailed information about the payment of hush money and other efforts to protect Nixon.

During the summer of 1973, the Watergate scandal became the focal point of national attention. Nixon continued to deny any involvement. He tried to appease critics by dismissing John Ehrlichman and H. R. Haldeman and appointing a special prosecutor to take over the haphazard Justice Department probe of the scandal.

In July 1973, the Ervin committee and Special Prosecutor Archibald Cox learned that Nixon had secretly recorded many of his Oval Office conversations, and they issued subpoenas for many of the tapes. Televised Senate hearings further eroded public confidence in the president's integrity. For the next year, Nixon fought doggedly to keep anyone from hearing the tapes. He claimed that "executive privilege" justified keeping secret his conversations with advisers. In reality, he hoped to keep the tapes private because they confirmed his involvement in numerous illegal activities.

Over several months, Nixon reluctantly surrendered a few tapes but refused to deliver the most incriminating evidence. In October 1973, he fired Archibald Cox for insisting on hearing the tapes. Public outrage forced Nixon to appoint a new special prosecutor, Leon Jaworski, who also demanded access to the tapes. In a series of rulings, federal courts dismissed Nixon's claims of executive privilege. On July 24, 1974, the Supreme Court unanimously ruled that while presidents had the authority to keep some information secret, Nixon must surrender the tapes because they were evidence in a criminal investigation.

Meanwhile, a scandal unrelated to Watergate further undermined the administration. On October 10, 1973, Vice President Spiro Agnew resigned and subsequently pleaded no contest to tax-evasion charges related to a bribery scheme. The Justice Department had discovered that Agnew, while governor of Maryland, had solicited kickbacks totaling $147,000 from contractors, including $17,000 he collected while he was vice president. Nixon quickly pushed Agnew out of office before talk of impeaching the vice president gained strength.

Implementing for the first time the Twenty-fifth Amendment to the Constitution, Nixon nominated House Minority Leader Gerald Ford of Michigan to replace Agnew. The moderately conservative and affable Ford was easily confirmed by Congress. But Nixon barely concealed his contempt for his eventual successor. In June 1974, during an Oval Office conversation with Nelson Rockefeller, Nixon asked, "Can you imagine Jerry Ford sitting in this chair?"

A month later, the House Judiciary Committee began discussing articles of impeachment against the president. According to polls, 75 percent of the American public believed Nixon had engaged in a criminal cover-up, and 66 percent favored his removal from office. On July 30, all the committee's Democrats, along with several Republicans, voted to impeach Nixon for obstruction of justice, abuse of power, and contempt of Congress.

Nixon's fate was sealed on August 5, 1974, when the White House released a long-sought tape made on June 23, 1972, five days after the Watergate break-in. This "smoking gun" tape confirmed that Nixon had conspired with his closest aides to cover up his ties to the Watergate burglars and had even tried to use the CIA and FBI as part of his effort to obstruct justice.

Republican support for Nixon in the House and Senate evaporated. Congressman Charles Wiggins of California, formerly one of the president's steadfast defenders, declared that "the public service of Richard Nixon must be terminated." Senator Barry Goldwater exclaimed, "There are only so many lies you can take and now there has been one too many. Nixon should get his ass out of the White House

—today." Even the ever-loyal Republican party chairman George Bush called on the president to resign.

Nixon delivered a televised speech on the evening of August 8 in which he announced his resignation. He acknowledged that "some of my judgments were wrong," but he denied committing any crimes worthy of impeachment. The president made the remarkable claim that he was quitting only because he lacked a "strong enough political base in Congress." As Nixon finished speaking, a boisterous crowd outside the White House gates chanted, "Jail to the Chief."

The next day, Nixon and his family flew home to California. The new president, Gerald Ford, declared: "My fellow Americans, our long national nightmare is over." Many Republicans feared that Watergate had consigned their party to permanent minority status. Yet, remarkably, it would not be all that long before a revitalized GOP pulled itself up out of the ashes of the Nixon presidency.

CHAPTER THREE

Stagnation, Malaise, and Conservative Revival, 1974–1980

The years 1974 through 1980 were characterized by widespread un-easiness among the American public. On July 15, 1979, President James E. "Jimmy" Carter confronted the nation's pessimistic mood in a televised address that became known as the "malaise speech." Carter, who originally had intended to discuss the nation's energy shortage and rising inflation rate, instead addressed what he called the country's "crisis of confidence." He claimed that this crisis posed a "fundamental threat to American democracy," because confidence was "the idea which founded our nation and which has guided our development as a people." The president insisted that this crisis would dissipate if Americans simply cultivated a more optimistic atti-tude. By contrast, Ronald Reagan and other Republicans blamed the country's malaise squarely on the failed leadership of President Carter and other Democrats. In fact, both Carter and Reagan were mistaken.

America's "crisis of confidence" in the 1970s resulted from con-crete, fundamental problems—not from psychological malaise nor from a lack of symbolic leadership. These problems included conflict over cultural values that had first exploded during the 1960s, public disillusionment over Vietnam and Watergate, economic stagnation and inflation, the federal government's inability to meet the increasing demands on it, and the decline of U.S. influence in global affairs. Hence, Americans' feelings of malaise were a result, not a cause, of these difficulties. By 1980, however, Reagan and other Republicans had successfully exploited these long-term structural troubles by blaming them on the recent policies of liberals and Democrats.

The first years of the 1974–80 period were characterized by public discontent over political deceit and economic stagnation. In 1976, Jimmy Carter, a relatively unknown Washington outsider, won the presidency by capitalizing on the era's reformist atmosphere, which had developed in reaction to the duplicity in government symbolized by the Vietnam War and the Watergate scandal. But victories by Carter and other Democrats in the mid-1970s represented only a fleeting public backlash against Republican scandals. Soon, voters shifted their concerns from political corruption to economic stagnation, which began in 1973 after three decades of unprecedented growth.

The political, social, and economic malaise of the 1970s generated new recruits for conservative Republicanism. The populist "New Right" reinforced socially conservative traditionalism, especially among southerners, at the grassroots level. Meanwhile, corporate America and "supply-side" economists reinvigorated a wave of fiscally conservative libertarianism. Finally, "neoconservative" intellectuals effectively criticized liberal polices at home and abroad. By the late 1970s, the expanding conservative movement had united behind the charismatic leadership of Republican Ronald Reagan.

As conservative Republicanism gained influence, Carter presided over the decline of Democratic and liberal influence. The breakdown of the New Deal coalition accelerated as southern conservatives increasingly left the party, while divisions widened between economic and cultural liberals. Conservative Republicans intensified discord among the Democrats by exploiting a backlash against liberal policies on such issues as race relations, crime, cultural values, feminism, the "rights revolution," "big government," and rising taxes. These domestic problems, as well as foreign-policy crises in Iran and Afghanistan, politically wounded Carter and the Democrats. In the 1980 elections, the GOP made important gains, including Ronald

Reagan's election as president and the attainment of a majority in the Senate. For the remainder of the twentieth century, conservative Republicanism would set the national agenda.

Watergate's Legacy, Political Reform, and Carter's 1976 Election

The mid-1970s were an era of political reform, a response to the political lies and corruption symbolized by the Vietnam War and the Watergate scandal. During his two years in office, President Gerald Ford sought to help America overcome this dispiriting legacy. Ford, a moderately conservative Midwestern Republican, projected an affable style that seemed well suited to bury the bitter Nixon-Watergate era. A month after Nixon's resignation, in September 1974, Ford attempted to close the book on Watergate, ending what he termed "our long national nightmare" by unconditionally pardoning his predecessor.

Ford's effort immediately backfired, permanently damaging his presidency. Pardoning the hated Nixon only reignited the issue of government corruption and caused Ford's public approval rating to plunge. Many observers criticized the new president for giving Nixon complete immunity from prosecution without having to even acknowledge any of his criminal acts. Others wondered if the pardon was part of a secret, prearranged bargain between Nixon and Ford. At the very least, the episode reinforced Ford's image as a bumbler. Journalist John Osborne spoke for many Americans when he wrote: "Gerald Ford is an awfully nice man who isn't up to the presidency."

In the 1974 midterm elections, Democrats won large, widespread victories by exploiting Watergate's legacy, Ford's pardon of Nixon, and a deep economic recession. In the House, Democrats made a net gain of 43 seats for a 291-144 margin, their second largest majority in nearly four decades. In the Senate, they added three seats for a 61-38 majority. At the state level, they gained an incredible 20 governors—the largest one-election increase in 36 years—for a commanding 36-13 majority. Democrats won many of these elections in solid Republican districts, especially in the suburbs and in the Midwest. Although these gains proved temporary, they stunned contemporary observers, especially Republicans who had hoped that Nixon's victories in 1968 and 1972 signaled the beginning of a permanent GOP majority.

The 1974 elections brought a new generation of politicians to Congress. Many in this "class of '74," which was the largest freshman group since 1948, had campaigned on a reform agenda. In the post-1968 dealignment atmosphere, these "Watergate babies" (as they became known) embodied a new political style that was less tied to traditional party loyalty. Party power and loyalty to party ebbed substantially among the new political generation. For example, party-line voting in the House dropped from 60 percent in the 1930s to 37 percent in the 1970s. As Democrat Richard A. Gephardt of Missouri put it, "There is nothing the [Democratic] leadership can offer me."

The public outrage ignited by the Watergate scandal helped this new generation of legislators initiate an era of political reform. Prodded by lobbying groups and public pressure, Congress enacted a series of changes in the mid-1970s designed to prevent future corruption. New congressional rules reduced the power of seniority and of committee chairs and set stricter rules for raising and spending campaign funds. Congress also passed a major campaign-reform law overhauling the existing system of financing election campaigns and enacted several other laws designed to guard against future presidential corruption and abuse of power.

Congressional reformers appeared especially eager to reign in the "imperial presidency" in foreign policy, hoping to prevent future Vietnam-type wars. In 1973, Congress passed, over Nixon's veto, the War Powers Act, which required the president to get congressional approval for any prolonged use of U.S. troops abroad. At the time South Vietnam fell, Congress also demonstrated its unwillingness to acquiesce to the "imperial presidency." American troops had left Vietnam in 1973, though U.S. economic and military aid to South Vietnam continued. In April 1975, Communists made their final assault on the capital of Saigon. Congress, reflecting the public's attitude, rejected Ford's last-ditch request for $1 billion in additional emergency aid, and the Communists soon conquered South Vietnam as U.S. personnel scrambled from the American embassy. The legislative challenge to the executive branch in foreign affairs was bolstered by congressional investigations revealing nefarious U.S. practices abroad, including several CIA-backed assassination plots against foreign leaders.

In the 1976 presidential campaign, Jimmy Carter rode the anti-Vietnam, anti-Watergate reformist wave all the way to the White House. Carter, the little-known former governor of Georgia, seemingly came out of nowhere to win first the Democratic nomination and then the general election. He ran primarily on the issue of restoring public trust in government, pledging reforms to make government more open and efficient and telling Americans that they deserved a "government as good as they were." A devout born-again Christian, Carter stressed the "character issue" and spurned the imperial presidency with his simple style. He also capitalized on his status as a Washington outsider, one untainted by corruption, proudly declaring: "I'm not a lawyer, I'm not a member of Congress, and I've never served in Washington." Most important, Carter directly addressed the public's sense of betrayal by Nixon and other leaders when he looked the American people in the eye and declared, "I will never lie to you."

Meanwhile, many conservative Republicans repudiated President Ford, despite his pro-business agenda. Most galling to them was Ford's appointment of their longtime nemesis, the moderate Nelson Rockefeller, as vice president. They also criticized the Ford administration for failing to attack the liberals' social agenda; indeed, First Lady Betty Ford was an outspoken supporter of abortion rights and other socially liberal causes. In addition, GOP conservatives denounced Ford for retaining Henry Kissinger as secretary of state and for continuing the Nixon-Kissinger policies of détente and nuclear-arms control with the USSR, policies they believed favored the Soviets. "Under Kissinger and Ford," charged Ronald Reagan, "this nation has become number two in a world where it is dangerous—if not fatal—to be second best."

In the 1976 Republican presidential primaries, conservatives rallied behind Reagan, the former governor of California. Ford tried to appease the right by removing Rockefeller from the ticket in favor of a conservative, Senator Robert Dole of Kansas. The president won most of the early GOP primaries in the Northeast and Midwest, but

Reagan ran especially well in the Sunbelt. In the end, Ford narrowly won the nomination by a margin of 1,187 to 1,070, the closest Republican contest in twenty-four years. The nomination of Ford marked the final time that moderates controlled the GOP; after 1976, Reagan and the conservative movement dominated the party.

In the general elections, Democrats recaptured the presidency and maintained their large majorities at all levels of government by again exploiting the Republican legacy of Watergate, Ford's pardon of Nixon, and economic insecurity. The main surprise was the closeness of the presidential contest. "We could run an aardvark this year and win," one Democrat had joked in early 1976. But Carter just barely edged out Ford by 50 to 48 percent in the popular vote and 297 to 240 in the electoral college—the smallest margin in six decades. Carter won by cobbling together the unstable remnants of the Democratic coalition, but he lacked stature as a party leader and displayed weak coattails. Democrats managed to add only a single seat in the House for a 292-143 lead, retained their 62-38 Senate majority, and gained one governor for a 37-12 margin over the Republicans. Carter's slim victory against a weak opponent was an inauspicious beginning for his administration. More significant, the mid-1970s represented merely an "Indian summer" of Democratic dominance.

Economic Stagnation: The End of the Postwar Boom

During the 1970s, Americans increasingly shifted their political concerns from the Watergate scandal to economic stagnation, as the U.S. economy slowed after decades of rapid growth. By 1979, nearly 70 percent of Americans viewed the economy as the country's most important issue, while fewer than 10 percent focused on social problems—a marked change from the 1960s and early 1970s. In November 1973, the postwar boom ended with an energy crisis and a subsequent recession that lasted seventeen months. It was the longest and deepest downturn since the Great Depression, and it proved to be the beginning of a lengthy period of slowed economic growth. The gross national product (GNP), which had expanded at an average annual rate of 4 percent in the

1960s, grew at less than half that yearly rate (1.8 percent) from 1973 to 1982.

These slower growth rates highlighted America's relative decline in the world economy, as the nation faced increasing competition from Western Europe, Japan, and East Asia. Alarmingly, the U.S. economy seemed less able to compete globally: productivity rose at an average annual rate of just 0.8 percent during the 1973–79 period, one-fourth the level of the 1960s. International competition proved especially worrisome in the crucial sectors of oil, automobiles, steel, and electronics. As a result, the 1970s saw the beginning of large and climbing U.S. trade deficits.

Rising inflation rates were the most prominent feature of the troubled economy. Inflation first took hold during the 1973 energy crisis. Two years later, America was suffering its highest peacetime inflation in history, and by 1980 the annual rate reached 13.5 percent. The real worth of the U.S. dollar fell by more than half from 1973 to 1981. These numbers stood in sharp contrast to those of the 1962–73 period, when inflation had averaged only 4.1 percent annually.

The inflation resulted mainly from soaring prices for energy, especially oil. In 1973, U.S. support for Israel during a Middle Eastern war provoked an embargo by Israel's enemies, the Arab members of the global oil cartel OPEC (Organization of Petroleum Exporting Countries), on the export of oil to the United States. The embargo eventually ended, but petroleum prices stayed high throughout the 1970s, and OPEC hiked prices again during the Iranian Revolution of 1979. Overall, oil prices increased eightfold in just nine years. The energy crisis rippled throughout the U.S. economy, which was based heavily on oil. It led to long lines at gas stations, soured the nation's love affair with large automobiles, threatened the "freedom" of the open road, prompted the government to reduce highway speed limits, and forced Americans to turn down their thermostats during what proved to be unseasonably cold winters. U.S. leaders could do little to influence the foreign sources of inflation, which aggravated public discontent. Conservatives attempted to use these problems to herald their antigovernment message. "Our problem isn't a shortage of oil," claimed Republican Ronald Reagan, "it's a surplus of government."

To make matters worse, the inflationary pressures occurred simultaneously with rising joblessness. Unemployment, which had averaged 4.7 percent from 1962 to 1972, grew to 7.4 percent during the 1973–86 period. In 1975, it reached 9.2 percent, the highest figure since the Great Depression. Typically, there had been a trade-off in the U.S. economy between inflation and unemployment: lower inflation resulted in higher unemployment, and vice versa. In the 1970s, however, economic stagnation and high unemployment combined with high inflation to create a novel phenomenon known as "stagflation," which confounded liberal Keynesian ideas about active management of the economy. The public became increasingly pessimistic about the future of the U.S. economy and the American lifestyle. For example, polls in 1980 revealed that 75 percent of Americans agreed with the statement, "We are fast coming to a turning point in our history. The land of plenty is becoming the land of want."

These national-level economic problems drove down the incomes and wages of ordinary Americans. After three decades of high growth, real (inflation-adjusted) median family income stagnated over the next two decades. By 1990, 80 percent of families had real incomes lower than in 1973. The working class bore the brunt of stagflation. The real hourly wages of the average worker, which had risen 75 percent from 1947 to 1973, dropped 9 percent between 1973 and 1998. Finally, unemployment in manufacturing sectors soared within the northern and Midwestern heartland, which became known as the Rustbelt.

Despite their lower real incomes, millions of Americans paid more in income taxes because inflation drove them into higher tax brackets (which were not adjusted for inflation). Being squeezed between stagnant real incomes, rising inflation, and higher taxes proved psychologically damaging, threatening middle-class dreams of rising living standards, social mobility, and home ownership. In 1980, only one-sixth of Americans felt "better off" economically, while two-fifths felt "worse off." As one observer asked, "What happens when the . . . growth machine begins to falter at the very moment when the population's appetites have been whetted and its expectations have reached unprecedented heights?"

One answer was that the American electorate punished what it viewed as presidential mismanagement of the economy. In the 1974 and 1976 elections, many voters blamed stagflation on the policies of

Republican presidents Nixon and Ford, showing their displeasure by voting for Democrats. In 1976, Jimmy Carter prevailed in part by faulting the Ford administration for the nation's high "misery index" (the combination of inflation and unemployment rates), which reached 12.7 percent on Election Day. Postelection polls showed that Carter won 75 percent of those voters whose primary concern was jobs. But the economic issue cut both ways. Continued stagflation under Carter helped the GOP make electoral gains, especially in 1980, when that same misery index hit 20.1 percent on Election Day.

The economic problems of the 1970s also transformed corporate behavior. Overall after-tax profits, which had been 10 percent in 1965, averaged only 6 percent from 1975 to 1979 and fell to 5 percent in 1980. To raise profits, corporations often adopted drastic measures. Many businesses gave up high-cost manufacturing in the United States, turning to foreign factories and spurring the deindustrialization of the economy. This resulted in the loss of 38 million industrial jobs during the 1970s, most of them in the Rustbelt, and further weakened the influence of organized labor. Corporate America also responded to its economic problems with an aggressive political mobilization behind the Republican party and the conservative movement, which was now undergoing a revival.

The Growing Conservative Movement

Economic discontent helped the conservative movement, which grew in organizational strength and popular appeal during the 1970s. The movement built upon the earlier conservatism of the 1960s, which had "fused" the right's main factions: socially conservative traditionalists, fiscally conservative libertarians, and anticommunists and antiliberals. But fusionist conservatives had never commanded a nationwide majority, as Barry Goldwater's 1964 trouncing confirmed. During the 1970s, however, each faction of the conservative coalition received reinforcements. Traditionalists enlisted recruits from the socially conservative New Right. Libertarians gained backing from fiscally conservative business leaders and supply-side economists. And anticommunists and antiliberals found allies among neoconservative intellectuals.

The New Right movement supplied reinforcements for socially conservative traditionalism. The older fusionist conservatism had tended toward elitism, disdained mass culture and politics, and focused on "national security, free market economics . . . and [opposing] U.S.-Soviet détente," observed conservative author Kevin Phillips. By contrast, the New Right tended toward populism and highlighted emotional social issues. Its strength was centered among white, southern, working-class and middle-class evangelical Protestants. Yet the differences between the brands of conservatism were less ideological than tactical. The New Right simply updated the message of earlier traditionalists to confront the new context of 1970s America. "There is not a great deal that is new about the New Right," conceded conservative organizer Richard Viguerie. "It is our emphasis that is different at times."

A key to the New Right's success was its development of new tactics and organizational methods, which enabled professional activists to mobilize a mass base for conservative causes. While working for the Goldwater and Wallace campaigns in the 1960s, Viguerie and other organizers had compiled huge computerized lists of individuals, businesses, and groups willing to finance conservative causes. By the 1970s, Viguerie's firm, RAVCO, and other fundraising companies were using these lists to underwrite right-wing efforts. In 1974, the New Right movement coalesced when RAVCO and like-minded groups began coordinating their activities. The movement's success showed that "conservatives have learned how to recruit, how to organize, and how to successfully market ideas," observed Viguerie.

New Right organizers exploited divisive cultural issues in their direct-mail fundraising appeals. These emotional "wedge issues" focused on opposition to such cultural changes as "easy divorce, abortion-on-demand, gay rights, militant feminism, unisex facilities, and leniency toward pornography, prostitution, and crime," noted the Rev. Tim LaHaye, chairman of the American Coalition for Traditional Values. New Right fundraising appeals were provocative and direct. The "shriller you are," admitted Terry Dolan of the National Conservative Political Action Committee, "the easier it is to raise funds." For example, one appeal read: "Dear friend, I am rushing you this urgent letter because the children in your neighborhood are in danger. How would you feel if tomorrow your child . . . was taught by a practicing homosexual?" Another fundraising letter urged: "Stop the baby killers. . . . These anti-life baby killers are already organizing, working and raising money to re-elect pro-abortionists. . . . Abortion means killing a live baby."

The New Right's exploitation of emotional wedge issues mobilized grassroots conservatives, especially the white, evangelical-fundamentalist Protestants of the "New Religious Right." A main issue for this group was the threatened termination of federal tax exemptions for racially segregated Christian schools. In 1978, the Internal Revenue Service (IRS) proposed strict new guidelines for receiving tax exemptions. The New Religious Right perceived the IRS ruling as intrusive, mean-spirited, and harmful.

Religious conservatives reacted to the IRS "attack" on their schools with large-scale political mobilization. "The Christian school issue was the one thing that turned everyone on," recalled Robert Billings, Sr., of the National Christian Action Coalition. "Moral Majority came on the heels of that." In 1979, the Christian school movement helped television evangelist Jerry Falwell to establish the Moral Majority, the New Religious Right's foremost political organization. "We're going to single out those people in government who are against what we consider to be the Bible, moralist position," Falwell declared.

GOP conservatives aggressively courted the support of the New Religious Right. In 1979, congressional Republicans prohibited the IRS from revoking the tax-exempt status of racially segregated Christian schools. A year later, the 1980 GOP platform promised: "We will halt the unconstitutional regulatory vendetta launched by Mr. Carter's IRS Commissioner against independent schools." The New Religious Right showed its appreciation by mobilizing behind the Republican party. In 1976, Democrat Jimmy Carter, himself a born-again Christian, had secured 56 percent of the white fundamentalist vote. Four years later, however, Republican Ronald Reagan, running against Carter, received 61 percent of their vote—including 85 percent of the self-described "most fundamentalist" of white Protestants.

While socially conservative traditionalists gained reinforcements from the New Right during the 1970s, fiscally conservative libertarians drew new strength from corporate America. Beginning in World War II, big business had cooperated with big government and big labor to promote economic growth. Until 1973, this "growth coalition" produced high corporate profits, rising wages and consumption, and increasing government spending and investment. In such profitable times, most business leaders felt little need to associate with such unpopular conservatives as Barry Goldwater. But the end of the postwar boom in 1973 spurred corporate America to transform its economic and political strategies. Executives worried by lower profits viewed themselves as being under attack from global competition, labor militants, and the consumer and environmental movements. They reacted by abandoning the growth coalition. "The leaders of industry," charged Douglas Fraser, president of the United Automobile Workers (UAW), "have broken and discarded the fragile and unwritten compact previously existing during past periods of growth and progress."

Corporate America also unified and expanded its political power. During the 1970s, big business overcame the narrow interests of individual industries and companies by creating umbrella lobbying organizations such as the Business Roundtable. From 1971 to 1982, moreover, the number of individual businesses with registered lobbyists in Washington skyrocketed from 175 to 2,445. Corporate America also became more directly involved in politics by funding candidates through political action committees (PACs). In 1980, for example, corporate PACs contributed $19 million to pro-business politicians.

In addition, corporations increasingly financed a conservative "counterestablishment" of nonprofit foundations and think tanks. Businesses shifted much of their funding from older, nonideological establishment institutions to newer right-wing organizations such as the American Enterprise Institute, the Heritage Foundation, and the Hoover Institution. In so doing, they created a conservative counterestablishment that intertwined corporate funding, right-wing intellectuals, and political power, especially within the Republican party. In return for this funding, conservative intellectuals provided pro-business, antilabor, antigovernment arguments for public consumption. The corporate mobilization behind the conservative movement proved successful; by the 1980s, business influence in politics had reached its highest level since the 1920s. UAW president Fraser aptly described the post-1973 corporate onslaught as a "one-sided class war."

An important component of the conservative counterestablishment was a group of maverick economists known as supply siders, who bolstered libertarianism by championing new rationales for fiscally conservative policies. In the late 1970s, the dominance of liberal Keynesian theories in the field of economics had been somewhat undermined by stagflation—stagnant growth and unemployment concurrent with inflation. Neither liberal Keynesians nor conservative monetarists could offer a painless solution to these twin problems. Rejecting both Keynesian and monetarist theories, supply-side economists proposed a politically popular, though economically dubious, answer to stagflation.

Supply siders advocated an unorthodox combination of cutting taxes to encourage growth while simultaneously tightening the money supply to reduce inflation. They based this policy on the premise that growth resulted primarily from stimulating the market's supply side rather than its demand side, a theory that directly challenged the Keynesian consensus that had prevailed since the Great Depression. If supply was indeed more important than demand, then it was imperative to encourage entrepreneurs and wealthy investors to put money into the marketplace by slashing their capital-gains and income taxes. Hence, "supply-side economics is frankly reactionary," as neoconservative Irving Kristol conceded.

A major problem with supply-side theory was the fear, expressed by most economists (especially orthodox fiscal conservatives), that vast tax cuts would create enormous budget deficits. Supply siders answered that lower tax rates would *increase* total tax revenues and hence *reduce* the deficit. This imaginative claim rested on the Laffer Curve, the brainchild of supply-sider Arthur Laffer, which purported to show that high tax rates curbed an individual's incentive to make more income and thus pay more taxes. By lowering the tax rate, Laffer claimed, individuals would invest, work, and earn so much more and make the economy grow so quickly that total tax revenues would increase. These exaggerated claims led skeptics to dismiss such arguments as "voodoo economics." Indeed, we now know that the Laffer Curve proved accurate only at extremely high tax rates,

nearing 100 percent. And indeed, the enactment of supply-side policies in the 1980s did result in enormous federal deficits, just as
Keynesians and orthodox fiscal conservatives had predicted.

In the late 1970s, however, the enticing political advantages of
supply-side economics overcame its deficiencies as economic science. The supply-side program promised to raise productivity and
growth, lower inflation, cut taxes, maintain funding for popular social
programs, and decrease the federal budget deficit. Supply-side ideas
were promulgated on the pages of libertarian journals and newspapers, especially the *Wall Street Journal*. In 1978, a group of libertarians asked GOP presidential candidate Ronald Reagan to endorse
supply-side economics. Convincing Reagan proved easy; supply
side's antitax emphasis and rosy predictions about economic growth
fit perfectly with Reagan's hatred of taxes and optimistic outlook.

As the New Right reinforced traditionalism, and corporate
America and supply-side economists bolstered libertarianism, neoconservative intellectuals strengthened the assault on liberalism.
Neoconservatives constituted a small but influential group of former
liberals and leftists who had grown disillusioned with the direction of
modern liberalism. They claimed that liberalism and the Democratic
party had been hijacked in the late 1960s by a well-educated "New
Class" that included government bureaucrats, peace activists, social
workers, radical professors, teachers' unions, and public-interest lawyers. The neoconservatives charged that this New Class had seduced
liberal Democrats into abandoning their core principles of unyielding anticommunism, merit-based social mobility, and traditionalist
values. "In fevered depravity the last Liberals ran riot through
the 1970s gibbering: consciousness-raising! self-realization! group-
therapy! human rights! animal rights!" complained neoconservative
R. Emmett Tyrrell, Jr. "This is light-years removed from the New
Deal."

In the late 1970s, most neoconservatives finally gave up on the
Democratic party and joined the GOP. As members of the intellectual
establishment, they made criticism of liberalism from the right ac-
ceptable among intellectuals. Neoconservative editor Norman Podhoretz later maintained that "if the grip of conventional liberal wis-
dom and leftist orthodoxy had not been loosened by the criticisms of
the [neoconservatives], . . . Ronald Reagan would in all probability

have been unable to win over the traditionally Democratic constitu-
ents." As conservative voters deserted the Democrats, they found a
new home in the GOP, which was increasingly dominated by the conservative movement.

The Decay of the Democratic Party
and the Backlash against Liberalism

As conservative Republicanism gained a larger following in the late
1970s, the Democratic coalition continued its steady decay. Many
contemporary observers assumed that Democratic victories in the
1974 and 1976 elections had restored the party's grip on national
power. For example, President Carter's pollster Patrick Caddell concluded after the 1976 election that "we find [the GOP] in deep
trouble." But it soon became apparent that many voters had only temporarily rebuked Republicans. Democrats made their largest inroads
among upper-middle-class citizens who traditionally voted for the
GOP but were now disgusted by Watergate. This support proved
short-lived, however.

The Democrats' post-Watergate victories masked the breakdown
of their party. "If this were France," remarked House Speaker Thomas P. "Tip" O'Neil, "the Democratic party would be five parties."
Most noticeably, conservative whites in the South and elsewhere continued their post-1964 shift to Republican candidates, especially
in presidential voting. This shift widened the partisan divide over
race, particularly in major metropolitan localities where the growth
of Democratic black power in the inner city provoked increased support for Republicans in surrounding white suburban areas. "A 'white
noose' was tightening" around black inner cities, historian James T.
Patterson later wrote.

In addition to its conservative-liberal split, the Democratic party
faced growing divisions between economic and social/cultural liberals. Economic liberals, found mainly among the working class, emphasized labor issues. Led by unions, they had formed the core of the
Democrats' coalition since the New Deal. But the power of economic
liberals weakened in the party and in society because union member-

ship continued its long-term decline, which had begun in the 1950s. Organized labor made its own troubles worse by proving too bureaucratized to respond effectively to the political assault by conservatives and corporate America after 1973.

Labor's power was also challenged within the Democratic party by social and cultural liberals. These "lifestyle liberals" tended to be members of the upper middle class who had been mobilized mainly by such social issues as civil rights, the antiwar movement, the counterculture, feminism, and environmentalism. Their growing influence helped George McGovern win the 1972 Democratic nomination. After the Democratic landslide in the 1974 midterm elections, the number of lifestyle liberals rose in Congress, where they spearheaded the reform efforts of the post-Watergate era. But their priorities often clashed with those of economic liberals. "If you're hungry and out of work, eat an environmentalist," read one popular union bumper sticker.

As the Democratic coalition disintegrated into individual factions, each bloc increasingly focused on its own concerns. Indeed, many Democrats shifted their main loyalty from the party to such single-issue lobbying groups as the AFL-CIO, the NAACP, the National Organization for Women, and the Sierra Club. Thus, they failed to defend the general interest and to address the larger concerns of society, allowing Republicans to depict single-issue Democrats as selfish "special interests."

It was Jimmy Carter's unfortunate fate to preside over the decay of the Democratic coalition in the late 1970s. During Carter's administration, conservatives and Republicans won converts to their cause by exploiting a growing backlash against a series of crises confronting American society—crises that they blamed on Democrats, especially liberals. In truth, most of these problems had long-term causes unconnected to any recent policies. Furthermore, the country's leadership, including President Carter, was hardly uniformly liberal. Yet liberals and Democrats responded ineffectively to these attacks, for they lacked a unified agenda that appealed to a majority of voters. Ronald Reagan spoke for many conservatives when he asserted that, "for the average American, the message is clear—liberalism is no longer the answer, it is the problem."

Reagan and other conservative Republicans profited from a growing voter reaction to liberal policies on such impassioned issues as race, crime, cultural and gender values, government spending, and taxes. Beginning in the 1960s, racial attitudes turned increasingly partisan, becoming a principal issue separating the two major parties. For example, 69 percent of Americans in 1980 said that the Democrats were likely to help racial and ethnic minorities, while only 11 percent said the same about Republicans (under the leadership of Ronald Reagan). Paradoxically, Reagan's strong opposition to affirmative action was taken as a given by the electorate, allowing him to employ race-neutral language. Thus, he appealed to segregationists without offending racially moderate whites.

In the late 1970s, Reagan and other conservative Republicans capitalized on a white backlash against racial preferences. After the enactment of civil rights laws in the 1960s, the main racial issue shifted from equal legal rights for historically oppressed groups to compensatory treatment for them through affirmative action and quotas. Most liberals supported these programs. "Conservative egalitarians," on the other hand, opposed racial preferences because they exemplified "reverse discrimination" against whites and supposedly undermined the American ideal of equal opportunity. Conservatives also portrayed minorities as whiny, selfish "special interests" who demanded preferred treatment. And they insisted that minorities should help themselves through self-discipline, education, hard work, and personal responsibility. "People—all people, black or white, rich or poor—may be unequally responsible for what has happened to them in the past, but all are equally responsible for what they do next," declared conservative sociologist Charles Murray.

Prodded by conservative rhetoric, whites increasingly (and overwhelmingly) rejected compensatory treatment for past racial discrimination. By 1980, polls found that two-thirds of whites opposed government "special help" to minorities, three-quarters rejected racial preferences in college admissions, and nearly nine-tenths opposed preferences in job hiring. Additionally, fewer than one in five Americans believed that the government should work to improve African Americans' social and economic position.

Race also became increasingly intertwined in the public mind with several other contentious issues, especially crime. Between 1960 and 1980, the number of reported crimes quadrupled, and violent-crime rates soared even higher. As the fear of crime became an urgent issue, especially in major cities, crime increasingly appeared to be connected to race in the public's mind. African Americans composed 11 percent of the population, but in victim surveys (the most accurate measure of crime), they represented 30 percent of the perpetrators of assault and 62 percent for robberies.

Conservatives exploited the growing white backlash against crime by blaming it on "permissiveness" toward criminals (especially blacks) by "liberal" politicians, judges, and lawyers. The right also criticized civil libertarians who demanded fairer treatment for defendants and prisoners. "We could adopt a better approach to crime control by showing criminals the same kind of mercy they show their victims," asserted conservative columnist Walter E. Williams. As crime rates soared, liberal views toward defendants and prisoners became extremely unpopular: "A conservative is a liberal who's been mugged," went one joke of the day. Influenced by conservative rhetoric and rising crime rates, attitudes toward criminal defendants hardened. In the mid-1960s, 48 percent of Americans believed that courts were "too lenient" toward defendants; by the late 1970s, this figure had soared to 83 percent. Meanwhile, opposition to the death penalty fell from 47 to 27 percent.

Just as conservatives blamed "liberal permissiveness" for tolerating crime, they condemned the counterculture for permitting behavior that traditionalists considered immoral or sinful. Although the mainstream media consistently denigrated hippies, the counterculture in fact reshaped America's popular culture beginning in the late 1960s by effectively promoting such values as tolerance, egalitarianism, self-expression, personal freedom, and individual fulfillment. The counterculture also angered traditionalists by questioning such authority figures as religious leaders, the military establishment, parents, and university administrators.

Conservatives hated the counterculture for creating what they saw as a widespread moral crisis. They also blamed middle-class lifestyle liberals for supposedly leading the poor astray by setting an example of recreational drug use, sexual experimentation, and non-traditional gender roles. "Our nation's moral fiber is being weakened by the growing homosexual movement and the fanatical [Equal Rights Amendment] pushers (many of whom publicly brag they are lesbians)," claimed conservative Congressman Philip Crane of Illinois. Howard Phillips of the Conservative Caucus argued that the only answer to America's moral crisis was to "resort to biblical law." This cultural war served as the primary issue mobilizing both the New Right and neoconservatives against "godless militant gays, liberal educators and vicious atheists [working to implement] a master plan to destroy everything that is good and moral here in America," in the overwrought allegations of the Rev. Robert G. Grant of the Christian Voice.

The most successful countercultural movement was feminism, which helped transform popular attitudes toward gender roles, sexuality, and family patterns. By the late 1970s, most women (and most men) agreed with feminism's basic goal: equal opportunity regardless of gender. A majority of Americans also supported abortion rights and the women's Equal Rights Amendment to the Constitution, which Congress had approved in 1972 and sent to the states for ratification (where it was narrowly defeated by a grassroots movement led by the antifeminist Phyllis Schlafly). Women also made remarkable strides toward equality in professional education and in the workplace during the 1970s. From 1973 to 1983, for example, the number of law degrees earned by women climbed from 8 to 36 percent, and the female proportion of new MBAs soared from 5 to 29 percent. Changing gender roles were similarly evidenced by the growing rates of abortion, divorce, and married women working outside the home. From 1972 to 1980, the annual number of reported abortions nearly tripled, from 600,000 to 1.6 million—an increase aided by the Supreme Court's 1973 *Roe* v. *Wade* decision legalizing abortion nationwide. Between 1965 and 1980, moreover, the divorce rate doubled, and the number of working wives grew from 36 to 51 percent.

Conservatives viewed all of these changes negatively and blamed them on feminist propaganda. "Women's lib has . . . left behind it a vast wreckage of broken and twisted lives," claimed neoconservative

Norman Podhoretz. In reality, many of the profound changes in gender roles and family structure resulted from long-term social trends occurring in all economically advanced nations during the twentieth century. Furthermore, conservatives were offering few genuine solutions to the "breakdown of the traditional family," because they refused to interfere with the capitalist market (the prime factor pushing mothers into the workplace) and opposed government programs designed to help families squeezed by market forces.

Nevertheless, the right thrived in the 1970s by inciting a backlash against a caricatured version of feminism. Conservatives portrayed feminism as a fad promoted by selfish, elitist liberal propagandists, while they identified antifeminism with "pro-family values" and "average families." In feminist thought, conservative Connie Marsher asserted, "family interferes with self-fulfillment." Televangelist Pat Robertson signed a fundraising letter that summed up the conservative view; in it, he described the feminist agenda as "socialist . . . encourag[ing] women to leave their husbands, kill their children, destroy capitalism and become lesbians."

The right similarly condemned liberal support for marginalized groups (in addition to racial minorities and women) who sought to expand their rights and privileges under the law. These groups included criminal defendants, prisoners, homosexuals, youths, American Indians, the poor, immigrants, and the mentally or physically disabled. Conservatives derided this "rights revolution." Liberalism has "decayed into the party whose doctrine of rights has soured every human relationship," wrote conservative publisher R. Emmett Tyrrell. Liberal victories expanding rights often came by decisions of judges and federal agencies rather than elected officials. Conservatives therefore charged that "unelected liberal elites" had usurped the power of ordinary people and their elected representatives. These charges helped sour public views toward government. By 1980, 49 percent of Americans considered government "too powerful," compared with only 15 percent who thought that it was "not strong enough."

In the late 1970s, antigovernment sentiment focused on soaring federal spending and climbing tax rates. From 1960 to 1980, federal expenditures skyrocketed from $92 billion to $590 billion (unadjusted for inflation). Yet Americans remained ambivalent in their views on government spending, as polls showed that most of the public approved of more federal funding for Social Security, Medicare, and social-welfare programs helping individuals to acquire jobs, higher education, and home or business loans. In fact, in 1980, at the height of antigovernment sentiment, a majority of Americans favored less spending in just two main federal programs: foreign aid (a tiny portion of the budget) and welfare.

Conservatives therefore focused middle-class anger at welfare spending on the poor. Indeed, the term *welfare* no longer applied in general usage to such popular, universal programs as Social Security and Medicare, which actually consumed the great majority of social spending. Instead, *welfare* now referred only to programs aiding poor and disproportionately minority Americans, such as food stamps and Aid to Families with Dependent Children (AFDC). Like other social spending, these welfare expenditures skyrocketed, as did the number of recipients. From 1965 to 1975, the number of families receiving AFDC more than tripled, and food-stamp recipients soared from 400,000 to 17 million. These increases led to a public backlash. By 1976, polls showed that support for welfare spending was at its lowest level ever, and it remained at this level through 1980.

Conservatives further inflamed the opposition to welfare programs by portraying them as unfair. For example, Ronald Reagan claimed that food stamps allowed "some fellow ahead of you to buy T-bone steak," while "you were standing in the checkout line with your package of hamburger." Reagan also repeatedly told a story about a "welfare queen" with "80 names, 30 addresses, [and] 12 Social Security cards" whose "tax-free income alone is over $150,000." Unbeknownst to his audiences (and Reagan himself), the "welfare queen" tale was completely fictional. Nevertheless, it effectively symbolized the supposed unfairness of government programs. Indeed, polls showed that the proportion of Americans who agreed that the "people running the country don't really care what happens to you" surged from 26 percent in 1966 to 60 percent in 1977.

The reaction against rising spending on social welfare was intensified by growing skepticism about whether these government programs worked as intended. Americans increasingly doubted that politicians, bureaucrats, and experts located in the nation's capital could analyze complex social problems throughout the diverse United States. "Liberals must divest themselves of the notion that the nation . . . can be run from agencies in Washington," argued neoconservative Daniel P. Moynihan, later a U.S. senator from New York. In fact, many conservatives claimed that all government programs resulted in counterproductive "unintended consequences."

According to this controversial theory, government programs inevitably *worsened* the social problems that they were designed to improve. For example, the unintended consequence of high welfare payments was to dissuade the poor from working. Similarly, financial support for single mothers with dependent children discouraged marriage; forced busing worsened inner-city schools by provoking middle-class "white flight" to suburbs; the burdens of racial preferences fell hardest on poorer whites; and bilingual education decreased immigrants' school performance. "Whether well-intentioned or not," argued conservative editor Mark Lilla, "the attempt to expand government activity simultaneously in many social spheres has been a counterproductive mistake."

This conservative evaluation of government social policies was debatable on many specific points, but it helped swell the reaction against federal programs. Accordingly, the proportion of Americans who believed that government officials were "smart people who know what they're doing" plummeted from 69 percent in 1970 to 29 percent in 1980. During those same years, the proportion believing that government would "do what's right most of the time" dropped from 56 to 29 percent.

A growing tax burden in the 1970s intensified the white middle-class backlash against government spending, especially on welfare programs designed to help poor minorities. As a result, Ronald Reagan and other conservative Republicans were able to exploit a racially tinged clash between mainly white taxpayers and disproportionately nonwhite tax recipients. In reality, the United States boasted the lowest tax rates of almost any advanced nation in the world. During the 1970s, however, Americans' traditional hatred of taxes was sharpened by the combination of stagnating real incomes, resentment against the perceived inefficiencies of government, and inflation-induced "bracket creep." By 1980, the proportion of Americans who viewed their federal income taxes as "too high" reached an all-time record. Making matters worse, soaring federal income taxes were more than matched by increased Social Security taxes, which rose with inflation. From 1960 to 1975, the maximum Social Security liability increased 473 percent (adjusted for inflation), while real income grew only 166 percent.

Despite a lack of convincing evidence, conservative Republicans also blamed high taxes and governmental regulation of business for economic stagnation, low productivity growth, inflation, and unemployment. Supply-side economists and other conservatives promised that growth would result from lowering individual and corporate income taxes and deregulating business and the market. This antitax message, which had always appealed to business and the wealthy, gained new popularity among a middle class squeezed by stagnant real incomes and rising income taxes. The result was a major attack on the "tax-and-spend" policies of liberal Democrats.

The ensuing "tax revolt" represented a turning point in American politics. It began in 1978 with California's Proposition 13, which cut soaring property taxes. The passage of Proposition 13 "triggered hope in the breasts of people that something could be done," Ronald Reagan later declared, "a little bit like dumping those cases [of tea] off the boat into Boston harbor" at the start of the American Revolution. The tax revolt spread throughout the nation after 1978, producing momentous consequences. It helped create a coalition against the liberal welfare state, gave the conservative movement a unifying issue, shaped an antigovernment ethic, and generated disaffection with the Democratic party. It also strengthened the links between ideological conservatives, business leaders, and the Republican party. "[T]his isn't just a tax revolt," observed Democratic pollster Pat Caddell. "It's a revolution against government."

Taxes were the main issue in the midterm elections of 1978. Early that year, Congress enacted a substantial reduction on capital-gains taxes and made permanent a temporary tax credit on investment. During the campaign, moreover, many Republican candidates ran on a tax-cut plan proposed by Representative Jack F. Kemp of New York and Senator William V. Roth, Jr., of Delaware. The Kemp-Roth plan called for reducing federal income taxes by one-third across the board. In the elections, Republicans made small gains at all levels of government. In the House, they added eleven seats but still trailed Democrats by 277 to 158. In the Senate, they reduced the Democratic majority by three seats, to 59-41. Conservative Republicans made their largest inroads in the Midwest, New England, and the South. The GOP also added six governors, reducing the Democratic majority to 32-18. Encouraged by their mild success in 1978, Republicans and conservatives stepped up their attack on liberalism, the Democratic party, and President Jimmy Carter during his last two years in office.

Ronald Reagan, Jimmy Carter, and the 1980 Election

It was ironic that the Democratic president, Jimmy Carter, was blamed for the decline of liberalism, because he was no liberal himself. A devout Christian from the Deep South, Carter was "the most conservative Democratic president since Grover Cleveland" in the 1890s, according to historian Arthur M. Schlesinger, Jr. However, Carter's administration did lean toward liberalism during his first two years in office. For example, Carter established the Consumer Protection Agency, strengthened the regulatory powers of the Federal Trade Commission, and created the Department of Education. The administration appeared most liberal in the rulings of its federal regulatory commissions, where the president had appointed assertive reformers to oversee occupational health and safety, consumer protection, and the environment. Conservatives and their business allies attacked all of these initiatives; "Jimmy Robin Hood," one conservative called the president.

Conservative nationalists also harshly criticized Carter's foreign policy. The 1976 campaign was the first presidential contest following the end of the U.S. debacle in Vietnam. A reformist candidate, Carter promised to restrain the imperial presidency, recognize the limits of U.S. power, promote human rights, pardon Vietnam-era draft resisters, and shun knee-jerk anticommunism. His record in achieving these goals was mixed. But his overall foreign-policy record from 1977 to 1979 was successful. Carter's greatest triumph was the Camp David Accords between Israel and Egypt. The president also pressed for Senate ratification of the Panama Canal treaties, which gradually turned the canal over to Panama and guaranteed the right of the United States to defend it afterward. Most important,

Carter built on the Nixon-Ford détente policies by negotiating a new strategic arms limitations treaty (SALT II) with the Soviet Union and by formally recognizing the People's Republic of China.

Conservative nationalists, led by Ronald Reagan, criticized all of Carter's foreign policies. When the president unconditionally pardoned all Vietnam-era draft resisters, the director of the Veterans of Foreign Wars called it "the saddest day in American history." Conservatives also condemned the Panama Canal treaty. They charged that it endangered U.S. security in Latin America, and Reagan rallied nationalist support on the Panama Canal issue by claiming, "We built it, we paid for it, it's ours, and . . . we're going to keep it." Most important, strident anticommunists contended that détente allowed the Soviets to increase their military strength and to meddle in the Third World. They further argued that Carter's condemnation of human-rights abuses by America's anticommunist allies was both "naive" and a "double standard."

In late 1979, conservative criticism of Carter's foreign policy intensified following two major international events: Iran's taking of American hostages and the Soviet invasion of Afghanistan. The Shah of Iran had served as America's regional policeman in the Middle East for 25 years, despite his well-documented abuses of human rights. In January 1979, a revolution overthrew his dictatorship, and a theocratic "Islamic Republic" was established under cleric Ayatollah Khomeini. Carter then allowed the self-exiled Shah into the United States for medical treatment, which angered the new Iranian government. On November 4, 1979, Iranian students reacted by taking 53 Americans hostage at the U.S. embassy in Teheran. For the next 444 days, the hostage crisis preoccupied the president and the American public. Following on the heels of the U.S. defeat in Vietnam, the Iranian crisis reinforced the feeling among American nationalists that their country seemed little more than a "pitiful, helpless giant," as Richard Nixon had warned. During the long crisis, ABC initiated a late-night news show whose title screamed "America Held Hostage."

A month after the Iran hostage crisis began, in December 1979, the Soviets invaded Afghanistan. Conservatives claimed that Carter's détente policies had encouraged Soviet aggression. With America's enemies seemingly on the march, militant nationalism mounted in the United States. The proportion of Americans agreeing that "too little" was being spent on defense, which had averaged 27 percent throughout the 1970s, shot up to 56 percent in 1980.

As the 1980 presidential election approached, Carter increasingly moved to the right in an effort to bolster his reelection prospects and undercut support for Ronald Reagan and other conservative Republicans. The president reduced funding for welfare programs and adopted a more conservative economic program based on fighting inflation while allowing unemployment to escalate. In July 1979, he appointed conservative Paul Volcker as chairman of the Federal Reserve Board. Volcker ruthlessly attacked inflation, reducing the money supply by pushing the prime interest rate up from 9.1 percent in 1978 to 21.5 percent in 1980. Though sanctioned by the president, Volcker's drastic measures caused the "Carter recession," damaging the president's reelection prospects by raising unemployment to the highest level since the Great Depression.

Carter also moved to the right in foreign policy. In April 1980, he ordered a military operation to free the American hostages held in Iran. The mission was a total failure, which only reinforced the president's desire to present a tough image. He pushed Congress to fund a new generation of nuclear missiles and to escalate military spending. Additionally, he harshly condemned the USSR for its invasion of Afghanistan, abandoned détente, and instituted several anti-Soviet policies.

Carter's turn to the right did little to help his reelection prospects. Conservatives continued to view him with contempt, while liberals were angered by his conservative rhetoric and actions. The nation's leading liberal, Senator Edward M. Kennedy of Massachusetts, responded by challenging Carter for the 1980 Democratic nomination. Many Democrats (and many other Americans) viewed Carter as a failed leader because he proved unable to overcome the two most visible challenges of his presidency: economic stagflation and the Iranian crisis. Nor was he helped by his uncharismatic personality. For example, the *Boston Globe* summarized a Carter speech with the headline "Mush from the Wimp." Nevertheless, Carter managed to hold off Kennedy's challenge in the Democratic presidential primaries.

Waiting for Carter in the general election was a more formidable candidate, Republican nominee Ronald Reagan. Reagan easily won his party's nomination in 1980, culminating a long journey for the 69-year-old politician. He had grown up in a small Midwestern town, and his speeches and stories recaptured the rural ideal of a bygone age. In truth, his childhood in a dysfunctional family was hardly idyllic, but it had inspired his remarkable ability to concoct escapist fantasies. His speechwriter Peggy Noonan later surmised that Reagan had come from a "sad house" and for the rest of his life "thought it was his job to cheer everyone up." Not surprisingly, the attractive and imaginative young man moved to Hollywood, where he became a film actor in the late 1930s. Though never a first-rank star, he enjoyed a successful and lucrative movie career.

Reagan's personal political journey paralleled that of many other Americans: from New Deal liberal in the 1930s to antigovernment conservative in the 1970s and 1980s. As a young man, he had idolized President Franklin D. Roosevelt and supported Roosevelt's New Deal and internationalist policies. His reverence for FDR's leadership never waned, and it showed in his own optimistic style. In the late 1940s, Reagan was a leading anticommunist liberal in Hollywood and even served as a secret FBI informer while president of the Screen Actors Guild. He claimed that he had discerned a "Communist plan . . . to take over the motion picture business" to brainwash American movie audiences.

Reagan's zealous anticommunism and staunch patriotism increasingly pushed him to the political right. During the 1950s, these conservative leanings were bolstered by his growing hatred of high income taxes on wealthy people like himself and by his marriage to actress Nancy Davis, who hailed from an affluent right-wing family. As his movie career waned in the late 1950s, Reagan sharpened his storytelling skills as a corporate spokesman for General Electric. His ties to GE executives and other businessmen strengthened his conservative beliefs, and he finally registered as a Republican after the 1960 election. "I didn't leave the Democratic party," he later claimed. "It left me."

During the 1960s and 1970s, Reagan became the nation's leading conservative Republican. He was a staunch supporter of Barry Goldwater during the 1964 campaign, and his speeches for Goldwater launched his own political career. Financed by his wealthy friends, Reagan won an upset victory in the race for the governorship of California in 1966, and he was reelected four years later. Like President Nixon, Governor Reagan combined pragmatic policies with hard-right rhetoric. He signed a bill legalizing abortion, raised taxes and spending, and expanded regulation of business and the environment. But he also proposed using American power to "level Vietnam," and he warned student protesters to "obey the rules or get out" of California's universities. By the late 1970s, he was an icon to the conservatives—"the man who can enunciate our principles to the people."

Reagan's greatest conservative achievement was papering over the differences between traditionalists and libertarians. In a 1977 speech, for example, he argued that the "time has come to see if it is possible to present a program of action based on political principle that can attract those interested in the so-called 'social issues' [which he identified as "law and order, abortion, busing, quota systems"] and those interested in 'economic' issues [such as] inflation, deficit spending, and big government. . . . In short isn't it possible to combine the two major segments of contemporary American conservatism into one politically effective whole?" In truth, his part in uniting the conservative movement was more emotional than intellectual. Reagan, observed journalist Sidney Blumenthal, "animated conservatives' intellectual theories with a resonant symbolism of idyllic small-town life of enterprising entrepreneurs whose success derived from moral character, and failure induced only by federal bureaucrats."

A key to Reagan's broad popularity was his ability to appeal personally to Americans, even to those who disagreed with his right-wing politics. From Herbert Hoover through Robert Taft to Barry Goldwater, conservative Republicans had been associated with gloomy personalities, a lack of compassion, and a strident moralism. By contrast, Reagan presented a softer, more affable image that enabled him to say harsh things in a good-natured manner. Unlike previous conservative GOP leaders, moreover, he embodied optimism, professed to accept a small welfare "safety net," and soft-pedaled talk of nuclear warfare. He thus projected strong leadership while avoiding the stereotype of a "mean, unfeeling" conservative.

In contrast to Carter's hand-wringing talk of limits and sacrifice, moreover, Reagan declared that "America's best days lay ahead." He scorned those who suggested that "the United States has had its day in the sun" and insisted it was "time for us to realize that we are too great a nation to limit ourselves to small dreams." His upbeat style captured the imagination of a public largely disillusioned by the malaise of the late 1970s. Without saying how, Reagan convinced many voters that he would tame inflation, cut taxes, and restore the world's respect for the United States. "This is the greatest country in the world," he proclaimed. "Now all we need is the leadership."

The victories by Reagan and other Republicans in the 1980 elections marked a new stage in the post-1968 GOP ascendancy. The presidential race remained close for much of the campaign, but Reagan eventually beat Carter handily, winning by 51 to 41 percent in the popular vote and by 489 to 49 in the electoral college. (Congressman John Anderson of Illinois, a moderate Republican, ran as an independent and won 7 percent of the popular vote.) Equally important, Reagan's strong coattails helped other GOP candidates. In the House, Republicans made a net gain of thirty-three seats, the biggest increase since 1966, to cut the Democratic majority to 243-192. In the Senate, they added twelve seats, the largest one-election gain in more than two decades, to regain a majority (53-47). It was the GOP's first Senate majority in twenty-eight years, ending the longest reign in history. Most of the newly elected Republicans were conservative, and several important liberal Democrats lost, including Senators George McGovern, Frank Church, and Birch Bayh. At the state level, Republicans added four governors to cut the Democratic majority to 27-23.

The 1980 elections marked a new phase in the Republican ascendancy that had begun with Richard Nixon's win in 1968. But the GOP victories did not represent a classic party realignment like the one that had occurred in 1932. Instead, the 1980 elections continued in the vein of dealignment: party loyalty was less important as most voters made their electoral decisions on a case-by-case basis about specific candidates. Most important, the election primarily symbolized a "landslide vote of no confidence in an incompetent administration," as political scientist Walter Dean Burnham concluded. Nevertheless, Republicans trumpeted their victories as a popular mandate for a conservative "Reagan Revolution."

CHAPTER FOUR

Ronald Reagan, George H. W. Bush, and Republican Ascendancy, 1981–1992

At his inauguration on January 20, 1981, President Reagan scoffed at talk of limits. Americans were a not people to dream "small dreams," he said. Reversing the central tenet of national politics since the formation of the New Deal, Reagan declared: "In the present crisis . . . government is not the solution to our problem, government is the problem." Symbolically, his first act as president was to temporarily freeze federal hiring.

Over the next twelve years, Republican Presidents Reagan and George H. W. Bush promoted policies designed to halt or roll back many of the New Deal's accomplishments. Reagan established a powerful bond with the public that transcended voters' opinions about his specific policies. He tapped a popular yearning to restore a sense of community, real or imagined, that had been lost since the 1960s. With his ruddy good looks, a tremor in his voice, and a twinkle in his eye, Reagan fulfilled a certain ideal of what a president should be. Whether or not they agreed with his programs, people enjoyed hearing his jokes and inspirational stories—which also served to deflect criticism and serious introspection. George Bush, who lacked comparable charm, was elected in 1988 largely on the good-will he had earned as Reagan's vice president. As long as the "good times" continued, President Bush enjoyed high levels of voter approval. But when economic troubles began in 1991, he quickly lost the trust of the American public, and Republicans suffered major setbacks.

To a large degree, the Republican agenda during the 1980s and early 1990s focused on reducing many Democratic programs. Both the Reagan and Bush administrations worked to shrink the social-welfare system, limit the role of federal courts in promoting civil rights and liberties, reduce government regulation of business and protection of the environment, slash income taxes, and foster a conservative social ethic in such areas as abortion rights, premarital sex, drug use, and the role of religion in public life. The two Republican presidents rejected the belief that the federal government should foster greater equality, insisting that market forces would create new wealth and assure its equitable distribution.

The "Reagan Revolution"

As a candidate and as president, Reagan focused on the general themes of national renewal, strength, and pride. He projected common sense, spoke of past heroes, and offered simple, reassuring answers to complex policy questions.

The president relied on a triumvirate of top policy advisers who served him well. In an astute move, he reached outside his inner circle of conservative Californians to appoint James A. Baker III, a close friend of Vice President Bush, as White House chief of staff. The more conservative and abrasive Edwin Meese, a close associate of Reagan from his days as California governor, became a presidential "counselor," an amorphous post without clear responsibility. Michael Deaver, a skilled public-relations expert personally close to the president and to First Lady Nancy Reagan, worked as deputy chief of staff, with responsibility for managing the president's image.

Reagan selected a cabinet composed almost entirely of white male Republicans who had served in the Nixon and Ford administrations or with him in California. Only two posts, Interior and Energy, went to members of the New Right—James Watt and James Edwards, respectively. Watt's provocative characterization of liberals as "un-American" and his criticism of non-Christians, as well as his effort to speed development of protected federal forest lands, forced the president to replace him before the end of the first administration. Initially, no women served in the Reagan cabinet, although UN ambassador Jeanne Kirkpatrick received honorary cabinet status. Reagan appointed an African American, Samuel Pierce, as secretary of housing and urban development. But the president cared so little about housing policy that he failed even to recognize Pierce the few times they met. In any case, Reagan seldom attended cabinet meetings, and often dozed off when he did.

The new president owed much of his initial success to the skill of Chief of Staff James Baker. During the first few months of the Reagan administration, while the Democrats remained in political shock, Baker concentrated on passing key legislation. He persuaded Reagan to push Congress for two items on the presidential agenda that were popular and that Reagan wanted most: tax cuts and a defense buildup. "If we can do that," Baker maintained, "the rest will take care of itself."

Reagan had long been critical of the progressive income tax. He believed that people should be rewarded for achieving wealth, not taxed at higher rates for doing so. He embraced conservative supply-side economics, which held that cutting the tax rate would pay for itself by stimulating business activity and economic growth. The Republican mantra against taxes also served to reduce the number of new government programs and to attract voters. According to leading Republicans, Americans could be divided into "tax payers" and "tax takers." In this view, tax payers were hardworking, mostly white Americans from whom the government took exorbitant sums of money. Tax takers were the "undeserving poor" and minorities, on whom Democrats supposedly lavished federal resources. Thus, GOP calls for "fairness" in taxation had the coded meaning of reducing aid to minorities. Tax cuts were also seen as a substitute for wage hikes at a time when working- and middle-class incomes were stagnating.

As the keystone of his agenda, Reagan asked Congress in January 1981 to enact steep cuts in federal income and business tax rates.

The president's proposal, based on a plan drawn up by Representative Jack Kemp of New York and Senator William Roth of Delaware, would reduce business taxes by 25 percent over three years and lower the top income tax rate from 70 percent (though the wealthy seldom paid this much because of numerous tax shelters) to 50 percent. To rein in both the power of the federal government and its expenditures, he called for shifting many social programs to state control, trimming Social Security benefits, and eliminating many business regulations and environmental protections. Reagan assured the public that these measures would balance the budget, create jobs, bring down inflation, make government less intrusive, and leave the American people with more money to spend.

In a diary entry, Reagan denied that he was secretly "trying to undo the New Deal." Instead, he hoped to "undo the Great Society. It was LBJ's war on poverty," he insisted, that had "led us to our present mess." Reagan complained that the Democrats' excessive deficit spending had "mortgaged our future and our children's future for the temporary convenience of the present." As the national debt approached $1 trillion, the new president called for lower social spending to save money and encourage people to help themselves.

Reagan relied upon David Stockman, the young and talented director of the Office of Management and Budget, to push his tax and budget bills through Congress. Stockman, who had been a left-wing activist before moving to the right, sincerely believed in reducing taxes as well as the size of government. In an unguarded moment, however, he admitted to a journalist that supply-side economics and across-the-board tax cuts were just a clever repackaging of the old Republican concept of "trickle-down" economics: the idea that some of the benefits lavished on the wealthy would eventually reach the poor. Reagan's small tax cut for the middle class, said Stockman, was a "Trojan horse" to make much larger reductions for the wealthy publicly palatable.

The president touted the supply-side theory that tax cuts would stimulate growth and boost tax revenue, but Stockman recognized that without big spending cuts, Reagan's program would generate huge budget deficits. To make matters worse, the new administration intended to increase defense spending significantly without making cuts in popular programs such as Social Security and Medicare. As a result, Stockman privately predicted a "budget hemorrhage" with annual shortfalls of $100 billion or more for the next four years, greater than any peacetime deficits run up by any Democratic president. Republican Senate majority leader Howard Baker of Tennessee agreed, describing Reagan's economic plan as a "riverboat gamble." The president ignored these concerns. He guessed, correctly, that most Americans would happily trade big deficits that had to be paid off by future generations for current tax cuts. In any case, if deficits mounted, he could place the blame on congressional Democrats.

Reagan rallied support for his program with direct appeals to the public and the press. Organized labor, already in decline, feared opposing Reagan after he summarily fired 12,000 striking federal air-traffic controllers whose work stoppage had violated their contract. Reagan also benefited from the humor and optimism he displayed when he was gravely wounded in an assassination attempt by a deranged gunman on March 30, 1981, just six weeks into his presidency. House Democrats, although holding a majority, hesitated to block popular tax cuts. Reagan also won support from sixty-three conservative, mostly Southern Democrats known as "boll weevils." In return for the president's promise to help get them reelected, they joined Republicans in voting for the Reagan economic program.

On August 13, 1981, President Reagan signed two major laws, the Economic Recovery Tax Act and the Omnibus Budget Reconciliation Act. The former slashed federal income tax rates by 25 percent over three years. The budget bill cut about $40 billion in domestic spending but left intact most popular big-ticket programs such as Social Security and Medicare. Funding for programs such as Amtrak (the national passenger rail service), synthetic fuels, low-income housing, school lunches, and other social services for the poor received small to medium cuts. Reagan spoke of pruning additional social programs, but Congress balked at making unpopular reductions after this first round. And the president's early victory in reducing federal appropriations turned out to be his last. By June 1982, with the budget deficit ballooning, Reagan bowed to congressional pressure and raised taxes.

The income tax cut received by most working- and middle-class taxpayers proved elusive. In April 1983, Reagan and Congress approved the proposal of a bipartisan panel to shore up the Social Security trust fund that paid pensions to millions of elderly Americans. The plan included a small reduction in benefits and an increase in the payroll taxes paid by workers. This levy consumed most of the small income-tax reduction passed in 1981. But the plan stabilized Social Security and removed it from partisan debate.

Reagan's New Cold War, 1981–1986

As a candidate in 1980, Ronald Reagan insisted that "there are simple answers" to complex international questions. Americans, he argued, suffered from a "Vietnam syndrome," a guilt complex that rendered them unwilling to use force to resist Communist threats or defend U.S. allies and interests abroad. He criticized his predecessors— Johnson, Nixon, Ford, and Carter—for arms-control policies that, he claimed, allowed the Soviets to gain military superiority. Instead of pursuing détente with Moscow, the headquarters of what he later called "the evil empire," Reagan pledged to resist Soviet pressures, aid anticommunist movements throughout the world, and restore American military dominance. This, he said, would bring the Soviets and their allies to heel. Reagan also blamed Carter's lack of resolve for increased terrorism against American targets.

The president's assertive foreign and defense policies marked a break from efforts by Republican Presidents Eisenhower, Nixon, and Ford to engage as well as confront the Soviet Union. From 1981 to 1986, Reagan presided over the biggest peacetime increase in defense spending in history. Annual expenditures rose from $144 billion in 1980 to a peak of $295 billion in 1986.

Reagan's huge defense budgets bought a larger navy, new generations of strategic and tactical missiles, and more tanks and combat aircraft. The most expensive program, the Strategic Defense Initiative (popularly known as "Star Wars") was an effort—ultimately abandoned—to build a vast antimissile shield. Reagan supplemented the hardware with tough rhetoric against terrorists, the Soviet Union, and communist movements elsewhere in the world. In practice, however, the administration shunned direct confrontation with Moscow.

Instead, the president encouraged his director of the Central Intelligence Agency (CIA), William Casey, to expand covert actions against pro-Soviet forces or governments in Africa, Afghanistan, the Middle East, and Central America. Despite Reagan's disdain for communism and personal admiration for the government of Taiwan, he maintained stable relations with the People's Republic of China. The PRC's anti-Soviet stance made it a valuable U.S. ally.

The Reagan-era interventions achieved mixed results. In Afghanistan, U.S.-supported Islamic guerrillas fought the Soviet army effectively, eventually forcing Moscow to withdraw. (Ironically, many of these fundamentalist warriors later turned their wrath against U.S., Israeli, and moderate Arab targets. On September 11, 2001, terrorists closely linked to radical Muslims in Afghanistan used hijacked commercial jetliners to demolish the World Trade Center Towers and damage the Pentagon.) In 1983, U.S. armed forces easily trounced a group of pro-Cuban thugs who had seized power on the tiny Caribbean island of Grenada. Reagan claimed that the Grenadian regime, besides its affinity for Moscow, threatened the safety of U.S. students attending a medical college on the island. These victories were offset by several foreign policy debacles. Reagan's dispatch in 1982 of U.S. Marines to intervene in Lebanon's chronic civil war proved disastrous. The U.S. force found itself caught between Christian and Muslim fighters and lacking a clear mission. Almost 300 marines were killed when their barracks were bombed in 1983. In Central America, Reagan's contempt for the Marxist Sandinista regime of Nicaragua led him to support a brutal anticommunist government in El Salvador and, over the objection of Congress, to aid anticommunist "Contra" guerrillas trying to overthrow the Nicaraguan government. This action led directly to the Iran-Contra affair, the largest scandal of Reagan's presidency, which is discussed below.

After 1986, Reagan altered his hard-line approach to foreign affairs. This resulted largely from his embarrassment over public revelations of his arms-and-hostages deal with Iran and the Contras, as well as from changes inside the Soviet Union. In 1985, reformer Mikhail Gorbachev assumed control in Moscow. He recognized that communism had reached a dead end, and that the survival of his country depended on democratic political reforms and creating a market-driven economy. Gorbachev hoped that improved relations with Washington and with his neighbors would provide the money and stability he needed to save the Soviet system. In the wake of the Iran-Contra debacle, Reagan accepted Gorbachev's outstretched hand. During 1987–88, the American and Soviet leaders signed a series of arms-control agreements, largely on U.S. terms. Gorbachev withdrew Soviet forces from Afghanistan and relaxed control over Eastern Europe, eventually permitting the region to throw out its Communist-led regimes.

In subsequent years, many Republicans, as well as some historians, attributed the Soviet collapse and the American "victory" in the Cold War to Reagan's confrontational rhetoric and his arms buildup, including the abortive antimissile program. But the Soviet demise was, in fact, the product of decades of slow rot, not a momentary crisis. Gorbachev's reforms failed to save the Soviet system, but they at least helped steer the Communist regime toward a relatively soft landing. Reagan's flexibility from 1986 on, rather than his earlier hard line, was probably what helped end the Cold War. In this regard, the president's need to recover from the public-relations disaster of the Iran-Contra scandal paid unexpected dividends.

The Reagan-Bush Economic and Social Record

The large tax cuts and defense buildup were the foundations of Republican governance in the 1980s, but the so-called Reagan Revolution and its aftermath during the Bush years was more a matter of perception than reality. When Reagan left office in 1989, the federal government was collecting about the same percentage of the nation's GNP—19 percent—in federal taxes as it had throughout the previous twenty years. Federal spending actually increased under Reagan, rising from about 7 percent of GNP to 8.2 percent. The biggest increases occurred in defense outlays, Medicare, and Social Security. Under Reagan and Bush, the gap between tax revenues and rising spending produced the largest budget deficits in U.S. history. Annual shortfalls ranged from $100 billion to over $250 billion. The cumulative national debt soared from $1 trillion in 1980 to $2 trillion in 1989 and $3 trillion in 1993. To make up the shortfall, Washington turned to foreign investors, who financed the debt by purchasing Treasury bonds and notes.

"Reaganomics" had a rocky beginning in 1981–83. The nation slipped into a deep economic recession soon after Congress approved Reagan's program. The downturn was caused partly by the actions of Federal Reserve Board Chairman Paul Volcker, who raised interest rates as high as 21.5 percent in order to stifle inflation. As a result, unemployment climbed to 10.8 percent, or 11.5 million jobless workers, while business failures, farm foreclosures, and homelessness increased dramatically. Conditions were especially severe in the Midwest's Rustbelt; it experienced the worst economic downturn since the Great Depression.

The recession impacted the 1982 congressional elections. Republican candidates enjoyed a better than 5 to 1 advantage in campaign funds ($215 million to $39 million), but Democrats still made substantial gains in Congress, picking up 26 House seats for an increased majority of 269 to 166. The Senate remained in GOP hands, 54 to 46; but Republicans lost seven governorships, giving the Democrats 34 state governors to the Republicans' 16.

The recession also drove down Reagan's approval rating, from 60 percent in mid-1981 to 41 percent by the end of 1982. Many media pundits and Democrats began describing Reagan as a likely one-term failure. The president, however, refused to alter his priorities and predicted economic recovery by 1984.

Reagan's forecast proved correct. After high interest rates squeezed inflation out of the economy, the Federal Reserve began cutting interest rates in 1983. Meanwhile, changes in world markets drove down petroleum prices, reducing the cost of imported oil for American motorists and industry. Additionally, Reagan's massive defense spending ignited a boom in high technology and the aerospace industries of New England, the Southwest, and the West Coast. The president also encouraged a commercial construction boom by easing rules governing savings and loan institutions. The economic expansion that began in 1983 continued until 1991.

Reagan's high public approval rating after 1983, along with his continued success at communicating his ideas and faith in America, gave the impression that the nation's economic problems were being swept away by waves of pride and optimism. Often, however, reality did not match the president's upbeat rhetoric. Not only did the nation's debt triple during the Reagan and Bush years, but economic expansion after 1983 proved highly selective. Prosperity flowed to both coasts, partly because of defense spending. So the Northeast and California boomed while the Rustbelt continued to lose high-paying industrial jobs.

Even in overall terms, the long economic expansion of the later Reagan and early Bush years was less impressive than Republicans boasted. Certainly, the economy performed better in the 1980s than it had in the "stagflation" years of the 1970s. But when measured against the entire 1945–80 period, the Reagan-Bush recovery appeared more modest. Unemployment during the two Republican administrations remained higher than in most years between 1947 and 1973, while growth slowed. Wages continued to stagnate, although the rising number of working wives and mothers whose earnings boosted total family income obscured this fact.

The most dramatic economic development of the Reagan-Bush era was the growth in wealth and income among the richest Americans, especially when compared to the economic decline among the poorest Americans and the relative lack of change among those in the middle. The rise in stock prices, new income tax laws, and other policies advantageous to businesses caused this change.

Reagan's tax cuts benefited the rich far more than the poor. In 1985, for example, the poorest fifth of taxpayers actually paid $137 more in taxes annually than they did before the Reagan tax reform. In contrast, the richest fifth paid $2,531 less. Meanwhile, the average weekly earnings of American workers declined from $378 in 1980 to $339 in 1992. In 1989, as Bush succeeded Reagan in the White House, the top 1 percent, or 834,000 households, held 37 percent ($5.7 trillion) of the net wealth in America. They possessed more wealth than the bottom 90 percent (84 million American households), with a net worth of $4.8 trillion. During the Bush presidency, the gap between rich, middle class, and poor in the United States became greater than at any time since World War II.

Early in his presidency, Ronald Reagan joked that the federal government had been fighting poverty for twenty years, and that "poverty won." As proof, he cited the nearly identical poverty rate of about 13 percent in 1963 and 1980. Reagan's humor obscured some dramatic changes. The elderly and disabled had constituted the bulk of the poor before the expansion of Social Security and Medicare under Presidents Johnson and Nixon. By 1980, these groups were much better off materially. In their place, women and children made up the bulk of the poor.

The so-called feminization of poverty grew more severe during the 1980s, partly because of the rising rate of children born to single mothers. The rate of children living with a never-married mother soared by 70 percent between 1983 and 1993. By the early 1990s, one of every four births in America was to an unwed mother. For African American and Hispanic women, the rate was about 50 percent and 33 percent, respectively. In 1992, 22 percent of all American children under the age of eighteen lived in poverty, including 47 percent of all African American children and 29 percent of Hispanics. Female-headed households, comprising 14 million people, accounted for 37 percent of the 37 million Americans living below the poverty line.

The Reagan and Bush administrations responded to the challenge of single parenthood (as well as to rising rates of sexually transmitted diseases such as AIDS) by admonishing teenage girls and unmarried women (males were largely ignored) to avoid sex. Internationally, the U.S. government stopped funding any organizations that even counseled women about abortion. Congress followed calls by both presidents to create "chastity clinics" as the major part of sex-education curricula in schools. Meanwhile, Reagan and Bush cut funding for food stamps, school lunch programs, and nutritional programs for poor mothers. A larger proportion of minorities depended on public assistance, so these reductions in funding affected only 2 out of 100 white households, compared to 15 of every 100 African American and 10 out of 100 Hispanic families. Reagan and Bush blamed welfare programs for perpetuating dependence, but neither president proposed an alternative to public assistance.

Government regulation of business, the environment, and financial markets in the 1930s had been one of the New Deal's most important innovations. Ever since the 1930s, conservatives and some business leaders criticized government interference with market forces, even though regulators argued that they had improved markets by keeping them honest. The Carter administration began to eliminate regulations that interfered with competition in the transportation and communication sectors, lowering prices in the airline, railroad, and trucking industries.

Reagan believed that unfettered market forces were best equipped to create and distribute wealth, and he saw deregulation as a cure-all for social and economic ills. In February 1981, he issued an executive order requiring federal agencies to perform cost-benefit studies of proposed new regulations to find the least costly alternatives. Reagan's appointees to federal agencies abolished many rules, ranging from requirements for stronger car bumpers to environmental restraints on offshore oil drilling. Budgets for regulatory agencies decreased by an average of 12 percent. The Environmental Protection Agency (EPA), the Occupational Safety and Health Administration (OSHA), and agencies overseeing the stock market and banking system received even steeper cuts.

The savings and loan (S&L) crisis that struck in the early 1990s resulted directly from these policies. Since the 1970s, savings and loan institutions, or "thrifts," had lost depositors because unregulated money-market funds paid higher rates of interest. To make banks and S&Ls more competitive, Congress in 1980 raised the federal insurance level to $100,000 on individual accounts and allowed these institutions to pay any interest rates they wanted. Two years later, Reagan convinced Congress to further deregulate thrifts. Previously, S&Ls made only low-risk loans for homes. With the new rules, they could invest depositors' funds in commercial real estate, shopping malls, or virtually anything else. If bad loans caused an S&L to collapse, depositors' accounts were protected by a government insurance pool, and owners had little liability.

S&L deregulation sparked a commercial construction boom during the mid-1980s. Unfortunately, some thrift executives, such as the notorious Charles Keating, head of Lincoln Savings and Loan in California, colluded with builders to drive up the cost of commercial projects, producing bigger fees for all the principals. Unscrupulous S&L executives also made dubious loans to business partners or paid themselves exorbitant salaries.

Then, in 1986, a major change in tax laws (discussed below) that was designed to close tax-avoidance loopholes reduced the inflated value of commercial properties built with S&L loans. This threatened to bury the industry under a mountain of bad debt. Timely intervention by federal regulators might have limited the cost of the debacle, but the Reagan administration and S&L executives found ways to keep the industry afloat. Five influential Republican and Democratic senators, including John McCain of Arizona, were later reprimanded for taking payments from Keating in return for lobbying on behalf of his Lincoln Savings and Loan. By 1989, when President Bush took office, hundreds of S&Ls had failed. To prevent a wider collapse, Congress created the Resolution Trust Corporation to take over a huge inventory of vacant buildings and obligations from the failed thrifts. At a cost to taxpayers of several hundred billion dollars, this was the biggest bank heist in the nation's history.

Like most conservatives, Reagan and to a lesser extent Bush, had criticized many Supreme Court decisions made since the 1950s. Both presidents, along with other Republican leaders, complained that rulings by liberal judges had encouraged a decline in morals, coddled criminals, promoted abortion and premarital sex, and banished religion from public schools.

Reagan was especially critical of efforts by the federal courts and Congress to promote civil rights for minorities. He had opposed landmark legislation such as the 1964 Civil Rights Act and the Voting Rights Act of 1965. Reagan was not racist in the narrow meaning of the term. But his perception of race focused on his personal feelings, not on the realities of life faced by minority groups.

Reagan and many other Republicans supported "conservative egalitarianism," the notion that government should oppose *both* racial discrimination and legal efforts to advance the rights of any group— even if members of the group had suffered past injustice. They also opposed "reverse discrimination" against whites. The 1980 Republican party platform, drafted with Reagan's approval, stated that true "equal opportunity should not be jeopardized by bureaucratic regulation and decisions which rely on quotas, ratios, and numerical requirements to exclude some individuals in favor of others, thereby rendering such regulations and decisions inherently discriminatory."

Reagan similarly used the language of equality to justify doing nothing to challenge existing racial and economic inequality. In practice, right-wingers cited the principle of conservative egalitarianism to oppose "special privileges" conferred by government in areas beyond race. For example, recognition of labor unions as the agents of workers, state and federal minimum-wage laws, the progressive income tax, welfare programs, and food stamps were all labeled special privileges that unfairly discriminated in favor of certain Americans.

Reagan's own discomfort with addressing racial problems and his implicit support for the Nixon-era "Southern Strategy" of expanding the GOP's appeal among white southerners showed in several ways. He endorsed a constitutional amendment to outlaw school busing, opposed a federal holiday honoring Martin Luther King, Jr., attempted to restore tax benefits to private segregated schools, and called for gutting the 1965 Voting Rights Act. Opposition by congressional Democrats and the Supreme Court ultimately blocked these initiatives; ironically, these failures blunted charges that Republicans were playing the race card to entice white southerners.

Reagan had better luck implementing his anti–affirmative action views through his executive appointments to the Justice Department and other federal agencies. The president's choice for attorney general, William French Smith, and for head of the Justice Department's Civil Rights Division, William Bradford Reynolds, reflected Reagan's opposition to affirmative action and similar programs. Smith and Reynolds vehemently opposed any special protection for groups or remedies based on rectifying past mistreatment, including voluntary school-busing programs based on race. Presidents Reagan and Bush also changed the direction of the federal Equal Employment Opportunity Commission and the Commission on Civil Rights by appointing conservative members who opposed most efforts to challenge racial discrimination or its legacies.

GOP leaders faulted federal courts for a series of decisions since the 1960s that expanded protections for criminal defendants, including informing defendants of their right to remain silent and to have an attorney, popularly known as "Miranda Rights," as well as other limits on evidence police could use at trial. Public fear over rising crime rates in the 1980s prompted both Republican and Democratic legislators at the state and national levels to mandate longer, mandatory prison sentences for many crimes, especially those related to the possession or sale of drugs. Reagan and Bush did not create this harsh anticrime wave, but they rode it skillfully for partisan purposes.

During the Reagan and Bush administrations, the war on crime merged with the war on drugs. Nearly every president since Woodrow Wilson had launched some type of war on drugs, and the Republicans of the 1980s were no exception. Middle-class Americans feared both drug abuse by their children and violence associated with "crack" cocaine, used mostly by urban minorities. Illicit drug use actually peaked around 1979, but several high-profile drug deaths in the mid-1980s and the emergence of crack in urban ghettos created a climate of fear that Reagan and then Bush used to prod Congress into escalating the federal war on drugs.

At her husband's urging, First Lady Nancy Reagan launched a "Just Say No" campaign to warn Americans against drug abuse. President Bush named the abrasive William Bennett as "drug czar." Bennett continued policies that ignored the role of prevention and the question of who uses drugs and why. Instead, he emphasized interdiction of drugs and harsh penalties for those found guilty of selling or possessing them. Virtually without hearings on the subject, Congress imposed strict, mandatory minimum sentences for a variety of drug-related offenses. Most states followed suit. By 1992, federal and state governments were spending nearly $15 billion annually on the drug war—mostly on police and prisons, not prevention or rehabilitation. The combined federal and state prison population increased more than 8 percent each year from 1985 to 1995, rising from 744,000 to 1,585,000. At the federal level, nearly half the new prisoners, most of them minorities, were serving time for drug offenses. Due in large part to the war on drugs, the United States had the highest incarceration rate in the world.

The most lasting impact that the Reagan and Bush administrations had on legal affairs came in the area of judicial appointments. Reagan appointed nearly four hundred federal judges—a majority of all those sitting in 1988—as well as a chief justice of the Supreme Court and three associate justices. Bush appointed two justices to the Supreme Court and many other federal judges. Especially under Reagan, the Justice Department carefully vetted potential judicial appointments to ensure they held conservative views. The Senate, under Republican control from 1981 to 1986, easily confirmed Reagan's first three Supreme Court appointments: Sandra Day O'Connor, the first female justice; the staunchly conservative Antonin Scalia; and William Rehnquist, promoted to chief justice.

The situation changed after the Democrats regained control of the Senate in 1987. That year, Reagan nominated Robert Bork to fill a Supreme Court vacancy. Bork was an outspoken conservative who as solicitor general in 1973 had defended Nixon's firing of the Watergate prosecutor Archibald Cox. Bork argued that the Constitution offered little protection for privacy, free speech, and the rights of women and minorities. Offended by his demeanor and views, a majority of senators voted down his nomination. Reagan then nominated Anthony Kennedy, a respected conservative judge, to the high court. The Senate easily confirmed him.

As the number of conservative justices increased after 1984, the Supreme Court whittled away at many earlier rulings that had expanded the rights of the accused and limited police powers. The Court also approved limitations on bail, affirmed most state death-penalty laws, and allowed prosecutors to present certain illegally seized evidence to juries. In addition, a conservative majority issued rulings that made it harder for women, minorities, the elderly, and the disabled to sue employers for job discrimination.

During the 1980s and early 1990s, American society seemed to pull in two directions regarding many social and religious issues. At one level, the nation appeared increasingly secular, liberal, and tolerant. Most single and married women now worked outside the home in a variety of professions. Sexuality in general was depicted much more openly in the arts and entertainment, and homosexuality was widely acknowledged, if not fully accepted, as part of the human experience. At the same time, however, the New Religious Right, led by flamboyant "televangelists," energized a crusade against abortion, gays, gender equality, pornography, sex education, and the teaching of the theory of human evolution, and demanded the resumption of organized prayer in public schools.

President Reagan's personal uneasiness with feminism pushed discussion of gender equality in more conservative directions. Besides his strident opposition to abortion, Reagan was the first president in half a century to oppose the principle of an equal rights amendment to the Constitution. A man in his seventies, he held views of gender roles that often seemed out of sync with trends in American life. For example, he questioned whether it was proper for mothers to work even though more than 50 percent of women held jobs outside the home. The president thought he was complimenting women by telling a conference of female administrators, "I happen to be one who believes that if it wasn't for women, us men would still be walking around in skin suits carrying clubs." His "compliment" drew audible groans from the audience.

Reagan counted no women among his close policy advisers. In 1983, as polls revealed a "gender gap" in which women voted for Democrats more often than did male voters, the president added two women to his cabinet: Margaret Heckler as secretary of health and human services and Elizabeth Dole as secretary of transportation. He described Heckler as a "good little girl" and sat quietly while aides lampooned Dole as "schoolmarmish."

Most Republicans rallied behind Reagan's conservative economic policies, but social issues such as abortion, school prayer, homosexuality, and the war on drugs divided the GOP. Libertarians, who complained about Democrats acting as the nation's "nanny," were uncomfortable with the Republicans' own notions of government intrusion into the sphere of private behavior. In contrast, religious conservatives supported greater use of government power to suppress behavior they considered sinful.

Reagan was the first Republican leader to recognize the key roles that the New Religious Right played in the GOP as faithful primary voters, campaign donors, and party activists. He spoke frequently to religious gatherings, befriended several televangelists, and invited prominent Christian leaders to private White House briefings. He endorsed calls for constitutional amendments to ban abortion and to permit prayer in public schools. He also supported teaching biblical "creationism" as an alternative to evolutionary theory and granting tax credits to parents who sent their children to private religious schools. Yet Congress enacted none of these proposals, and Reagan never spent any of his political capital to push them harder.

The president and key GOP fundraisers were especially impressed by the large following commanded by televangelists such as Jerry Falwell, Jimmy Swaggart, Jim Bakker, and Pat Robertson. In the mid-1980s, their electronic ministries brought in almost $1 billion annually. Reagan's Justice Department refused to investigate complaints that televangelists flouted tax laws by using some of these religious contributions to support Republican candidates and political causes. As one presidential aide put it, "We want to keep the Moral Majority types so close to us they can't move their arms."

It was difficult to fathom the depth or sincerity of Reagan's belief in the agenda of the New Religious Right. After all, he was the first divorced president, seldom attended church, and maintained close friendships with gay actors from his days in Hollywood. Opinion surveys revealed that many socially liberal voters believed that Reagan was "winking" at them when he denounced gays, divorce, premarital sex, and so forth. Yet Christian conservatives took his statements at face value. In 1987–88, when scandals engulfed several of the more flamboyant televangelists, such as Jimmy Swaggart and Jim Bakker, Reagan quickly distanced himself from them. However, self-described Christian conservatives remained the GOP's most loyal supporters. In the 1984 presidential election, they voted for Reagan over Walter Mondale by a margin of 78 to 22 percent. Even though some among the New Religious Right questioned George Bush's allegiance to their cause, he received nearly the same overwhelming proportion of votes from Christian conservatives in 1988 as had Reagan in earlier elections. Congressional Republicans throughout the 1980s and 1990s could rely on similar margins of support from these voters.

Reagan's 1984 Reelection and Second Term

By 1984, falling inflation, lower oil prices, increased defense spending, and the S&L-fueled construction boom had restored economic growth—and Ronald Reagan's political fortunes. For average Americans who enjoyed a few more dollars in their pockets, abstract difficulties such as the budget deficit had little immediate impact. Democrats insisted that only the wealthy had made substantial gains under Reagan and that a worker voting for a Republican "was like a chicken voting for Colonel Sanders." In spite of these arguments, 80 percent of Americans told pollsters they were better off economically in 1984 than they had been four years earlier.

In the election contest of 1984, Reagan's team shielded their seventy-three-year-old candidate from normal campaign rigors. They relied largely on televised commercials that repeated the theme "America is back" or that portrayed the president in patriotic settings, such as his speech on the cliffs above the Normandy battlefield in June 1984. In his speech paying homage to the heroes of D-Day, Reagan quoted from a letter sent to him by the daughter of a veteran. Saluting the American heroes who had helped crush Hitler, he declared: "We will always remember. We will always be proud. We will always be prepared so we may always be free." Millions of Americans gulped as he brushed a tear from his eye.

Reagan's Democratic challenger, Walter Mondale (who had been vice president under Carter) emphasized his many years of government experience and his endorsement by organized labor and other liberal groups. With his rumpled demeanor and nasal voice, Mondale was not a telegenic candidate. Republicans portrayed his celebration of the glory days of the Democrats and his search for endorsements as proof that he was an old-fashioned "tax-and-spend" liberal pandering to "special interests." Mondale selected Congresswoman Geraldine Ferraro of New York as his vice-presidential candidate, the first woman nominated for the national ticket by a major party. But the GOP undermined Ferraro's appeal by spotlighting tax problems surrounding her husband's real-estate business.

Mondale tried to run a campaign based on issues, speaking about runaway deficits, an out-of-control arms race, environmental disasters, and the unfairness of Reagan's economic policies. His most dramatic campaign line was: "He'll raise taxes, so will I. He won't tell you, I just did." Commentators briefly praised Mondale's political courage, but within a week they decided that he had committed political suicide.

Reagan's only misstep came in the first of two televised campaign debates. On October 7, 1984, Reagan, appearing distracted and confused, rambled through his prepared remarks. Mondale privately told an aide that the president seemed "senile." Even Nancy Reagan, her husband's greatest fan, described his performance as a "disaster." But the president bounced back in a second debate two weeks later. When asked if age might impede presidential performance, Reagan quipped that he would not exploit his fifty-six-year-old challenger's "youth and inexperience" as a campaign issue. As millions of viewers laughed, a dejected Mondale recognized he had just lost the election.

In addition to Reagan's personal appeal, Republican candidates in 1984 could coast on a huge financial cushion. Between 1977 and 1984, GOP fundraising groups took in about $771 million, nearly four times the Democrats' total of $201 million. The Democrats had to use their paltry funds to pay routine expenses such as rent and utilities, while Republicans could commission polls, purchase computer support equipment, and employ high-priced consultants such as Richard Wirthlin to conduct frequent surveys among test groups of voters. This preparation helped assure a GOP victory in 1984.

In the presidential race, Reagan carried every state except Mondale's home state of Minnesota, amassing 59 percent of the popular vote and a record 525 electoral votes. In the South, the Democrats' pre-1964 stronghold, Mondale received only 25 percent of the white vote, further evidence of the success of the GOP's "Southern Strategy." Nationally, the only groups giving Mondale a majority of their votes were African Americans, Jews, and those who earned less than $10,000 annually.

The size and scope of Reagan's victory confirmed the Republican party as the dominant force in presidential politics. Yet Reagan's triumph was more personal than partisan. In the Senate, the GOP actually lost two seats, reducing its majority to 53-47. In the House of Representatives, Republicans gained 14 seats, an unusually small number given the size of the Reagan landslide, and Democrats retained a large majority, 253 to 182. Republicans elected only one additional state governor. These results suggested that while Reagan appealed to a broad coalition of voters, congressional Republicans had failed outside the South to win over large numbers of blue-collar, Catholic, and white ethnic Democrats.

During Reagan's second administration, internal staff changes and foreign-policy reverses diminished his luster. His triumvirate of close advisers left the White House. Chief of Staff James Baker and

Counselor Edwin Meese became, respectively, treasury secretary and attorney general. Assistant Chief of Staff Michael Deaver went into private business. Treasury Secretary Don Regan, a less politically astute aide, became the president's chief of staff. Without direct guidance from Baker, Deaver, and Meese, the president lost direction.

During Reagan's second term, Congress approved only two major pieces of domestic legislation backed by the White House. In 1986, Congress passed a major tax-reform bill drafted by a coalition of Democrats, Republicans, and Treasury officials. Neither "liberal" nor "conservative," the new tax code lowered top rates from 50 percent to 28 percent, closed many loopholes, and eliminated taxes for 4 million of the poorest Americans. The sudden removal of tax breaks for investors in commercial real estate practically killed the savings and loan industry, which had poured money into office buildings and strip malls, many of which stood vacant.

That same year, Congress tackled immigration reform. Since 1965, when Congress had repealed ethnic quotas, almost 90 percent of new arrivals in America came from Asia and Latin America, compared to only 10 percent before. In addition, as many as 13 to 15 million undocumented (illegal) immigrants, many of them from Mexico and Central America, lived in the United States. In 1986, Congress passed the Simpson-Rodino Act, named for Senator Allan Simpson, a conservative Republican from Wyoming, and Representative Peter Rodino, a liberal Democrat from New Jersey. The law conferred legal status on undocumented migrants already in the country, but it discouraged future illegal entrants by imposing fines on employers who hired them. The Simpson-Rodino bill permitted about 1 million immigrants to enter the United States annually, historically a very high number.

The other major Reagan-backed law was a balanced-budget bill. In a move coordinated with the White House, Republican Senators Phil Gramm of Texas and Warren Rudman of New Hampshire joined with their Democratic colleague from South Carolina, Ernest F. Hollings, to push the Gramm-Rudman-Hollings Act through Congress in 1986. The law mandated an end to the massive deficit by calling for reduced federal expenditures during each of the next five years. But the approach was ineffectual. It contained no enforcement mechanism, so deficits actually increased during Reagan's final years and got even bigger under the administration of President George H. W. Bush.

In 1986, Republican congressional candidates again failed to capitalize on the public's affection for Reagan and their party's substantial funding advantage over Democrats. Democrats actually regained control of the Senate and increased their majority in the House. Six Republican senators elected in 1980 lost their seats, and three other incumbents fell to Democratic challengers. Only one Democratic seat changed hands, in Missouri. Democrats now held a 55-45 majority in the Senate. Democratic challengers did especially well in southern states—winning six of seven seats—by portraying the GOP incumbents as tools of the national Republican party with little interest in local affairs. In the House, the GOP suffered a net loss of five, giving Democrats an expanded margin of 258 to 177. Republicans fared better at the state level, winning eight governorships (many of them in the South) and pulling nearly even with the Democrats. But the Democrats actually increased their representation in state legislatures.

Controlling once again both branches of Congress after 1986, Democrats blocked Republican efforts to cut social programs further, expand defense spending, and intervene more directly in Central America. The Democrat-controlled Senate rejected Reagan's nomination of Robert Bork to the Supreme Court, and Congress again rebuffed proposed constitutional amendments to ban abortion and permit school prayer.

In November 1986, Reagan suffered a major blow to his image when word leaked out of his direct involvement in the Iran-Contra scandal. This bizarre scheme involved illegally trading weapons for hostages with Iran and using profits from the deal to fund anticommunist guerrillas in Central America. A panel selected by Reagan and a separate congressional probe condemned the president for violating his word, breaking the law, and tarnishing the nation's reputation. As a result, public support for the president fell below 50 percent.

As members of Congress muttered threats of impeachment and the press lambasted Reagan as an incompetent manager, unexpected help from the "evil empire" helped rescue the president. Soviet reformer Mikhail Gorbachev, desperate to reduce defense spending and attract Western financial aid, endorsed American proposals to limit intermediate-range nuclear missiles and conventional forces. Reagan's positive response to this dramatic change in Soviet behavior persuaded many critics and ordinary Americans to overlook the president's legal and ethical lapses in the Iran-Contra affair.

During his final years in office, Reagan visited the Soviet Union, hosted Gorbachev in the White House, and reached important disarmament agreements with Moscow. The only harsh criticism of Reagan's actions came from the most right-wing Republicans, who distrusted Gorbachev and called the president a "useful idiot" controlled by the Kremlin. Nearly all other Americans applauded Reagan's flexibility. When he stepped down in January 1989, he enjoyed a 68 percent job-approval rating, higher than any president leaving office since FDR.

George H. W. Bush, Michael Dukakis, and the 1988 Election

Despite serving eight years as vice president, George Bush remained relatively unknown to the public. He was not especially close to Reagan, telling one interviewer that he had never even been invited into the family wing of the White House. Nor had Bush played much of a part in setting the domestic or foreign-policy agenda. Until being tapped as Reagan's running mate in 1980, he had supported abortion rights and disparaged Reagan's budget plan as "voodoo economics." These past lapses, along with his "preppy" mannerisms and what some viewed as a wimpy "Mr. Rogers" personality, made Bush the object of mistrust and derision among the Republican right wing. In the contest to succeed Reagan, more conservative challengers, including Reagan aide Patrick Buchanan, televangelist Pat Robertson, and Senator Robert Dole, stressed these points and accused Bush of being an unauthentic conservative, more "Eastern Establishment liberal" than rugged individualist. One wag dismissed Bush's claim to being a Texan as "all hat and no boots."

The son of a wealthy Republican senator from Connecticut, Bush had left college during World War II to become the youngest fighter pilot in the U.S. Navy. After the war, he graduated from Yale, then moved to Texas and made a fortune in the oil business. As a moderate in an increasingly conservative Republican party, he served two terms in the U.S. House of Representatives from 1967 to 1971. As a proponent of strong government aid to Planned Parenthood, Bush was sometimes called by his nickname, "Rubbers." Defeated in 1970 for a Senate seat from Texas, Bush was appointed to a number of posts by Presidents Nixon and Ford, including chairman of the Republican National Committee, U.S. representative in China, and director of the CIA.

After Bush secured the 1988 GOP nomination, he worked to highlight and enhance his conservative credentials. He selected Senator Dan Quayle of Indiana, a favorite among Christian conservatives but otherwise considered a political lightweight, as his running mate. At the Republican convention, Bush brought delegates to their feet by borrowing a line made famous by actor Clint Eastwood. "Read my lips: no new taxes," he declared. Nevertheless, he never won the full trust of the GOP right.

Democrats approached the 1988 election factionalized and uncertain. Eight candidates battled for the nomination, and by the spring of 1988, two remained in play. The Reverend Jesse Jackson, the first African American presidential candidate to win a substantial following, led a "Rainbow Coalition" that championed traditional liberal causes. But Massachusetts governor Michael Dukakis, a relative unknown, eventually outpolled Jackson, who was dogged with a "radical" image. Dukakis shunned the "liberal" label and promised to achieve nationally the rapid economic growth that his state had experienced during his efficient stewardship.

Despite his impressive resume and eight years as vice president, Bush was seventeen points behind Dukakis in opinion polls in the summer of 1988. The GOP nominee set out to alter the public's favorable view of Dukakis as a moderate technocrat sensitive to the needs of ordinary Americans. Adopting a slashing strategic plan crafted by his campaign manager, Lee Atwater, Bush promised to oppose abortion, cut taxes, promote prayer in public school, and get even tougher on drug users. He also "demonized" Dukakis as a "high tax, high spending, proabortion, card-carrying member of the American Civil Liberties Union." In short, Bush depicted Dukakis as an "unrepentant sixties liberal."

Much of the GOP attack focused on Dukakis's veto of a Massachusetts law requiring schoolteachers to lead students in the Pledge of Allegiance to the American flag. Bush also criticized the governor for granting a prison furlough to a murderer named Willie Horton, who then raped a woman. The fact that Horton was African American and his victim was white added to the emotional nature of the incident. Bush said of Dukakis: "I don't understand the type of thinking that lets first degree murderers . . . out on parole so they can rape and plunder again, and then isn't willing to let teachers lead the kids in the Pledge of Allegiance."

Dukakis proved a wooden candidate, unable to refute Bush's charges or to articulate a program to regain the support of conservative Democrats who had supported Nixon and Reagan. Bush won the election with 54 percent of the popular vote and with majorities in forty states, running especially strong among white men and in the South. Yet Bush was also the first candidate since John F. Kennedy to win the presidency while his party actually lost seats in the House of Representatives. In that body, Democrats made a net gain of 2 seats, for a majority of 260-175. Republicans also fared poorly in Senate races, where Democrats won 19 of 33 contested seats and retained their 55-45 majority. In state elections, Democrats picked up one governorship and made substantial gains in several state assemblies. The results of this status quo election showed that GOP dominance of national politics centered on the White House.

As a candidate, Bush had pledged to preside over a "kinder, gentler America," an implication that he intended to govern with more concern for meeting people's needs than for achieving ideological purity. This stance helped him win over moderate swing voters, but it put Bush on a collision course with the more conservative elements of the Republican party.

From 1989 through 1991, continued economic expansion, the collapse of the Soviet Union, and quick success in the Gulf War sustained the popularity of Bush as president. His abrasive chief of staff, former New Hampshire Governor John Sununu, worked hard to keep the White House on good terms with the New Religious Right. Bush himself cooperated with the Democratic majority in Congress to pass several important pieces of legislation for the environment and the disabled. The Americans with Disabilities Act of 1991 was designed to assure that government, business, and educational institutions provided equal access to the physically handicapped. Revisions of the Clean Water Act and the Clean Air Act expanded laws first passed in the 1970s that set federal and state standards for water and air purity, regulated automobile and industrial emissions, and funded sewage systems. The Radiation Exposure Compensation Act provided payments for victims of atomic mining and testing during the Cold War. The Native American Graves Repatriation Act forced museums to return certain human remains and cultural artifacts to Indian tribes. In 1991, Bush signed a civil rights bill that permitted racial and gender goals in hiring. He also favored federal initiatives in setting local education standards. His support for these "good-government" measures infuriated more-conservative Republicans.

Their anger intensified when economic circumstances forced Bush to retreat from another pillar of the Reagan Revolution: the commitment to not raise taxes. Faced with a growing deficit and complaints from foreign creditors worried about the value of the dollars owed to them, the president and the Democratic leadership of Congress agreed to a budget deal in 1990, that called for modest tax hikes along with small spending cuts in social programs and defense. Now, conservatives led by Representative Newt Gingrich of Georgia condemned Bush for breaking his "read my lips: no new taxes" pledge. Meanwhile, some liberal Democrats balked at their leadership's approval of a plan that imposed regressive sales taxes on beer and cigarettes, taxes that hit the poor hardest. Together, this unlikely coalition blocked the budget deal and forced a three-day shutdown of the federal government in October.

Congress eventually approved a reconfigured budget that included small tax hikes for high-income Americans and a small reduction in spending. Nevertheless, Bush's actions had outraged Gingrich and his right-wing followers, and the president never regained their trust. Democrats expressed their own contempt for the president, charging that his waffling on taxes and spending proved that he was an ineffective leader who lacked principles.

By now it was clear that Bush, unlike Reagan, did not believe that "government" was the enemy. He also tried to work with the Democratic congressional majority to pass needed legislation. In contrast, Gingrich and a group of more conservative House Republicans advocated a "take no prisoners" strategy of politics, denouncing Democratic motives and opposing everything their political opponents attempted to accomplish. As the newly selected House Republican whip (a party officer charged with enforcing discipline), Gingrich favored confrontation as the best way to undermine the Democrats' built-in advantage of incumbency.

During the 1980s and early 1990s, many of the Republicans' most important gains came at the state and local levels. By the mid-1990s, in fact, the GOP held gubernatorial control in nine of the nation's ten largest states, and more than 70 percent of the American population lived in states led by Republican governors. Many differences existed among these GOP state leaders, but they generally governed more moderately than Presidents Reagan and Bush or congressional Republicans.

Most big-state GOP governors were fiscally conservative but socially moderate. Michigan's John Englar and Wisconsin's Tommy Thompson, for example, supported both tax cuts and increased state funding for education, as well as welfare reform. Other socially moderate Republican governors, such as Tom Ridge of Pennsylvania, George Pataki of New York, and Christie Todd Whitman of New Jersey (all elected in 1993 or 1994), backed "pro-choice" policies despite the GOP's strident opposition to abortion rights. And some, including Ohio's George Voinovich, were against abortion but refrained from vigorously opposing the *Roe* v. *Wade* decision issued by the Supreme Court in 1973.

Among big-state Republican governors in the 1990s, only Texas's George W. Bush (elected in 1994 and 1998) and his brother, Florida's Jeb Bush (elected 1998), were outspokenly conservative. But the Bush brothers governed southern states and held presidential aspirations. These factors probably underlay their vocal support for controversial positions in the Republican national platform that were near and dear to social and religious conservatives (especially southerners), including firm opposition to abortion rights and gun control, approval of capital punishment, expansion of military spending, and criticism of liberal judges.

In contrast to pragmatic GOP governors, congressional Republicans increasingly assumed an unyielding conservative posture during the 1980s and 1990s. Except for a handful of Northeastern senators and a larger contingent of representatives, moderate, or "accommo-dationist," Republicans became an endangered species in Congress. Conservative southern and southwestern Republicans dominated the GOP leadership by the mid-1990s, epitomized by Representative Newt Gingrich of Georgia and Senator Trent Lott of Mississippi.

In 1989, Democrats provided unintended assistance to Gingrich when the Senate rebuffed Bush's nomination of former Texas senator John Tower as secretary of defense. Tower, who was disliked by senators from both parties, faced embarrassing criticism from Demo-crats for his problems with alcohol, womanizing, and business ethics. Gingrich used the rejection of Tower to rally House Republicans and justify his own blistering attack on the ethics and fundraising prac-tices of House Speaker Jim Wright, a Democrat from Texas. Wright, a flamboyant personality who had violated House procedures, re-signed under pressure in 1989.

In contrast to Wright, Democrat Thomas Foley of Washington, the new House Speaker, was a model of probity. Nevertheless, he had to defend himself against charges of homosexuality spread by Re-publican National Committee chairman Lee Atwater. The RNC peddled a report titled: "Tom Foley: Out of the Liberal Closet," which accused the Speaker of being both liberal and gay—equally grave faults in the opinion of much of the New Right. Bush, who hoped to cooperate with Foley in passing legislation, apologized for the smear and reprimanded Atwater. This further angered Gingrich, and mem-bers of Congress from both parties accused the other side of numer-ous moral, ethical, and legal transgressions during the next two years.

Despite the growing partisan rancor in Congress, voters returned nearly all incumbents on Election Day in November 1990. Only one of thirty-two Senate incumbents seeking reelection—Republican Rudy Boschwitz of Minnesota—lost his seat, and 98.5 percent of House incumbents won reelection. Democrats held an increased ma-jority in the Senate (56-44) and gained eight seats in the House (267-165). Although most incumbents were returned to office, public dis-taste for congressional feuding expressed itself in other ways. Colorado became the first state to impose term limits on federal of-fice holders. Voters in California, Colorado, and Oklahoma placed similar caps on service by state legislators. The balance of Republican and Democratic governors changed little in 1990, but fourteen statehouse majorities switched from one party to the other, and more incumbent governors were defeated than in any election year since 1970.

Controversies over individual rights continued to strike discordant notes. Abortion rights remained an especially charged issue. In two Supreme Court decisions, *Webster* v. *Reproductive Services Of Missouri* (1989) and *Planned Parenthood* v. *Casey* (1992), the justices held, by 5-4 vote margins, that states could strictly regulate but not absolutely ban abortions.

Liberal concerns and conservative hopes for the future direction of the Supreme Court intensified when Associate Justices William Brennan and Thurgood Marshall retired. The departure of these stalwart liberals gave Bush an opportunity to tip the ideological balance of the Court. To replace Brennan in 1990, the president nominated the virtually unknown David Souter of New Hampshire, who had served for only a few months on the federal bench. Unlike Robert Bork, Souter had not expressed himself publicly on controversial issues such as abortion, the right to privacy, and the death penalty. He maintained silence on these matters during the Senate confirmation process and easily won approval. To the surprise of nearly everyone, once on the high court, Souter emerged as a voice of moderation on abortion and other issues.

After disappointing conservatives with Souter, Bush filled the Supreme Court vacancy left by the retirement of Thurgood Marshall —the Court's first African American justice—with a high profile conservative. The "most qualified American" to replace Marshall, Bush claimed, was Clarence Thomas, a forty-three-year-old African American federal appeals court judge. Thomas, a staunch conservative, had criticized many past Supreme Court rulings on abortion, school prayer, privacy rights, and the death penalty. Nevertheless, he appeared headed for speedy confirmation until a journalist revealed that he once had been accused of sexual harassment by law professor Anita Hill and other former colleagues.

After Professor Hill agreed to testify before Congress to detail her charges against Thomas, the all-male Senate Judiciary Committee reluctantly interviewed her in a tense, televised hearing. Hill's detailed allegations, Thomas's vehement but vague denial, and the committee's condescending treatment of Hill made a sorry spectacle. The Senate ultimately confirmed Thomas, who unlike Souter, proved a reliable conservative, but the whole episode aroused strong misgivings, especially among feminists, over Bush's judgment in making the nomination. The incident became an important factor in the revival of Democratic fortunes in 1992.

The End of the Cold War
and Bush's "New World Order"

The years 1989 through 1992 witnessed the most dramatic changes in global politics since 1945. The United States and the Soviet Union ended their rivalry, and communism collapsed throughout Eastern Europe. Bush had the good fortune to preside over the peaceful dissolution of the Soviet empire and the demise of communism as a global force. But he also deserved credit for steering these events in peaceful directions.

In 1989, Soviet leader Mikhail Gorbachev permitted free parliamentary elections for the first time since 1917. He then announced that the "satellite" states of Eastern Europe were free to run their own affairs without Soviet interference. In November 1989, the highly symbolic Berlin Wall was brought down, and the unification of Germany followed the next year. Peaceful revolutions soon toppled communist regimes in most of the rest of Eastern Europe. In November 1990, Bush and Gorbachev jointly declared the Cold War over.

Despite Gorbachev's reform efforts, the Soviet Union spiraled toward collapse. An abortive coup by Communist hard-liners in August 1991 weakened central authority and prompted non-Russian ethnic groups in the Baltic and Central Asian regions to declare independence from Moscow. Gorbachev signed a decree on December 25, 1991, dissolving the Soviet Union and transferring power to Boris Yeltsin, the democratically elected president of the Russian Republic.

Even as the Soviet empire dissolved, new challenges to U.S. interests emerged. The first foreign military intervention by the Bush administration took place in Panama, where military strongman and former CIA paid informant Manuel Noriega had taken power in

1983. The Reagan administration had tolerated Noriega's known ties to Colombian cocaine cartels in exchange for his cooperation with the CIA in the war against the leftist regime in Nicaragua. But Noriega became an embarrassment to Washington after that conflict ended in 1988 and the Bush administration began its high profile "war on drugs." Then, in 1989, Noriega voided the results of an election won by his opponents and sent thugs to beat up his critics and some U.S. citizens residing in Panama. In response, Bush concluded: "Enough is enough. This guy's not going to lay off. It will only get worse," and dispatched an invasion force of twelve thousand U.S. soldiers to Panama. After three days of sporadic fighting, the U.S. military arrested Noriega and installed the winner of the election as president. The American public strongly approved of this intervention, and a U.S. jury later convicted Noriega of drug trafficking, despite his claim that the Reagan administration had been his silent partner.

The U.S. national interest faced a far greater challenge after August 2, 1990, when Iraq seized the tiny, oil-rich sheikdom of Kuwait in the Persian Gulf region. Iraqi leader Saddam Hussein annexed Kuwait in order to enrich Iraq, gain influence in the Arab world, and play a major role in setting global petroleum prices. Saddam may have expected the United States to tolerate his actions, because both Reagan and Bush had authorized generous loans to Iraq, aided Saddam in his war with Iran during the 1980s, and ignored his past use of chemical weapons and efforts to acquire atomic and biological weapons.

The tiny nation of Kuwait was no democracy, but it was a sovereign state and a member of the United Nations. The United States and its allies feared that if the Iraqi seizure of Kuwait went unchallenged, Saddam would be in a position to intimidate, or even to invade, Saudi Arabia. This would give him control over a major part of global oil reserves and the power to destabilize the industrialized world. To prevent this, Bush persuaded the UN to impose a tight economic embargo on Iraq and sent half a million U.S. troops to Saudi Arabia as part of a coalition force from twenty-eight nations. Even the Soviet Union, Iraq's former arms supplier, supported the sanctions. For the first time since the Japanese attack on Pearl Harbor,

Congress debated a president's formal request to authorize military retaliation. Only ten Democratic senators—including Al Gore and Joseph Lieberman—endorsed the proposed use of force, but Congress gave approval by a narrow margin on January 12, 1991.

Five days later, after diplomatic efforts to liberate Kuwait had failed, Bush ordered U.S. and coalition planes to begin bombing Iraqi targets and troops. In launching the attack code named "Desert Storm," Bush paraphrased the words of President Woodrow Wilson, declaring that "we have before us the opportunity to forge for ourselves a new world order." On February 23, after five weeks of aerial attack, U.S. and coalition troops launched a ground offensive, which liberated Kuwait and drove deep into Iraq in less than a hundred hours. When Bush accepted Saddam's plea for a cease-fire on February 27, only 223 allied troops, including 148 Americans, had been killed, compared to tens of thousands of Iraqis. Kuwaiti sovereignty (not democracy) was restored, and Saudi oil reserves were secured. Nine in ten Americans, a Gallup poll reported, approved of Bush's job performance at that time.

George H. W. Bush, Bill Clinton, and the 1992 Election

In spite of the president's boast that the United States had, at last, "kicked the Vietnam syndrome," the Gulf War victory proved to be a limited one. Coalition forces had stopped their push on to Baghdad before driving Saddam Hussein from power. Bush and his advisers feared that if the Iraqi tyrant were toppled, he might be replaced by even more threatening Islamic fundamentalists. Even though as part of the cease fire Saddam agreed to accept UN personnel in his country who were supposed to make sure he did not reacquire nuclear, chemical, or biological weapons, the Iraqi regime continued to threaten its neighbors and to frustrate and eventually drive out the international inspectors. By the end of 1992, a growing number of Americans criticized Bush's failure to "finish off" Saddam, and over the next decade, the president's action undermined GOP claims of being a better manager of foreign policy than the Democrats.

The lack of clear direction after the end of the Cold War and the murky outcome of the Gulf War were somewhat abstract problems to most Americans. Indeed, the onset of a steep economic recession in 1991 proved far more tangible and damaging to the Bush administration and GOP fortunes. Conservative Republicans angrily attributed the downturn to the president's reversal of Reagan's tax policies. Bush, who privately called the recession an economic "free fall," felt trapped between the massive federal deficit of almost $300 billion and GOP conservatives prepared to denounce him for any display of moderation. Afraid to raise taxes in order to reduce the deficit or boost spending (to stimulate the economy), the president appeared paralyzed. Democrats charged that Bush's lethargy indicated that he was ineffective and that Reaganomics had been proved a failure.

As the recession extended into 1992, the public blamed a variety of villains. Without the demon of communism and the Soviet Union to unify the country, some condemned America's industrial allies for unleashing a barrage of automobiles and electronic goods onto the open U.S. market. The "good news is that the Cold War is over," quipped Paul Tsongas, a Democratic senator from Massachusetts. "The bad news is that Germany and Japan won."

By early 1992, the fading glow of the Gulf War victory and the worsening recession tarnished Bush's halo. Criticism by Democrats of the president's apparent apathy toward domestic issues, along with harsh denunciations by conservative Republicans for the breaking of his 1988 "Read my lips, no new taxes" pledge, drove down Bush's job approval rating from about 91 percent in March 1991 (immediately following the Gulf War) to 44 percent in February 1992. That spring, over 80 percent of Americans told the Gallup Poll that they were unhappy with the state of the nation. Bush's proud phrase "new world order" became an object of popular derision.

Despite his plummeting popularity, Bush won renomination for a second presidential term in the summer of 1992. Patrick Buchanan mounted a strident conservative attack on Bush's record but lost every primary. Even though Buchanan collected fewer than a hundred delegates, he wounded the incumbent by portraying him as an insincere conservative and an incompetent administrator.

Since 1968, Democratic presidential candidates had lost five of six elections, including three straight landslide trouncings in the 1980s. Political pundits and academic specialists speculated that the

GOP had secured a lock on the White House as a result of Republican strength in the southern and southwestern Sunbelt states, the Rocky Mountain region, and the upper Midwest. These states possessed about 250 electoral votes, just twenty fewer than the 270 needed for victory. A related argument held that a majority of voters were strongly attracted to certain symbolic and cultural positions held by GOP candidates. These included the espousal of patriotic nationalism and "traditional moral values," along with opposition to taxes that paid for government programs for the poor and minorities. Democrats, in contrast, seemed beholden to minorities, labor unions, and "liberal values" outside the mainstream of American culture.

Beginning in the late 1980s, a small but influential group of Democrats worked to reshape their party's positions on issues of patriotism and moral values, challenging the perceived GOP advantage. Calling themselves New Democrats, these reformers established the Democratic Leadership Council (DLC). Most DLC members came from the moderate and conservative wings of the party; most were from the South; and most had close ties to corporations. They included Senators Al Gore of Tennessee, Joseph Lieberman of Connecticut, Sam Nunn of Georgia, and Joseph Biden of Delaware, as well as Governor Bill Clinton of Arkansas.

New Democrats worked to distance the party and its candidates from their traditional embrace of liberal policies and their close identification with labor unions and racial and ethnic minorities. Through past efforts to satisfy these constituencies, they argued, Democrats had alienated a larger group of white voters, especially males, who lived in the nation's suburbs and in the South. To win the presidency, a Democrat would have to attract these centrist voters by adopting relatively conservative proposals on issues such as welfare reform, crime, free trade, and defense. By distancing themselves from labor unions, New Democrats also hoped to obtain vital corporate campaign contributions. More traditional party leaders such as Jesse Jackson viewed New Democrats as GOP clones and joked that "DLC" stood for "Democrats for the Leisure Class."

Yet New Democrats, unlike Republicans, still believed that the federal government should play a major role in many areas of American life. These included job training, national service, environmental protection, and investments in education, health, transportation, and housing. New Democrats also supported a woman's right to choose an abortion. As mentioned, Republicans since Reagan had identified the federal government as "the problem" and called for turning many public functions over to state and local officials or to the private sector and charities. New Democrats, on the other hand, spoke of "reinventing government" to make it smaller, more efficient, and more responsive.

While governor of Arkansas, Bill Clinton had served as the DLC chairman, and he based his 1992 campaign for the presidency firmly on New Democrat themes. As one friendly observer noted, he "stressed economic mobility rather than wealth transfers, took a tough-minded line on crime, welfare dependency and international security issues, and called for a new ethic of personal responsibility to temper demands for entitlements."

Surprising many journalists and party traditionalists, Clinton won most of the Democratic state primaries and secured the party's presidential nomination despite rumors of his marital infidelity and draft "dodging" during the Vietnam War. As the recession worsened, Clinton skillfully added an element of economic populism to his campaign. This appealed to organized labor, liberals, and nonunion working-class Americans who felt passed over by both Bush and the New Democrats. Now, Clinton led a unified party and focused on an economic message. In reply to what the election was about, his campaign declared "It's the economy, stupid." And, he denounced "savings and loan crooks" who profited while "workers were losing their jobs."

Meanwhile, Ross Perot, a flamboyant Texas billionaire who personally hated Bush, entered the presidential race as a self-funded independent. Promising to slash the soaring deficit and shake up the system, the mercurial candidate attracted slightly more Republican than Democratic voters.

For his part, President Bush ran a lethargic reelection campaign. Clinton's relatively conservative position on issues such as the death penalty and crime made it hard to paint him as a bleeding-heart liberal. The end of the Cold War also muted the effectiveness of the standard GOP charge that Democrats were soft on communism and defense. Instead, Bush unleashed a relentless attack on Clinton's character, including his rumored womanizing, youthful marijuana use, and avoidance of the Vietnam-era draft. But these accusations fell flat as the public responded enthusiastically to Clinton's pledge to improve the economy.

On Election Day, voters turned Bush out of office. Clinton carried thirty-two states, won 370 electoral votes, and received 43 percent of the popular vote, compared to Bush's 38 percent. Perot, who had quit and then reentered the race, received 19 percent of the popular vote, nearly the most ever for an independent candidate and enough to seal Bush's defeat.

The outcome of congressional races also showed a desire for change. Record numbers of women, African Americans, and Hispanics were elected. Four women, including one African American, were elected to the Senate, where the Democrats now enjoyed a 55-45 majority. Retirements, redistricting, and voter discontent led to a 25 percent turnover in the House, where Republicans scored a net gain of 10 seats, leaving the Democrats with a 258-176 majority. Few governorships changed hands, but voters in fourteen states imposed congressional term limits (which the Supreme Court later held were unconstitutional).

Clinton's victory and the reelection of Democratic majorities to both houses of Congress dashed GOP hopes of institutionalizing the Republican ascendancy begun under Nixon and solidified during the Reagan and Bush administrations. In retaking the White House for the Democrats, Clinton owed a great deal to the high unemployment rate during the 1992 recession that followed twenty years of stagnant incomes for 80 percent of American families. Reversing a trend begun in the 1960s, Clinton won six southern and border states and swept the Pacific West, becoming the first Democrat since 1964 to secure California's fifty-four electoral votes. As a moderate, Southern Democrat, Clinton had restitched the tattered but resilient New Deal coalition. Reduced racial tension, the end of the Cold War, and economic recession caused millions of working-class, southern, and Catholic whites to return to the Democratic presidential fold. Whether the Democrats had reversed their decline remained unclear. As Clinton's tart-tongued campaign strategist James Carville remarked, "We didn't find the key to the electoral lock . . . we just picked it."

Above: Ronald Reagan (right) campaigning for Barry Goldwater (left) in 1964, the year that the right came together behind Goldwater, who won the Republican presidential nomination. The Goldwater campaign was also the starting point of Reagan's own political career. Courtesy Ronald Reagan Library

Overleaf (top): Richard Nixon was elected president in 1968, after a remarkable political comeback that astonished friends and foes alike. Courtesy Richard Nixon Library and Birthplace

Overleaf (bottom): After winning re-election in 1972 by an historic margin, the Watergate scandal had reversed Nixon's political fortunes once again. Here in 1974, protesters march in front of the White House. Courtesy Washington D.C. Public Library

Top: Senators shown on the Capitol steps in 1976 who ran for president or vice president (left to right): Strom Thurmond (1948), Edmund Muskie (1968), Robert Dole (1976, 1996), Barry Goldwater (1964), George McGovern (1972), and John Sparkman (1952). Courtesy U.S. Senate Historical Office

Bottom: President Carter (right) and Vice President Walter Mondale took office in 1977 with a number of unresolved problems including stagflation, high unemployment, an adverse trade balance, and increasing dependence on foreign energy sources. Courtesy Jimmy Carter Library

Ronald Reagan was the first Republican leader to recognize the key roles that the New Religious Right played in the GOP as faithful primary voters, campaign donors, and party activists. Reagan befriended televangelists including Pat Robertson (top) and Jerry Falwell (bottom). Courtesy Ronald Reagan Library

Opposite top: President Reagan with (from right) Caspar Weinberger, George Schultz, Ed Meese, and Donald Regan discussing the president's remarks on the Iran-Contra affair, November 25, 1986. Courtesy Ronald Reagan Library

Opposite bottom: Soviet reformer Mikhail Gorbachev, Ronald Reagan, and George H. W. Bush at the White House. Reagan's positive response to the dramatic change in Soviet behavior helped detract attention from his involvement in the Iran-Contra affair. Courtesy Ronald Reagan Library

Opposite top: President George H. W. Bush and his Vice President Dan Quayle, 1989. Courtesy George Bush Presidential Library

Opposite bottom: Operation Desert Storm: General Colin Powell, chairman of the Joint Chiefs of Staff (second from left); Secretary of Defense Richard B. Cheney; and General Norman Schwarz-kopf in the command center, Saudi Arabia. Courtesy Defense Department

Above: The inauguration of William Jefferson Clinton, January 20, 1993. Courtesy of the Clinton White House

Top: U.S. Secreatary of State Colin Powell (left) and U.S. National Security Adviser Condoleezza Rice (right) after a speech by President George W. Bush, May 1, 2001, in which he vowed to deploy a shield against ballistic missile attacks and, in turn, reduce nuclear forces. © AFP/CORBIS

Bottom: President George W. Bush addresses a crowd as he stands with firefighters and search crews at the site of the World Trade Center Towers, September 14, 2001. © Reuters NewsMedia, Inc./CORBIS

CHAPTER FIVE

New Democrats and Republican Revolutionaries, 1993–2000

On January 23, 1996, President Bill Clinton declared in his State of the Union address: "The era of big government is over." The Democratic president continued his speech by embracing other conservative themes that Republicans had espoused since the 1960s: balancing the federal budget, reforming welfare, toughening crime laws, and strengthening "family values." Seven months later, just weeks before his reelection, Clinton signed and took credit for a law "ending welfare as we know it." And in 1998, he presided over a White House ceremony celebrating fiscal discipline and the first federal-budget surplus in three decades.

Clinton's adoption of many of his opponents' popular issues in 1996 and afterward contrasted with the early years of his presidency, when first Democrats and then Republicans had undertaken ambitious, controversial programs. In 1993–94, the Clinton administration overextended itself by trying to enact wide-ranging proposals designed to please both moderate and liberal Democrats. The president's program and its many failures disappointed his supporters and provoked a fierce reaction from conservatives. In the 1994 midterm elections,

Republicans capitalized on voter disapproval of Clinton to win both houses of Congress for the first time in four decades. House Speaker Newt Gingrich and other GOP leaders proclaimed that their victories represented a conservative "Republican Revolution" that gave them a popular mandate to transform the federal government and American society. Both Clinton's New Democrat strategy and Gingrich's Republican Revolution "were conscious attempts to break the mold, change the program, alter the coalitions, shift the order, and end the Era of Divided Government," observed political scientist Byron E. Shafer.

Like Clinton's New Democrats, Gingrich's Republican Revolutionaries overreached once in power and failed to establish a new permanent majority. Clinton stymied this Republican effort by seizing the political center, commandeering the GOP's popular issues, and winning reelection in 1996. The failures of the Clinton and Gingrich programs renewed the political stalemate that had characterized American politics since 1968. During his second term, Clinton shunned an ambitious agenda and embraced small, often symbolic policies while touting his management of the booming economy. Republicans, who lacked overwhelming popular domestic or foreign issues, responded with intensified personal assaults on Clinton, eventually impeaching him in December 1998 after a sex scandal. Two years later, the 2000 election, one of the closest in history, epitomized the political deadlock between Republicans and Democrats that characterized the late twentieth century.

Republicans versus Clinton, 1993–1994

A month into his presidency, on February 17, 1993, Bill Clinton unveiled his administration's agenda. For moderate New Democrats, he called for reforming the welfare system and ratifying the North American Free Trade Agreement. For populist and liberal "Old Democrats," he proposed expanding the Earned Income Tax Credit for low-paid workers and raising income taxes on the richest 1.5 percent of Americans. Additionally, both New and Old Democrats could support the president's proposals for health-care reform, a middle-class tax cut, federal investment to stimulate economic growth, and increased aid for education and job training. But the huge federal budget deficit—a whopping $290 billion for 1993—constricted Clinton's agenda. Congress, Federal Reserve Chairman Alan Greenspan, Wall Street, and Ross Perot's independent movement all demanded reducing the deficit. Most New Democrats agreed, forcing the president to trim his program.

Clinton's compromise budget passed Congress in August 1993. It shrank the deficit by $500 billion over five years, decreasing spending by $250 billion and increasing tax revenues by the same amount. Conservative Republicans protested the budget's tax hikes on the wealthy. For example, a *National Review* editorial warned that "the income tax rate increase . . . will dampen investment, reduce national savings, slow business and job creation, and most importantly will fail to add a penny of revenues to the federal Treasury." Each of these conservative predictions proved spectacularly wrong in the booming economy that followed. Nevertheless, every Republican in both houses of Congress voted against Clinton's 1993 budget. In addition, deficit reduction forced the president to abandon his promised middle-class tax cut and to slash his economic-stimulus package. These actions revealed how much the political spectrum had shifted to the right on economic matters since the 1970s. "Where are the Democrats?" Clinton complained to advisors. "We are Eisenhower Republicans here, and we are fighting Reagan Republicans. We stand for lower deficits and free trade and the bond market."

Despite his political centrism, Clinton provoked nothing but hatred from conservative Republicans. Beginning in the 1992 campaign, they denounced him as a lying, corrupt, self-pitying narcissist and "a philandering, pot-smoking draft dodger," in the words of Bush adviser Mary Matalin. Other conservatives were more vicious. Judge Jim Johnson, a longtime Clinton foe from Arkansas, vilified the president as "a queer-mongering, whore-hopping adulterer; a baby-killing, draft-dodging, dope-tolerating, lying, two-faced, treasonist activist."

Although Republicans unrelentingly attacked Clinton's "immoral" character, his behavior and his personal history seemed comparable to that of a typical baby boomer. Most middle-class males of his generation, including several prominent GOP conservatives, had avoided service in Vietnam and smoked marijuana during their college years. And his womanizing proved far from unique among politicians; tabloid newspapers in the late 1990s exposed the adultery of seven high-ranking Republicans who had criticized the president's morals. Moreover, criticism of Clinton's personality appeared inconsistent. Many foes portrayed him, like his wife Hillary Rodham Clinton, as a conceited intellectual snob from Yale who personified the Washington-Northeastern elite. At the same time, however, they mocked the president, nicknamed "Bubba," as a hamburger-loving, "white-trash redneck" from the Deep South.

As this inconsistency revealed, the right's hatred for the Clintons was motivated by more than their personal shortcomings. Conservative Republicans believed that the Clintons personified the legacy of the 1960s counterculture, the right's hated foe in the "culture wars." To right-wing billionaire Richard Mellon Scaife, who financed several anti-Clinton projects, the president "was an embodiment of the sixties antiwar leftist movement that is immoral through and through," recalled a Scaife associate. Similarly, Republican Gingrich called the Clintons "countercultural McGoverniks." Conservatives' personal and cultural hostility to Clinton was aggravated by the president's political style. Republicans derided what they viewed as "Slick Willie's" overriding ambition, cynical opportunism, and slippery ways. "What is Clinton, beyond a desire to win?" sneered GOP speechwriter Peggy Noonan. Instead of adhering to principle, Republicans charged, the president "permanently campaigned," using a "war room" and a "spin machine" to attack opponents, commandeer their agenda, and manipulate the news media.

The main reason Republicans so vehemently opposed Clinton was that they perceived him, a Democrat, as an unworthy usurper of the presidency. Since 1968, conservatives had viewed the White House as a GOP entitlement, so Clinton's victory shocked Republicans, who saw it as somehow "illegitimate." After the 1992 election, Senate Minority Leader Bob Dole declared that he would represent the 57 percent majority who had voted for Bush and Perot. Newt Gingrich, the House Republican leader, refused to acknowledge Clinton as the "legitimately elected president of the United States," and Dick Armey, the second-ranking House Republican, referred to him as "your president." GOP leaders also vowed to obstruct this "il-legitimate" pretender in any way they could.

Fear and loathing of Clinton proved useful in uniting the diverse conservative coalition. The right of the 1990s included executives at multinational corporations, small-business owners, conservative academics and journalists, the religious right, right-to-life activists, home-schooling parents, anti-environmentalist loggers and miners, antitax advocates, radical libertarians, gun enthusiasts, anti-immigration activists, white supremacists, and antigovernment militias.

Opposition to Clinton helped these disparate groups work in concert. A weekly strategy session at Grover Norquist's Americans for Tax Reform brought together conservative activists from think tanks like the Heritage Foundation and Empower America, grassroots lobbying groups such as the Christian Coalition and the Eagle Forum, and single-issue causes like the National Rifle Association and U.S. Term Limits. The conservative movement further developed and disseminated its line through an array of media sources: magazines and newspapers that included the *National Review,* the *American Spectator,* the *Washington Times,* and later the *Weekly Standard;* syndicated columnists like George F. Will, Robert Novak, and Charles Krauthammer; such talk-radio hosts as Rush Limbaugh, James C. Dobson, and G. Gordon Liddy; and later, television cable channels like Fox News and Internet muckrakers led by Matt Drudge. "The radical right have their own set of press organs," Clinton charged. "They make their own news and then try to force it into the mainstream media." Many conservative activists also developed close relationships with the GOP's congressional leadership. Finally, the movement received funding from such wealthy organizations and individuals as the Bradley and Olin Foundations, the Coors and Koch families, Rupert Murdoch, and Richard Mellon Scaife. Scaife, for example, gave an estimated $400 million over forty years to conservative causes.

The right's unrelenting attacks on Bill and Hillary Clinton focused on uncovering, publicizing, and investigating several of their alleged scandals. In 1993, four Arkansas state troopers who had served as Governor Clinton's bodyguards published lurid gossip about him, prompting a short-lived "Troopergate"; Richard Mellon

Scaife secretly financed these troopers. One of their published stories involved a government employee named Paula Corbin Jones, who then sued Clinton for sexual harassment. Also in 1993, administration officials, possibly acting on behalf of Hillary Clinton, fired the White House travel office staff, spawning the so-called Travelgate. Another supposed scandal was "Filegate," the discovery of 900 FBI background files—many on Republicans—in the White House. Most absurdly, many conservatives blamed the Clintons for the July 1993 "murder" of Deputy Counsel Vincent W. Foster, Jr. This scurrilous myth remained a touchstone for Clinton-haters and conspiracy buffs—despite the fact that five separate federal investigations ruled Foster's death a suicide.

The main Clinton scandal was Whitewater. It involved a series of arcane real estate deals carried out in the early 1980s by the Clintons' unstable business partner, James McDougal. Critics also questioned the propriety of Hillary Clinton, an attorney, representing McDougal's bank before an Arkansas regulator as well as her making $100,000 on a $1,000 investment. The Clintons' reluctance to discuss their personal finances angered political opponents and journalists, who viewed it as stonewalling. The first family's contempt for reporters only worsened their media image. In January 1994, GOP leaders pressured Attorney General Janet Reno to appoint Republican Robert B. Fiske, Jr., as special counselor to probe the Whitewater dealings. Seven months later, a panel of conservative judges replaced Fiske with Kenneth W. Starr. Ultimately, the independent counsel's seven-year, $56 million (of taxpayers' money) investigation uncovered no conclusive evidence implicating the Clintons. But Starr's probe ranged far beyond Whitewater to delve into the president's sex life and culminated in the president's impeachment. Beginning in 1995, moreover, several GOP-chaired congressional committees investigated the Whitewater real-estate dealings. They, too, discovered no criminal evidence against the first family.

Still, allegations of presidential corruption made for big news, and the media and Republicans kept the "scandals" alive despite a lack of hard evidence to support conservatives' allegations. Eventually, each case—Troopergate, Paula Jones, Travelgate, Filegate, Foster's "murder," Whitewater—was dismissed for lack of evidence. More pertinently, each scandal appeared insignificant when compared to the abuses of presidential power by Nixon in Watergate or Reagan in Iran-Contra. Yet Republicans clung tenaciously to allegations of corruption. In 1997, an exasperated Hillary Clinton called their fixation on Whitewater "a never-ending fictional conspiracy that honest-to-goodness reminds me of some people's obsession with UFOs."

The administration helped its opponents with its amateurish start. Most observers judged Clinton the most skillful politician of his generation, but he made a rocky transition into the presidency. After announcing early on that homosexuals would no longer be discharged from the armed forces, the administration quickly retreated to a "don't ask, don't tell" compromise. But "gays in the military" became the foremost symbolic issue for cultural conservatives who saw the president as a raving liberal threatening the honor and unity of the armed forces. Clinton's choices to fill administration positions provoked controversy, too. "For women, minorities, and those on the left, Clinton's appointments seemed almost literally to provide a long-sought seat at the table; for the right, they represented the worst of 'political correctness' and the politicization of administration," noted political scientists Virginia Sapiro and David T. Canon. In response to stiff Republican criticisms, Clinton dropped several of his cabinet nominees. By June 1993, only 36 percent of Americans approved of Clinton's handling of the presidency, the lowest figure ever recorded after four months in office.

Health-care reform represented the Clinton administration's main failure. By 1992, health-care costs accounted for 14 percent of the nation's gross domestic product. Yet 37 million Americans carried no medical insurance as the United States remained the only developed country without national health care. The president appointed a task force headed by his wife to confront the issue. In September 1993, after months of secret deliberations, Hillary Clinton's task force presented a 1,342-page plan to Congress. It outlined a complex formula relying on health maintenance organizations (HMOs) to control medical costs. Additionally, the plan proposed that most businesses would be required to provide insurance coverage for their employees. At first, the proposal received a favorable response from the public, large insurance companies, and big corporations.

Soon, however, voices rose in opposition to it. Small businesses disliked its employer mandate, and many Americans worried that the plan would force them into HMOs. Small insurance companies played on these fears by waging a negative ad campaign. Some Republicans initially recommended compromising with the president. But conservative strategist William Kristol argued that national health care would become another popular program that "will relegitimize middle-class dependency for 'security' on government spending and regulation. It will revive the reputation of the party that spends and regulates, the Democrats." Following Kristol's advice, Republicans denounced the plan as "big government" or even "socialized medicine" (which it was not). Congress's rejection of health-care reform dealt a damaging blow to the Clinton presidency. Obviously, it also left unsolved America's health-care problem. By 2000, market forces had forced most Americans into HMO plans without government encouragement, while the number of uninsured Americans had risen to 44 million.

The administration did secure several legislative victories during its first two years, when the Democrats controlled both houses of Congress. Clinton succeeded in passing a family and medical leave act, motor-voter registration, and the Brady Bill, which established a five-day waiting period for handgun purchases. The administration's most important victory was congressional ratification of the North American Free Trade Agreement (NAFTA), which created a free-trade zone including Canada, Mexico, and the United States. NAFTA was a quintessentially New Democrat policy, having been negotiated earlier by President George Bush and backed by most Republicans and business groups. By contrast, most labor unions, environmentalists, and liberal Democrats opposed NAFTA because it failed to protect jobs, workplace safety, or the environment. After heavy lobbying by the administration, Congress ratified NAFTA in November 1993. GOP votes proved crucial, as 75 percent of House Republicans voted for ratification, compared to just 40 percent of Democrats.

Newt Gingrich, the 1994 Elections, and the "Republican Revolution" of 1995

From the start of his presidency, Clinton ran into firm Republican opposition led by Representative Newt Gingrich of Georgia, a master of political warfare. The son of an army officer, Gingrich had married (and divorced) his high school geometry teacher, avoided service in Vietnam, and earned a Ph.D. in history from Tulane University in 1971. He taught at a small college before winning election to the House in 1978. In Congress, he specialized in using guerrilla tactics against the Democratic majority. As a GOP backbencher, he frequently enraged Speaker Edward P. "Tip" O'Neill of Massachusetts, who denounced one of his stunts as "the lowest thing that I have ever seen in my thirty-years in Congress." After O'Neill's retirement, Gingrich turned his sights on Democratic Speaker Jim Wright of Texas, filing ethics charges that forced Wright's resignation.

A talented political entrepreneur, Gingrich developed a core of congressional followers through his political think tanks and fundraising organizations, including the Conservative Opportunity Society, GOPAC, and the Progress and Freedom Foundation. He used these groups to finance likeminded candidates and to publicize his ideas, which were a strange blend of old-fashioned apocalyptic conservatism with New Age faith in high-tech futurism. He was "the only [Republican] who can give us a run for our money on the vision thing," admitted Clinton.

Gingrich remained a conservative ideologue even after he ascended to the GOP House leadership in the late 1980s. He maintained close ties with right-wing organizations, refused to compromise with Democrats, and led a failed Republican mutiny against President Bush's 1990 tax hike. Declaring that politics was "war without blood," he denounced liberals as "the enemy of normal Americans" and distributed a list of terms for Republicans to use publicly about Democrats, including "pathetic," "sick," "corrupt," "traitorous," and "criminal." Gingrich's hardball tactics helped produce a vicious partisan atmosphere in Washington. Even a fellow conservative, Congressman Dan Coates of Indiana, admitted that

"Newt's belief that to succeed you almost had to destroy the system . . . was kind of scary stuff."

Gingrich both profited from and escalated an increase in partisanship both among voters and in Congress. Beginning in the Great Depression, voters and members of Congress demonstrated high levels of party loyalty. As the Depression's crisis atmosphere dissipated and new divisive issues arose in the 1960s, however, partisan loyalty declined markedly, especially among white conservative Democrats in the South. The mid-1970s marked the low point for party unity in Congress, after which partisanship reasserted itself. In the electorate, polls showed that voters increasingly perceived "important differences" between the Democratic and Republican parties, with the proportion soaring in 1980 and again in 1984 and reaching an all-time (post-1952) high in 1996. In Congress, similarly, the GOP's ideological shift to the right and congressional Republicans' devotion to Reagan's conservative agenda after 1981 helped to unite both parties and pit them against each other. By the 1990s, party loyalty among both voters and Congress had reached the highest levels since the 1950s.

In this partisan atmosphere, Gingrich's main priority was recapturing the House for the GOP. It was a formidable task. In 1993–94, Democrats controlled the House by a 258-176 margin and had retained their majority for four consecutive decades and fifty-eight of the past sixty-two years. Indeed, some observers argued that the party held a "lock" on the House. According to this theory, the public preferred Democratic positions on such policies as Social Security, health care, education, and the environment. Most voters also believed that Democrats were more likely to bring home pork-barrel projects, thus boosting local economies.

Gingrich therefore concluded that winning the House required a unified strategy and a cohesive ideology. His plan for 1994 relied on two main elements. First, he thought that Republicans could ride the antigovernment wave that had proven so advantageous for Ross Perot in 1992 because the Democrats' lengthy control of the House, Gingrich believed, identified *them* in the public's mind as "the government." By 1994, the public's disapproval of Congress exceeded its approval by 51 percentage points, and hostility was often deep. For example, a congressional term-limits group sent out a fundraising letter reading: "You don't have to look very far to see the source of your problems. Career politicians at every level who have built little empires at your expense [through] corruption [and] . . . taxpayer funded perks and privileges that would make a Third World autocrat blush." The second element of Gingrich's strategy involved making the national, presidential-level issues of patriotic leadership and traditional cultural values, which favored the GOP, the key issues at the local, congressional level.

To do this, Republican candidates ran on an explicit agenda: Gingrich's "Contract with America." Playing to antigovernment sentiment and Perot voters, the Contract included calls for congressional term limits, reduction of the federal government, a balanced-budget amendment to the Constitution, large tax cuts, and a presidential line-item veto of multiple-item bills. Embracing patriotism and traditionalist values, the Contract proposed increasing defense spending, radically changing welfare, and toughening anticrime measures. It deliberately avoided divisive and less popular social issues such as abortion, but its $500-per-child tax credit temporarily mollified the religious right. Most voters remained unaware of the Contract, but it gave Gingrich a national platform and kept the GOP united with conservative activists.

The Republicans' main asset in 1994 was the unpopularity of President Clinton, whose disapproval rating reached 64 percent by election day. The GOP exploited "Clinton's disregard of campaign promises on welfare and taxes, his overreaching on health care, and his initiatives on gays in the military," wrote journalist John B. Judis. Opposition to Clinton disproved the maxim that "all politics is local" in congressional races, and many Republican challengers used television ads that "morphed" a picture of their Democratic opponent, whomever he or she was, into one of Clinton. Only 39 percent of eligible Americans voted, but those who did included many enthusiastic conservatives: the Christian Coalition claimed to have distributed 33 million voter guides. Most "angry white males" and Ross Perot followers also supported Republicans. Clinton, remarked Dan Fierce of the Republican National Committee, "had activated each and every [conservative] group." Meanwhile, many Democrats stayed home, frustrated by Clinton's perceived failures. Scholar Robert Erickson summarized voters' attitudes: "Half were upset because they didn't like [Clinton's] policies, and the other half were upset because he couldn't enact his policies."

The 1994 GOP victories marked a new stage in U.S. political history. In the House, Republicans added 52 seats, the biggest gain in nearly half a century, for a 230-204 margin—the first GOP majority in forty years. This tally included 73 freshmen, the biggest class in almost five decades. Republicans defeated 34 Democratic incumbents, including House Speaker Tom Foley, and they won 21 of 31 open seats previously held by Democrats, the highest proportion ever. Early in 1995, House GOP ranks swelled when five Democrats from Texas, Mississippi, and Louisiana switched parties. In the Senate, the GOP added 9 seats to retake the majority (53-47), this after Democrat Richard Shelby of Alabama became a Republican. A few months later, Colorado Democrat Ben Nighthorse Campbell also joined the GOP in the Senate. At the state level, Republicans gained eleven governorships, for a nationwide majority of 30-19. Prominent liberal Democratic incumbent governors such as Mario Cuomo of New York and Ann Richards of Texas were swept aside. Republicans also won a nationwide majority of state legislative chambers for the first time since Reconstruction. Most remarkable of all, not a single GOP incumbent lost in any House, Senate, or gubernatorial race. The election of 1994 represented "the most shatteringly one-sided Republican victory since 1946," declared Gingrich, the new speaker of the House. For the first time since Reconstruction, the GOP controlled both houses of Congress and a majority of governorships and state legislatures.

The 1994 elections culminated the Republican ascendancy that had begun with Richard Nixon's 1968 victory. From 1972 through 1988, GOP presidential candidates won by an average landslide margin of 440-97 in the electoral college and by 54-44 percent in the popular vote. But Democrats continued to control government outside the executive branch throughout the 1970s, holding an average majority of 270-163 in the House and 58-40 in the Senate. From 1980 through 1992, Republicans became competitive in the Senate and in governorships, though they continued to lag behind in the

House and in state legislatures. The 1994 elections marked the breakthrough for Republicans at all levels of government. The process of Republican ascendancy also revealed itself in long-term shifts in party identification toward the GOP. From 1978 to 1994, the proportion of voters who identified themselves as Democrats fell from 54 to 48 percent, while Republican-identifiers rose from 32 to 41 percent. The trend toward the GOP was most pronounced among conservatives, white men, and white southerners.

By 1994, consequently, the Democratic "Solid South" in Congress had crumbled. Since the late 1930s, the Republican proportion of the non-southern congressional vote had remained between 45 and 55 percent. But the GOP's southern vote rose steadily. In the 1930s and 1940s, Republicans won a little over 20 percent of the congressional vote in the South. Their proportion increased to just under 30 percent during the 1950s, to under 40 percent during the 1960s, to over 40 percent during the 1970s and 1980s. In 1994, Republicans won a majority of the southern vote for the first time ever. As a result, the GOP's proportion of southern congressional seats also increased steadily. Republicans constituted 8 percent of the House southerners after the 1954 elections, 15 percent in 1964, 24 percent in 1974, 36 percent in 1984, and 53 percent in 1994. In the Senate, Republicans representing the South climbed from zero percent after the 1954 elections to 15 percent in 1964, 35 percent in 1974, 46 percent in 1984, and 58 percent in 1994. Not since Reconstruction had a majority of senators and representatives from the South belonged to the Republican party. "The party of northern aggression has become the party of southern dominance," boasted Karl Rove, adviser to Republican George W. Bush, the new governor of Texas.

Newt Gingrich believed that the pivotal 1994 elections signaled the first stage of a far-reaching conservative transformation. Under his leadership, the GOP would "revolutionize" first the House, then the entire federal government, and eventually the United States itself. "What is ultimately at stake is literally the future of American civilization," he declared. The seventy-three House freshmen served as the backbone of Gingrich's Republican Revolution, receiving unprecedented power in return. Most of those GOP newcomers to Congress were relatively young, and many were antigovernment activists with little or no legislative experience. They included such right-wingers as Helen Chenoweth of Idaho and Steve Stockman of Texas, both with ties to radical militia groups; Robert L. Barr, Jr., of Georgia, who gave speeches to the John Birch Society and white-supremacist groups; and Fred Heineman of North Carolina, a staunch foe of government regulation of business who believed that $750,000 a year constituted a "middle-class" income. The 1994 freshmen together with the forty-four Republicans first elected in 1992 made up more than half the GOP caucus. These hard-core conservatives were devoted to Gingrich—as long as he maintained his uncompromising stance toward Clinton and the Democrats.

In the first ninety-three days of the 104th Congress, the House, led by Gingrich, passed every major item from the Contract with America except one: a constitutional amendment for congressional term limits, which required a two-thirds majority. Some of the Contract items were nonideological reforms. They subjected congressional employees to the laws that applied to other Americans, banned gifts to legislators, and reduced the power of the House committee chairs. Several conservative items from the Contract eventually won enactment, too. They included a ban on unfunded federal mandates on states and localities, abolition of farm subsidies (though large-scale "emergency" subsidies continued), six anticrime bills, and the dismantling of welfare as a federal entitlement. All told, this legislation represented the extent of Gingrich's Republican Revolution. Although the House passed several other conservative measures, the bills were rejected by the Senate, vetoed by the president, or declared unconstitutional by the Supreme Court.

The End of the "Republican Revolution" and Clinton's 1996 Reelection

The Republican Revolution stalled after April 1995 because GOP conservatives overreached, falsely believing that they enjoyed a popular mandate to transform the government. For example, House Republicans tried to gut federal regulation of environmental protection, workplace safety, and business procedures. The Environmental Protection Agency was "the Gestapo of government," charged Republican Tom DeLay of Texas. But a March 1995 poll showed that 70 percent of Americans opposed rolling back years of protective legislation, so the GOP's more extreme deregulation bills failed to win enactment. Conservative Republicans also reinforced their image as intolerant cultural crusaders. They proposed constitutional amendments criminalizing late-term abortions and outlawing flag "desecration," and they repealed both the ban on automatic weapons and the Brady handgun law. House Republicans also angered mainstream middle-class Americans by voting to cut funding for Medicare, the National Endowment for the Humanities, the National Endowment for the Arts, the Public Broadcasting System, and the Department of Education.

Once in power, moreover, House Republicans quickly discarded their populist promises of creating a "citizen legislature." They brazenly allowed business lobbyists to write deregulation bills and refused to cut corporate welfare. Many Americans viewed this conduct as the same old corrupt cronyism in Congress. "If they legislate for special interests," GOP strategist William Kristol had presciently warned, "it's going to be hard to show the Republican Party has fundamentally changed the way business is done in Washington."

Speaker of the House Newt Gingrich's unpopularity worsened the Republicans' image. Gingrich lacked charm, and he made several public blunders. The House Ethics Committee fined him $300,000 for transgressions relating to his fundraising activities, and negative publicity forced him to return a $4.5 million book advance from conservative publisher Rupert Murdoch. Then, on Gingrich's first day as Speaker, CBS televised an interview with his mother, who confided that he had told her that Hillary Clinton was a "bitch." Soon after that, he mused publicly about placing more children in orphanages, which shocked the public and reinforced his media caricature as an uncaring "Grinch," as *Newsweek* had labeled him. The media, which had savaged Clinton for two years, was now turning its sights on Gingrich, too. By September 1995, 58 percent of Americans disapproved of Congress's performance under Gingrich's leadership.

Outside Congress, meanwhile, antigovernment violence helped discredit extreme demands for "revolutionizing" the government. In the 1980s and 1990s, right-wingers bombed several abortion clinics, and armed militias resisted federal agents enforcing gun-control, child-support, and environmental laws. In 1993 at Waco, Texas, agents from the Bureau of Alcohol, Tobacco, and Firearms (ATF) laid siege to an armed cult, the Branch Davidians, after they shot and killed ATF personnel. As federal agents stormed the compound on April 19, seventy-four Davidians, including many children, died in a fire ordered by the cult's leader, David Koresh.

The Waco tragedy galvanized right-wing extremists, who blamed federal law enforcement for the deaths. The National Rifle Association (NRA), for example, called ATF agents "jack-booted government thugs." In protest, former president George H. W. Bush resigned from the NRA, and conservative William Bennett criticized the organization for "saying . . . cops are bad, cops are the enemy." Indeed, anti-law-enforcement sentiment seemed at odds with the right's traditional demands for strict "law and order." Nevertheless, right-wing radio hosts such as G. Gordon Liddy, Bob Grant, Chuck Baker, and Bob Mohan continued to condone antigovernment violence. Conservative Republicans took up the rough talk, too. Congressman Steve Stockman accused Attorney General Janet Reno of "premeditated murder" at Waco, and Senator Jesse Helms warned Clinton that he "better have a bodyguard" if he visited North Carolina's military bases.

On April 19, 1995, the second anniversary of the Waco fire, antigovernment zealot Timothy McVeigh used a truck bomb to destroy the Murrah federal building in Oklahoma City, Oklahoma. The explosion killed 168 people, including nineteen children in a day-care facility. The homegrown terrorism by McVeigh, a former army soldier who maintained ties with right-wing militias, not only shocked the public but also helped discredit antigovernment sentiment. Polls showed that the proportion of Americans "satisfied with [their] government" soared from 29 to 49 percent after the bombing.

As a result, President Clinton regained the political initiative. Clinton's stature rose after the Oklahoma City bombing when he comforted the nation and the victims' families. A month after the tragedy, in May 1995, his public favorable rating reached a majority at 51 percent and continued to rise thereafter. Equally important, the Republican Congress provided him with a convenient public foil: "a very fat punching bag in the person of Newt Gingrich," quipped Senator Bill Bradley of New Jersey.

The 1995 budget battle symbolized the turning point in Clinton's efforts to stymie Gingrich's Republican Revolution. The GOP's proposed budget called for eliminating three cabinet agencies and more than 200 federal programs. It also reduced the increase in Medicare spending by $270 billion while cutting taxes—primarily for the wealthy—by $245 billion. Thus, the GOP proposals enabled Clinton to argue that Republicans took billions of dollars from needy seniors and gave it to the rich. Gingrich then unintentionally helped his opponents by predicting that the agency running Medicare would "wither on the vine." Still, the GOP leadership believed that the president would capitulate to their budget demands. Gingrich later admitted that Republicans viewed Clinton as a "weak President who would ultimately feel required to sign an agreement with us for a balanced budget with tax cuts." Moreover, Republicans speculated that if Clinton stood firm, a shutdown resulting from the impasse would be blamed on him or (believing their own rhetoric) the public would thank Republicans for closing the federal government. Instead, the six-day shutdown in November 1995 enraged the public, who faulted the GOP. Soon thereafter, Gingrich claimed that Clinton had caused the showdown by disrespecting the Republican leadership, including a supposed snub of Gingrich on Air Force One. These petulant comments also backfired, igniting a firestorm of derision; "Cry Baby" read one headline. Frustrated Republicans implored their leadership to "tell Newt to shut up!" The budget impasse caused a second government shutdown in early January 1996.

Eventually, Bob Dole and other GOP Senate leaders convinced Gingrich to compromise with Clinton. In the resulting budget deal, Democrats protected Medicare, Medicaid, education, and the environment, while Republicans received Clinton's agreement to balance the budget within seven years. Most House conservatives finally voted for the compromise, but they felt betrayed by Gingrich. The budget battle proved a bruising defeat for the GOP. As Gingrich later admitted, grassroots conservatives were "all gung ho for a brutal fight over spending and taxes. We mistook their enthusiasm for the views of the American people."

Having thwarted the Republican Revolution, Clinton positioned himself for reelection in 1996 by employing a strategy of "triangulation" devised by his political adviser Dick Morris. This centrist approach allowed Clinton to distance himself from liberal Democrats, portray the Gingrich-led GOP as extremists, and appear conciliatory toward Republican moderates. Declaring that "the era of big government is over," the president focused on small issues, hoping to win over moderate swing voters—who in 1996 were symbolized by the suburban "soccer mom." This tactic also allowed him to take advantage of the "gender gap": the tendency of women to favor Democrats. Clinton endorsed a wide range of popular, though minor, programs designed to promote "family values" and to protect children's safety. He also took a centrist position on race, rejecting quotas but promising to "mend, not end" affirmative action. For their part, congressional Republicans, chastened and facing reelection, moderated their image by supporting such Democratic initiatives as raising the minimum wage and making health care "portable" for workers who changed jobs.

Welfare reform and an omnibus crime bill represented the most significant legislation of 1996. The removal of a welfare safety net for poor Americans (half of whom were children) appalled many liberals. But welfare reform lay at the core of Clinton's New Democrat agenda. It also appealed to centrist swing voters. After signing the bill, the president eagerly took credit for "ending welfare as we know it." He also signed a harsh crime bill, which disturbed civil libertarians but undercut the Republicans' advantage on issues of "law and order."

To challenge Clinton, the GOP selected veteran senator Bob Dole as its 1996 presidential nominee. A traditional Midwestern conservative, Dole had little in common with the new generation of fire-breathing right wingers. Yet he embraced much of the right's agenda to defeat his main primary challengers, social conservative Patrick J. Buchanan and fiscal conservative Malcolm "Steve" Forbes, Jr., a millionaire publisher. Dole's shift to the right hurt him in the general election against Clinton. Dole's strongest personal attribute was his World War II service, which had left him partially disabled. But it also highlighted his main liability: his advanced age of seventy-three.

In one revealing gaffe, he referred to the "Brooklyn Dodgers": the Dodgers, of course, had left Brooklyn in 1958. And he seemed anything but a scintillating candidate. "Bob's sooo boring," joked Buchanan. Most important, Dole never presented a compelling reason for voters to oust Clinton. The Republican candidate initially pushed a 15 percent income-tax cut and chose as his running mate the prominent supply sider Jack Kemp, a former New York congressman and Housing and Urban Development secretary under George H. W. Bush. But the tax issue never gained much traction, because most voters feared that tax reductions would cause the federal deficit to balloon. By default, Dole's principal theme became Clinton administration scandals. But this tactic held little appeal among centrist swing voters, leaving a dumbfounded Dole to complain: "Where's the outrage?"

Clinton, by contrast, ran a skillful campaign. After appearing so vulnerable in 1994, he reemerged as a formidable candidate two years later. He was helped by a strong economy, a shrinking federal deficit, and the lessening of crime and other social problems. In his campaign, the president positioned himself as a moderate against GOP "extremism." He attempted to seize the Republicans' key issues of welfare, crime, values, the deficit, and taxes. He also stressed such popular Democratic issues as Medicare, education, and the environment. And his call to "build a bridge to the twenty-first century" contrasted with Dole's backward-looking references to the World War II generation. Meanwhile, Democrats highlighted Dole's alliance with Gingrich and his opposition to popular federal programs. A week before the election, however, the news media revealed Clinton's unseemly fundraising methods. These included overnight stays in the Lincoln Bedroom of the White House for large campaign donors, questionable contributions from foreign nationals, and reliance on unlimited "soft money" (funds exempt from federal limits) from the Democratic National Committee.

The 1996 elections reaffirmed the status quo. The revelations of Clinton's campaign fund-raising transgressions tightened the presidential contest, but he still defeated Dole by 49 to 41 percent in the popular vote and 379 to 159 in the electoral college. Ross Perot, this time at the head of the Reform party, won 9 percent of the popular vote. Clinton beat Dole among women, in all age groups, among independents, and within all regions except the South, where the two candidates tied. The president lost only narrowly among men and whites, traditional GOP constituencies. But his nonpartisan "triangulation" strategy precluded any coattail effect. In the House, Republicans lost 3 seats but retained a 227-207 margin. In the Senate, they added 3 seats, for a 55-45 majority. With a prosperous economy and the thwarting of both Clinton's and Gingrich's ambitious agendas, the country settled back into political stalemate after 1996.

The Impeachment of William Jefferson Clinton

During his second term, Clinton maintained his centrist strategy, which he called the "Third Way" because it supposedly "transcended" both the right's unrestrained capitalism and the left's "big government." The administration's "Third Way" budget for 1997 included conservative proposals for balancing the budget and for cutting capital-gains taxes and inheritance taxes. It also contained liberal propositions for an education tax credit, health insurance for 2 million children, and a tax cut for lower-income families. Generally, in "his fourth and fifth years in office, Clinton's opportunistic centrist strategy worked well," concluded political scientists Paul J. Quirk and William Cunion.

In early 1998, Clinton attempted to renew his moderate agenda, while Republicans focused on tax cuts. The president proposed antitobacco legislation, a "bill of rights" for HMO patients, extended Medicare coverage, tax breaks to help working parents pay for child care, and a higher minimum wage. He also recommended putting the year's federal budget surplus—the first in three decades—into Social Security. By contrast, congressional Republicans sought to overhaul the Internal Revenue Service and proposed using the budget surplus for a 10-year, $792 billion income-tax cut. But a presidential sex scandal, which ultimately led to Clinton's impeachment by the Republican Congress, soon overshadowed all other political issues.

The impeachment culminated years of GOP assaults on Clinton. Republicans viewed him as an unworthy usurper who twice had "stolen" the presidency through "lies" and campaign-finance "corruption." Additionally, historian David A. Bell observed, "[t]o 1990s conservatives, Clinton symbolizes the dark side of the America of the 1960s: irresponsible, amoral, unpatriotic, untrustworthy, and profligate." Beginning in the 1992 campaign, GOP conservatives spread wild accusations about the president through books, talk radio, videos, and the Internet. "The far right tried to convince the American people that I had committed murder, run drugs, slept in my mother's bed with four prostitutes, and done numerous other things," the president complained.

Clinton's impeachment also culminated the practice of manipulating the legal system for political ends. By the 1990s, argued conservative authors Benjamin Ginsburg and Martin Shefter, electoral competition had been eclipsed by "a major new technique of political combat—revelation, investigation, and prosecution." The news media and the federal judiciary abetted this process. Conservatives like Ginsburg and Shefter viewed independent counsels as especially dangerous. A response to Nixon's Watergate scandal, independent counsels were granted the power to investigate and prosecute high-ranking federal officials for criminal and civil offenses. During the Reagan and Bush administrations, several top Republican officials had been targeted by independent counsels. With a Democratic administration in power, however, many Republicans voted in 1994 to renew the independent-counsel law. It resulted in investigations of the president, the first lady, and five cabinet secretaries. Meanwhile, right-wing legal activists such as Larry Klayman of Judicial Watch harassed Clinton aides through depositions and subpoenas.

Congressional Republicans also wielded their legal powers against the Clinton administration. Their hearings "soon settled into a predictable pattern," observed Clinton partisans Joe Conason and Gene Lyons. "[O]ne Republican or another would level broad cha[r]ges of corruption and cover-up against the Clintons and their allies. Reporters for the *New York Times,* the *Washington Post,* and their followers at the TV networks would gravely repeat each accusation, warning of shocking evidence to come. Subsequent testimony would either fail to support or actually disprove the damning charge." Nevertheless, as journalist Jeffrey Toobin pointed out, "the very existence of the inquiries . . . was seen as proof [by the media] that they were justified."

Elite news organizations abetted the scandal-mongering. "Some of the coverage reads as if the reporters or editors were committed to finding something wrong—as if they had an investment in the story," commented journalist Anthony Lewis. The *New York Times*—scooped twenty years earlier on Watergate by the *Washington Post*—was determined to expose a major presidential scandal. For its part, the *Post* created an investigative unit solely to probe the Clintons. And the *Wall Street Journal* seemed obsessed with uncovering administration corruption. "In the harsh light cast by the media," observed media analyst Howard Kurtz, "Clinton was a slippery, dishonest, cash-obsessed opportunist who, by sheer dint of his political skills, had managed to fool the voters, co-opt the Republicans, and outrun the prosecutors."

In their search for scandals, media outlets often relied on questionable sources. As pro-Clinton journalists Conason and Lyons noted, accusations usually originated from "longtime Clinton adversaries . . . an angry gallery of defeated politicians, disappointed office seekers, right-wing pamphleteers, wealthy eccentrics, zany private detectives, religious fanatics, and die-hard segregationists." And Anthony Lewis pointed out that "the press too often seem[ed] an eager accomplice of the accusers." Nevertheless, scandal-mongerers had come up empty by late 1997. Independent Counsel Kenneth Starr's investigation was winding down, too.

In January 1998, however, Republicans, the media, and Starr's office eagerly pounced on a new Clinton scandal that proved far more damaging. The scandal followed a convoluted story line. In 1991, then-governor Clinton had allegedly propositioned Arkansas state employee Paula Corbin Jones. Three years later, Jones sued Clinton for $700,000 on charges of sexual harassment. On May 27, 1997, the Supreme Court ruled that the president could indeed be sued while still in office. Jones's lawyers then sought out government workers with whom Clinton might have engaged in sex—even consensual sex—to demonstrate a "behavioral pattern."

In December 1997, right-wing sources alerted Jones's lawyers to Monica Lewinsky, a young former White House intern and secretary.

Lewinsky's friend Linda Tripp had secretly taped conversations the two had about Lewinsky having engaged in oral sex with the president. Tripp gave the tapes to the Clinton-hating literary agent Lucianne Goldberg, who informed *Newsweek*'s Michael Isikoff and several conservative lawyers who called themselves "the elves" for their secretive help to Starr's office. The elves passed Lewinsky's story to Jones's lawyers. "Their involvement was a classic demonstration of the legal system's takeover of the political system," wrote lawyer-journalist Jeffrey Toobin. The elves "used the [Jones] lawsuit like a kind of after-the-fact election, to use briefs, subpoenas, and interrogations to undo in secret what the voters had done." Meanwhile, Clinton had asked his friend, lawyer Vernon L. Jordan, to find Lewinsky a job. In January 1998, Lewinsky in an affidavit and Clinton in a deposition both lied to Jones's lawyers about their sexual relationship. The president then discussed the case with his secretary Betty Currie, a possible witness to the Clinton-Lewinsky relationship. After being notified by the elves, Starr's office convinced Attorney General Janet Reno to broaden the Whitewater investigation to include the Clinton-Lewinsky matter.

In late January, the Internet's *Drudge Report* and *Newsweek*'s Michael Isikoff disclosed the Clinton-Lewinsky affair, generating an unprecedented media frenzy. Particularly on cable news, it was "all Monica, all the time," remarked media critic Eric Alterman. During a midday news conference, Clinton told the American people, "I did not have sexual relations with that women, Miss Lewinsky." But media pundits predicted an outpouring of outrage that would force his resignation. Instead, the public remained calm, and Clinton's job-approval rating rose to 69 percent. Most women continued to support the president, partly because the first lady, who blamed "a vast right-wing conspiracy" for the family's troubles, stood by him. On April 1, moreover, U.S. District Court Judge Susan Webber Wright dismissed Paula Jones's lawsuit for lack of evidence.

On July 28, after a six-month delay, Starr's office gave Lewinsky immunity from prosecution in return for her cooperation in the investigation of the president, which included handing over a dress on which there was DNA evidence of Clinton's semen. Starr's delay "illustrated a larger truth about Clinton's enemies," argued Jeffrey Toobin. "Starr and his team . . . were convinced [Lewinsky] was withholding additional evidence of Clinton's criminality. This belief was pervasive among those who tried to drive the president out of office—that some grander conspiracy was sure to be uncovered, just over the horizon. Of course, this evidence was never located because it didn't exist."

On August 17, Clinton gave a televised speech after testifying before Starr's grand jury. The president admitted his affair with Lewinsky and said it "was wrong," but he denied lying in his deposition. He then denounced Jones's "bogus lawsuit" and Starr's conduct. "Even presidents have private lives," he insisted. "It is time to . . . get on with our national life." This line of argument struck a chord with most Americans, who by this time were sick of the Clinton-Lewinsky story anyway. By contrast, media pundits condemned the president's defiant speech, and House GOP Whip Tom DeLay initiated "The Campaign" to mobilize Congress to impeach Clinton and then remove him from office.

On September 9, Starr submitted his impeachment referral to Congress. The "Starr Report," released over the Internet, alleged eleven impeachable counts and contained graphic accounts by Lewinsky of her ten sexual encounters with the president. Ten days later, House Republicans released a videotape of Clinton's grand-jury testimony. Once again crushing GOP hopes, the president's measured performance boosted his public standing.

Congressional Democrats and most of the public rejected Republican calls for an impeachment inquiry. Most Democrats condemned Clinton's behavior but denied that it could be categorized as "high crimes and misdemeanors," the constitutional standard for impeachment. Bolstering this judgment, more than 800 historians and legal experts signed statements saying that they had concluded that Clinton's conduct failed to constitute grounds for impeachment. Polls showed that most Americans agreed and that they faulted the GOP and the media for overreacting to Clinton's transgressions.

Party loyalty generally held throughout the impeachment process. Democrats consistently denounced Starr. "Yes, there is a threat to society here, but it is from the tactics of a win-at-all-costs prosecutor determined to sink a president of the opposition party," charged

Congressman John Conyers of Michigan. On October 5, 1998, the House Judiciary Committee, chaired by Republican Henry J. Hyde of Illinois, voted 21 (all Republicans) to 16 (all Democrats) to begin an impeachment inquiry. Three days later, the entire House sanctioned an inquiry.

Most observers viewed the 1998 congressional elections as a referendum on the Clinton impeachment. In October, Republican leaders acceded to the president's budget agenda, which outraged conservatives. Meanwhile, Gingrich authorized an anti-Clinton ad blitz, but it backfired. After the November elections, Republicans maintained their 55-45 Senate majority. In the House, they lost 6 seats to retain a slim 221-213 majority, marking the first time since 1822 that a president's party had gained congressional seats in the sixth year of his presidency. Enraged, Republicans now revolted against Gingrich, who had predicted a GOP gain of twenty seats. After Robert L. Livingston, Jr., of Louisiana challenged him for the speakership, Gingrich resigned, saying: "I am willing to lead, but I won't allow cannibalism."

Despite their rebuke by voters, House Republicans continued down the road to impeaching Clinton. In late November, the House Judiciary Committee held impeachment hearings. Starr, the only witness, presented his case against Clinton. He also announced that his office had uncovered no impeachable offenses related to Whitewater, Travelgate, or Filegate. The next day, Samuel Dash, the famed Watergate investigator, resigned as Starr's "ethics adviser," charging that the independent counsel lacked objectivity. On December 11 and 12, the House Judiciary Committee—again, with no Democratic votes—approved four articles of impeachment. Article I accused Clinton of committing perjury before Starr's grand jury. Article II charged him with perjury in the Jones case. Article III accused him of obstructing justice by influencing the testimony of Lewinsky and Betty Currie. Finally, Article IV charged Clinton with abusing his presidential power. A week later, as the House debated impeachment, Bob Livingston, aware that his own philandering was about to be revealed to the public, announced his resignation. The nondescript J. Dennis Hastert of Illinois replaced him as speaker, though the strident conservative Tom DeLay remained the power behind the Republican throne.

Livingston's shocking resignation underscored the dangers that "sexual McCarthyism" posed to Republicans as well as Democrats. Ironically, the media exposed several Clinton-haters as adulterers themselves, including conservative GOP congress members Livingston, Henry Hyde, Dan Burton, Bob Barr, and Helen Chenoweth. The media also accused the most recent Republican presidential nominees, George H. W. Bush and Bob Dole, of conducting extramarital affairs, and Newt Gingrich later admitted to carrying on a secret adulterous relationship since 1993. But Republicans claimed that their behavior differed from Clinton's. Impeachment was "not a question of sex," Hyde maintained. It was "a question of the willful, premeditated, deliberate corruption of a nation's system of justice."

The impeachment saga played out in late 1998 and early 1999. On December 19, 1998, the House of Representatives impeached the president by passing Article I (perjury before Starr's grand jury) and Article III (obstruction of justice). Only five Democrats voted for impeachment. After the votes, House Democrats rallied with the president at the White House. Three weeks later, on January 7, 1999, the Senate's trial of Clinton began, with Chief Justice William H. Rehnquist presiding. Republicans needed sixty-seven votes to convict and remove the president but they held only fifty-five seats. The thirteen Republican House "managers" wanted to present a full trial. But GOP senators knew they did not have the votes to convict Clinton and feared a circus atmosphere, so they engineered a limited trial without any live witness testimony. On February 12, the Senate acquitted Clinton on both counts. All Democrats and a few moderate Republicans voted for acquittal, and polls showed that 68 percent of the public agreed with the verdict. A month later, Clinton declared: "I do not regard this impeachment vote as some great badge of shame. . . . I do not believe it was warranted."

Other Clinton scandals also ended anticlimactically. In October 2000, Starr's successor as independent counsel, Robert W. Ray, announced that he lacked evidence to indict Bill or Hillary Clinton for Whitewater, Filegate, or Travelgate. In January 2001, Clinton agreed to a plea bargain for his misleading testimony, receiving a $25,000 fine and a five-year suspension of his law license. The Paula Jones matter also ended indecisively. In October 1998, Jones appealed her case, and Clinton settled for $850,000 without admitting wrongdoing. Jones always maintained that she had sued Clinton solely to prove that she "wasn't that kind of a girl." In December 2000, however, she posed nude for *Penthouse* and confessed that her lawsuit had been "used by a lot of people to get to [Clinton]."

U.S. Foreign Relations during the Clinton Era, 1993–2000

Foreign relations played a relatively minor role in U.S. politics during the Clinton years. The American victory in the Cold War and the collapse of the Soviet empire in the early 1990s had ended a long era in U.S. foreign policy. The forty-year confrontation with communism had provided the United States and the GOP with a national purpose, an obvious enemy, a structured and largely predictable conflict, and a rationale for global engagement and leadership. When these certainties disappeared, so did the consensus over U.S. foreign policy.

The GOP, now lacking a threatening anticapitalist enemy abroad, split into three factions during the 1990s. One group, including hawkish Republicans such as Senator John McCain of Arizona, called for more defense spending and favored military interventions abroad. A second bloc, which included Governor George W. Bush of Texas, focused on promoting U.S. business globally. These Republicans encouraged, for example, trade and investment with China, even though they remained suspicious of its Communist leadership. Unlike the McCain group, they usually opposed military action overseas, though they, too, favored a defense buildup and a national missile-defense system. The third GOP faction was composed of right-wing nationalists such as Pat Buchanan and Senator Jesse Helms of North Carolina. They embraced almost isolationist sentiments and opposed foreign imports, immigration, and the United Nations and other international organizations. They were especially wary and contemptuous of Communist China. Divisions among these three main blocs caused Republicans to act inconsistently with respect to foreign policy. Often, they supported Clinton's actions; at other times, they harshly denounced them. Yet they never presented a coherent alternative policy of their own.

Republicans, focused on domestic issues, opportunistically criticized Clinton's foreign policies. One of their main charges was that the Democratic administration had responded ineffectively to foreign threats. After four decades of nuclear terror, most Americans looked forward to an era of international cooperation. But GOP conservatives viewed international cooperation as naive and dangerous, and they opposed reducing the U.S. arsenal of thousands of nuclear weapons. Senator Jesse Helms, chairman of the Senate Foreign Relations Committee after 1994, led Republican opposition to arms control and to cooperation with the United Nations. Helms blocked Clinton's efforts to pay the United States' UN dues, boost aid to poor countries, and reduce nuclear warheads, and he also helped defeat congressional ratification of the Comprehensive Nuclear Test Ban Treaty.

In addition, Republicans accused Clinton officials of coddling Chinese Communists, echoing the GOP's McCarthyist tactics of the early 1950s. Beginning in 1997, congressional committees chaired by Fred Thompson in the Senate and Dan Burton and Christopher Cox in the House charged that Clinton had endangered national security by soliciting campaign contributions in 1996 from Chinese representatives in return for overlooking theft of U.S. nuclear secrets. In January 2000, Cox released a scathing report charging that Chinese spies had stolen the "crown jewels" of the U.S. nuclear arsenal. This espionage supposedly would allow China and possibly Communist North Korea to develop missiles and warheads capable of reaching the United States.

Few of these charges held water. Some Chinese donors had given relatively small contributions to Democrats, but few funds originated from Communists in the People's Republic of China. Most "Chinese money" came from anticommunist Taiwanese businessmen, and it was GOP candidates who received the bulk of these contributions. Most important, no evidence surfaced linking foreign contributions to Clinton's policy decisions. Furthermore, China obtained most of its nuclear information from open sources, and the Chinese and

North Korean arsenals remained small and unsophisticated, while the United States commanded several thousand technically advanced intercontinental ballistic missiles. Thus, GOP warnings about stolen nuclear secrets seemed intended mainly to frighten the public into supporting an expensive (and probably unworkable) national missile-defense system.

Republicans also charged that the Clinton administration had reduced U.S. defense capability by employing the armed forces in risky new missions. The president did call for using the military to stop war, forced starvation, and genocide. In practice, however, he only hesitantly and reluctantly employed force for humanitarian or peace-keeping missions. Still, Republicans scorned the president's efforts as "nation building," a label that seemed disproportionate to the actual scale of U.S. interventions. In late 1993, Clinton ended a U.S. mission in Somalia, which had been launched by President George H. W. Bush, after several American soldiers were killed. Republicans harped on Clinton's "draft dodger" image by blaming the Somalia debacle on his lack of military experience. This was nonsense, but thereafter the president appeared to be more cautious about deploying the armed forces. In fact, no more U.S. troops were killed in overseas combat missions during the rest of Clinton's presidency.

Clinton's main area of concern was a humanitarian catastrophe in the former Yugoslavia. In Bosnia, Serb troops had conquered ethnic-Serb areas and were expelling Croats and Muslims in a gruesome "ethnic cleansing," which cost an estimated two hundred thousand lives. Hawkish Republicans denounced Clinton for allowing genocide. In August 1995, the president ordered NATO bombing against Serb troops, which then prompted GOP isolationists to accuse him of trying to police the world. Three months after the bombing began, the administration brokered a peace deal, the Dayton Accords, which created a Bosnian state protected by an international force that included six thousand U.S. troops. In 1999, the Bosnian situation was replayed in Kosovo, a province of Serbia. President Slobodan Milošević of Serbia sanctioned grisly counterterrorism actions against Kosovar rebels seeking independence. In response, NATO planes (overwhelmingly American) bombed Serbia. Again, most Republicans opposed U.S. intervention. But the bombing eventually compelled the Serbs to withdraw and contributed to Milošević's fall from power a year later.

As had the Bush administration, Clinton used economic embargoes or military force to contain perceived threats from small anti-American nations such as Cuba, Iraq, North Korea, Iran, and Libya. The president also ordered the bombing of Osama bin Laden's al-Qaeda terrorist sanctuaries in Afghanistan and the Sudan, and he authorized $1.3 billion in military aid to Colombia to fight drug producers. Republicans alleged that Clinton exploited foreign conflicts to divert voters' attention from his domestic difficulties. But the GOP presented no coherent alternative to any of his specific strategies.

Under Clinton, the United States took leadership roles in attempting to resolve several international conflicts. The administration negotiated agreements to find "Nazi gold" and to compensate Holocaust survivors. In 1996, the president appointed former Senator George Mitchell to chair negotiations over Northern Ireland. These talks resulted in the Good Friday Accords of April 1998, which created the structure for Catholic-Protestant power sharing. In the Middle East, however, Clinton failed to broker a peace settlement between Israel and the Palestinians, despite several summits.

But throughout his eight years in office, Clinton stressed economic diplomacy more than military interventions or peacemaking. His emphasis on free trade and globalization drew support from most Republicans, business executives, and economists. By contrast, liberal Democrats, labor unions, and environmentalists insisted that U.S. trade agreements should protect jobs, wages, and the environment at home. Rejecting liberal demands, the Clinton administration, with strong GOP support, secured 270 free-trade treaties, the most important of which were the North American Free Trade Agreement, the General Agreement on Tariffs and Trade, and the World Trade Organization, which supervised and expanded global trade. The administration also worked to alleviate international financial panics due to economic crises in Mexico in 1995 and in Asia two years later. Overall, U.S. exports rose by 50 percent during Clinton's presidency. "One of his legacies most surely will be the elevation of trade and economics as foreign policy instruments, in a contemporary version of 'dollar diplomacy,'" observed political scientists Emily O. Goldman and Larry Berman.

George W. Bush, Al Gore, and the 2000 Election

As the 2000 elections approached, each major party united behind a presidential candidate. For the Democrats, Vice President Al Gore stood as Clinton's anointed successor, and he easily defeated his sole primary challenger, former senator Bill Bradley. Clinton bequeathed Gore peace and prosperity. The real (inflation-adjusted) gross national product grew by 40 percent during Clinton's eight years in office, the longest peacetime boom in history. Both real wages and median household income rose steadily after two decades of stagnation. The Clinton years also saw the highest home ownership ever, a tripling of the stock market to record highs, 22 million new jobs, and the lowest rates of inflation, unemployment, poverty, and welfare recipients since the 1960s. The robust economy helped produce the first consecutive budget surpluses in forty-two years. "This is the best economy I've ever seen in 50 years," Federal Reserve Chairman Alan Greenspan told the president.

Yet Clinton's economic management failed to assure Gore's victory. Only 15 percent of Americans gave the president primary credit for the boom, compared to the 24 percent who attributed it to the technology companies of the "new economy." And media pundits gave the credit to Alan Greenspan. In addition, argued economist Ray Fair, "[t]he economy, while it has been good, is not the best it's ever been. . . . [The growth rate] has been higher in previous elections." The markets, especially technology stocks, dipped in early 2000 after an uninterrupted boom lasting years. As a Democrat, moreover, Gore "had to rally a base of voters who had not actually prospered very much during the nineties," noted journalist William Greider. "This might explain why Gore was reluctant to brag about the boom—his own principal constituencies were the losers."

Clinton left his vice president a less favorable legacy on noneconomic issues. The presidential scandals culminating with the impeachment reinforced the Democrats' perceived weaknesses on moral issues. Additionally, the news media and Republicans portrayed the administration as having failed to fulfill its promised agenda. Yet political scientist Carolyn M. Shaw concluded that 69 percent of Clinton's proposals were "fully or partially comparable to his campaign promises." This percentage ranked first among all post-1960 presidents. But most ordinary Americans and most experts graded Clinton as a mediocre president. For example, a poll of historians ranked him just twenty-first out of forty-one presidents. Many media pundits went further, claiming that his legacy hurt Gore's candidacy with voters—a sentiment dubbed "Clinton fatigue." The president's job-approval rating was more than 60 percent, one of the highest second-term ratings ever, but his personal-approval rating was about 30 percent, one of the lowest ever. For that reason, Gore shunned the president's campaign help, although polls showed little real evidence of Clinton fatigue. Gore reinforced his decision to "run as [his] own man" by choosing as his running mate Senator Joseph Lieberman of Connecticut. Lieberman was an Orthodox Jew, popular with conservative "virtuecrats" who consistently scolded Clinton, and the first prominent Democrat to rebuke the president for the Lewinsky affair.

Meanwhile, most Republicans rallied behind Governor George W. Bush of Texas. Despite his relative inexperience, Bush enjoyed high name recognition as the namesake of his father, the former president. And as a governor, he could dissociate his candidacy from unpopular Republicans in Washington. Helped by his father's connections, he secured the backing of the GOP establishment, which flooded his campaign with contributions. "It was just one massive hug around this guy they thought was the most likely to deliver a Republican White House," said GOP pollster Frank Luntz. Bush also gained the endorsement of the far right. In public, he usually kept his distance from militant conservatives. In private, however, he capitulated to their demands. "He went to every [right-wing constituency] and got them signed up or neutralized, including me, two years before the election," confided antitax activist Grover Norquist.

Bush enjoyed a huge lead in the polls over his Republican rivals, so he ran a careful primary campaign. He stayed "on message," piled up a record $193 million war chest, and spent it liberally. After several candidates fell away, Senator John McCain of Arizona was left to challenge Bush. McCain, a Vietnam War hero who ran on his signature issue of campaign-finance reform, became a media darling and drew moderates and independents to his cause, despite his conservative voting record. After a strong start, however, his candidacy eventually faded.

As the Republican nominee, Bush worked to distance himself from unpopular right wingers. Controversial conservatives such as the GOP congressional leadership and Christian right leaders Pat Robertson and Jerry Falwell maintained a low profile while quietly supporting Bush. In contrast, conservative Pat Buchanan quit the GOP and took control of the Reform party, running on a right-wing platform. Bush also rejected appeals to racism, spoke of "inclusion," and publicized his reliance on two African American advisers, retired General Colin Powell and national-security expert Condoleezza Rice. At the 2000 GOP convention, it appeared as if every black and Hispanic delegate were given a front-row seat before a televison camera. Bush also buried contentious issues such as his opposition to abortion rights. It presented a strong contrast to past Republican conventions: in 1992, for example, Pat Buchanan had declared a "cultural war" on liberal Democrats. Most important, Bush's message of "compassionate conservatism" made it difficult for Gore to portray him as a right-wing extremist.

Bush, a self-proclaimed "new kind of Republican," promised to enhance such core Democratic programs as Social Security, Medicare, Head Start, federal aid to education, and regulation of HMOs. Downplaying the details of his plans, he tried to reassure Americans who depended on these programs. He also trumpeted his proposed ten-year, $1.6 trillion tax cut—but de-emphasized the fact that in his plan, $700 billion would go to the richest 1 percent of Americans. Gore criticized these proposals as watered-down versions of his own plans. Bush tried to dismiss his opponent's critique as "fuzzy math," but exit polls after the 2000 election showed that voters who prioritized issues over a candidate's personal characteristics supported Gore by a 55-39 percent margin.

Gore's upper hand on policy questions compelled Bush to stress the "character" issue. The Republican nominee insisted that his candidacy was meant "to usher in the responsibility era . . . [and] to restore honor and dignity to the Oval Office," a reference to Clinton's misbehavior. Bush also mocked the personal style of Gore, who presented an easy target. The vice president projected a wooden image, and his desire to appear as the "smartest kid in class" worsened his tendency to exaggerate his many real accomplishments. For example, Bush ridiculed Gore's reputed boast that he had "invented the Internet." The Bush campaign also claimed that Gore "would say anything to get elected."

Still, it remained puzzling why the "character" issue favored Bush. Gore's biography read like a book of virtue: devoted son of a respected senator, still married to his teenage sweetheart, Harvard graduate, Vietnam veteran, divinity student, investigative journalist, congressman by age twenty-eight, senator at thirty-six, vice president at forty-four. Although his unseemly fundraising episodes in 1996 had tainted his image, Gore remained "Mister Clean," as journalist Howard Kurtz observed, "a boy scout, an upright if boring figure."

In contrast, Bush's life story raised serious questions about his character. An indifferent student at Yale, he evaded Vietnam service, never denied snorting cocaine, was convicted of drunk driving at age thirty, married late, drank heavily and failed at all his business endeavors until age forty, and succeeded afterward only with the help of his father's friends. Yet he dismissed it all with a smirking quip: "When I was young and irresponsible, I was young and irresponsible." Commentators also questioned whether he possessed the experience, judgment, and temperament to serve as president. "George W. Bush is simply unqualified for the job," concluded Ron Reagan, the former president's son. "What is his accomplishment? That he's no longer an obnoxious drunk?" But Bush's "spin machine" succeeded in winning the "character war." Exit polls showed that voters who viewed candidates' "personal qualities" as most important favored Bush by a 61-36 percent margin.

The 2000 presidential campaign ended with what *Time* magazine called "the wildest election in history." The outcome hinged on who had won in Florida. On election night, television networks incorrectly called the state for Gore and then for Bush. The confusion caused Gore to concede and then withdraw his concession. Eventually, Bush led in Florida by 537 votes out of 6 million cast, a difference of less than a hundredth of 1 percent. The closeness of the election highlighted voting irregularities. In Palm Beach, a heavily Democratic county, a confusing "butterfly" ballot probably cost Gore thousands of votes. Voting machines there failed to read another 10,000 ballots, and Gore insisted that these "undervoted" ballots should be counted by hand. Irregularities occurred in other heavily Democratic areas, and many African Americans complained that poll workers had unfairly inhibited their voting access. An analysis by the *Miami Herald* concluded that Gore would have won Florida by 23,000 votes in a flawlessly run election.

For five weeks, the nation remained without a president-elect, while Florida roiled in turmoil, swarmed over by the media, political operatives, and lawyers. Bush sought to preserve the count favoring him by thwarting Gore's request for a manual count of undervoted ballots. He received crucial help from Republican allies in Florida. His brother Jeb Bush was governor; Florida's Secretary of State Katherine Harris ruled for him in every decision she made; a GOP mob convinced Miami-Dade county's canvassing committee to forgo a manual count of the ballots; and the Republican-controlled state legislature threatened to name Bush's electors even if Gore won. Eventually, the all-Democratic Florida Supreme Court upheld Gore's suit requesting a manual count in three heavily Democratic counties. Bush then appealed to the U.S. Supreme Court, which surprised legal experts by issuing an immediate stay order that stopped the count.

On December 12, the Republican-dominated U.S. Supreme Court voted 5-4 to overturn the Florida Supreme Court's decision, effectively handing Bush the presidency. The court's five conservatives, each appointed by a Republican president, voted as a bloc. Their majority opinion appeared to be based on politics rather than the law, because it spurned such core conservative principles as states' rights and judicial restraint. The decision provoked widespread outrage. In his dissent, Justice John Paul Stevens declared that the real loser was "the nation's confidence in the judge as an impartial guardian of the rule of law." Most legal experts agreed, and "[e]ven many Republican lawyers were taken aback by the majority's weak legal reasoning," wrote journalist Jonathan Alter. But Gore conceded, saying, "while I strongly disagree with the Court's decision, I accept it."

With Florida's 25 electoral votes, Bush won the presidency by a 271-266 margin in the electoral college. In the popular vote, however,

Gore won by more than half a million votes and a margin of 48.4 to 47.9 percent. It marked only the fourth time in history that a candidate had won the popular vote but lost the presidency. Reform party candidate Pat Buchanan gained 1 percent of the popular vote. Leftwinger Ralph Nader of the Green party received 3 percent nationally, but he won 97,000 votes in Florida, probably costing Gore the presidency.

Other election contests in 2000 proved nearly as close. In the House, Republicans retained a slim 221-212 majority. In a series of exciting Senate races, several conservative GOP incumbents lost close races; and Hillary Clinton became the only first lady to win political office, capturing a Senate seat from New York. Democrats gained five Senate seats for a 50-50 tie, the first since 1881, though Republicans retained a majority in that chamber by the vote of new Vice President Richard B. Cheney. At the state level, the GOP maintained a 29-19 nationwide majority in governorships. (Two governors were independents.) Candidates had spent a record total of $3 billion—and the result was continued stalemate.

The Rise and Fall of Republicans' Conservative Strategies, 1968–2001

During his 1968 campaign, Republican Richard Nixon correctly predicted that his election as president would end the Democratic age that had begun in 1932 and usher in an era of GOP ascendancy. From Nixon in the 1970s through Ronald Reagan in the 1980s to Newt Gingrich in the 1990s, the Republican ascendancy derived from the party's increasingly popular agenda of assertive anticommunist nationalism combined with social and economic conservatism. By 2000, however, this program had lost much of its momentum, which compelled presidential candidate George W. Bush to declare himself a "new kind of Republican." Nevertheless, Bush owed his victory that year to his identification with the GOP's traditional conservative agenda.

Immediately following the 2000 elections, Republicans held small majorities at all levels of government. But it seemed uncertain whether they had established a permanent majority based on their traditional conservative strategies. Moreover, the GOP coalition of moderates, libertarians, and economic and social conservatives remained unstable. Some Republican strategists argued that this coalition, together with many independents, could unite behind "National Great-ness," a less ideologically conservative strategy. The National Great-ness strategy's prospects for success were bolstered by the great out-pouring of patriotism following the September 11, 2001, terrorist attacks on America. Most likely, however, the post-2000 era will be characterized by continued stalemate between Republicans and Democrats. Also, government officials will probably address the next generation's major issues through pragmatic policies rather than rigid ideological programs.

Republicans and the "Party System" of 1968–2001

Many political scientists and a few historians contend that U.S. his-tory operates in cycles or stages. The most popular approach is the party-system theory. It posits that American political eras, or "party systems," last for about thirty-six years, with each system being iden-tified by its particular major policy issues and unique partisan align-ment. In most versions of this theory, party systems are separated by a "critical election," which elevates new issues to a central position and realigns partisan supremacy. According to this model, the first party system began with the founding of the Republic in 1788 and survived until the initial explosion of popular democracy in 1824 dur-ing Andrew Jackson's first presidential campaign. The Jacksonian era persisted until Abraham Lincoln's election in 1860, which turned on the slavery issue. The third party system began with the Civil War and ended with the economic depression and social upheavals of the early 1890s. In 1896, the election of William McKinley as president ushered in a period of Republican dominance that continued until the Great Depression. Franklin Roosevelt's victory in 1932 then com-menced an age of Democratic control lasting until 1968, when the election of Republican Richard Nixon launched the era examined in this book.

As we have seen in previous chapters, the most significant parti-san change during the post-1968 party system was the steady shift of conservative whites, especially in the South, from the Democratic to the Republican party. The 1968 presidential campaign laid the foun-dation for this shift. In that year, Nixon sought to end thirty-six years of Democratic dominance by pursuing a "Southern Strategy." This plan entailed taking conservative stances on race relations and other polarizing cultural issues such as religion, crime, education, welfare, drugs, the sexual revolution, feminism, and homosexuality. Nixon calculated that these divisive, emotional issues would serve as "wedges" to pry conservative southern whites from their traditional loyalty to the Democratic party. Nixon's foreign policy reinforced his Southern Strategy by embracing the southern traditions of staunch patriotism, assertive nationalism, and anticommunist interventionism abroad.

Nixon's adoption of the Southern Strategy and assertive nationalism helped him win the presidency and furthered the long-term migration of white southern conservatives into the Republican party. In the 1968 presidential election, the former Confederacy split between Nixon and George Wallace of the American Independent Party, as Democrats won no southern states for the first time ever. Below the presidential level, however, most southerners continued to support Democrats throughout the 1970s. Additionally, President Nixon pursued a centrist and sometimes liberal fiscal program—even embracing the Keynesian label—and he initiated détente with the major Communist powers, China and the Soviet Union. By the late 1970s, however, a prolonged recession had discredited liberal economic policies, and Soviet aggression in Afghanistan had ended the United States' tentative cooperation with Moscow.

In 1980, Ronald Reagan won the presidency with a campaign that reaffirmed Nixon's Southern Strategy but stressed a stronger commitment to economic conservatism and strident anticommunist nationalism. Reagan and his successor, George H. W. Bush, both benefited from and accelerated the shift of conservatives, especially white southerners, to the GOP. In 1994, Newt Gingrich's "Republican Revolution" culminated the transformation of southern politics that had begun in the 1960s, enabling the GOP to recapture both houses of Congress for the first time in four decades.

The Decline of the Republicans' Conservative Strategies in the 1990s

Based on the theory of thirty-six-year cycles, as described above, the next party system ought to begin in 2004. But it should be remembered that each recent political realignment has been preceded and shaped by at least one of the following: a major war, an economic depression, or a cultural upheaval. It remains to be seen whether the events of late 2001—including the beginning of an economic recession, the terrorist attacks of September 11, and the start of the U.S. war in Afghanistan—will trigger another political realignment by 2004. Of course, as the joke goes, historians are trained to predict the past, not the future. Other experts, however, were less cautious about forecasting the future of American politics during the 2000 election campaign.

Many Republicans predicted that the GOP would dominate the next political generation. Karl Rove, George W. Bush's chief adviser, saw parallels between his candidate and William McKinley. Rove claimed that, like McKinley in 1896, Bush in 2000 would launch a decades-long GOP reign. Other Republicans agreed. "I think it's entirely possible that Bill Clinton will be as aberrational to a period of Republican dominance as [Democrat] Woodrow Wilson was" during the 1896–1932 period, ventured GOP strategist Ralph Reed during the 2000 campaign. "Clinton never changed the underlying demographics fueling Republican victories. Whether it was the rise of the Sunbelt as a political force, the increasingly conservative views of ethnic Catholics, or the fact that Jews and minorities under age 40 are less certain to be liberal Democrats than their parents and grandparents. These things still favor us." At first glance, the 2000 elections seemed to confirm these Republican hopes. In its wake, the party controlled, for the first time since Reconstruction, all branches of government: the presidency, both houses of Congress, the Supreme Court, and a majority of governorships and state legislatures. "We are the majority party in this country," GOP Congressman Tom DeLay boasted after the elections.

But it was premature to view the 2000 sweep as heralding a new era of Republican dominance. For one thing, GOP majorities remained narrow and tenuous at each level of government. Indeed, the party lost control of the Senate in June 2001. More important, it appeared doubtful that Republicans could maintain and extend their majorities based on the agenda that had proven so successful during the 1968–2000 period: assertive anticommunist nationalism, antigovernment economic conservatism, and the culturally and racially conservative Southern Strategy.

By 2000, the U.S. victory in the Cold War, the collapse of international communism, and the disintegration of the Soviet empire had undermined Republican foreign-policy views, which posited anticommunism as the main rationale for U.S. intervention overseas. "If you have knocked down the Berlin Wall and the Evil Empire has disappeared, it makes it a little bit difficult to run on a platform of 1956 or 1960," GOP tactician Karl Rove conceded during the 2000 campaign. Without a threatening anticapitalist enemy abroad, the Republicans' unity on trade issues and military assertiveness weakened.

In fact, the major parties had "traded places" on support for overseas intervention during the 1990s, political scientist Lawrence F. Kaplan argued in 2000. With Clinton as president, most Democrats supported interventionist military policies, while many Republicans questioned them. "An issue or crisis comes up, and [many GOP congressmen's] reaction is almost Pavlovian: Don't send troops," complained Senator John McCain. Similarly, prominent conservatives such as Pat Buchanan and Senate Foreign Relations Committee chairman Jesse Helms professed almost isolationist views, and George W. Bush's campaign criticized Clinton for being "too quick to reach out to the military instrument." By 2000, public-opinion polls showed that the GOP had lost its large advantage over Democrats on foreign policy. In 1990, voters had preferred Republicans' international approach by twenty-six percentage points. A decade later, the GOP enjoyed only a five-point advantage. "Basically, we're still trying to find our post–Cold War voice," Republican James Spears, a former Reagan-Bush official, admitted during the 2000 campaign.

With George W. Bush as president beginning in 2001, Republicans sought to regain the foreign-policy advantage that they had enjoyed with the public from the late 1960s through the mid-1990s. Some Republicans, especially Christian conservatives, worked to rekindle Cold War tensions with Communist China. Their effort was bolstered in early 2001 by a mid-air collision off China's coast between a Chinese jet and a U.S. surveillance plane. But the GOP's corporate wing, with its ties to China's businesses and hopes to penetrate Chinese markets further, quickly rebuffed attempts to use the incident to worsen U.S.-China relations. Consequently, Republicans needed to look elsewhere for a foreign enemy to serve as the unifying antagonist for their nationalistic foreign policy.

The horrific attacks on September 11, 2001, by foreign-born Islamic terrorists reinvigorated nationalistic, interventionist sentiments within both the GOP and the U.S. public. Americans immediately rallied behind President Bush. Polls showed that the public again preferred Republicans by a wide margin over Democrats on the issue of foreign policy, although the Democrats supported Bush's anti-terrorist foreign and domestic policies. Several Republicans, including the president and Defense Secretary Donald Rumsfeld, sought to connect the new struggle with the traditional cornerstone of GOP international strategy by comparing the fight against terrorism with the Cold War crusade against communism. The analogy seemed strained, however, since terrorist networks represented a much more amorphous enemy than the Soviet Union or China had during the Cold War. Furthermore, the United States desired better relations with many Islamic-majority nations, which undermined an all-out crusade comparable to the earlier U.S. anticommunist campaign. Finally, it remained to be seen whether the public's embrace of the foreign policy of Bush and the GOP after September 11, 2001, represented a permanent shift or a fleeting patriotic sentiment of rallying behind Amer-ica's president during a time of crisis.

By 2000, the GOP's conservative economic agenda appeared to be losing its public appeal as well. During the 1980s, Reagan Republicans won elections by espousing a popular program that included supply-side tax cuts favoring the wealthy, deregulation of business, curtailed social programs, and escalated defense spending. By the early 1990s, however, these policies had lost much of their rationale. "An economic slowdown, aggravated by huge budget deficits, had undercut the argument for supply-side tax cuts; [and] the savings-and-loan debacle had dimmed public enthusiasm for deregulation," wrote journalist John B. Judis. "The economic strategy of cutting taxes and slashing social programs had become irrelevant, if not harmful."

Yet the GOP of the 1990s continued to champion a Reagan-style economic agenda. In 1998, congressional Republicans proposed a

$792 billion tax cut favoring the wealthy, and George W. Bush put forth his own regressive $1.6 trillion tax-reduction plan two years later. Although Congress narrowly passed Bush's plan in 2001, it generated a tepid response from an electorate fearing a return of large deficits. "In the early '80s, when the tax revolt was in full bloom and the economy was in recession, this was good politics," observed Judis in 2000. "But, in the last decade—as the economy has boomed and the average American's tax burden has fallen—the tax-cut constituency has dwindled to Wall Street speculators and Sun Belt nouveau riches." Similarly, the failure of the Gingrich revolution demonstrated that the public wanted to retain most government programs. From 1996 to 2000, Congress actually *increased,* by 17 percent, the funding of the sixty-five largest federal programs targeted for elimination in the GOP's 1995 budget.

In short, the Republicans' conservative economic agenda no longer gave them a decisive edge over Democrats. In 1990, polls showed that Americans favored GOP management of the economy by nineteen percentage points. By 2000, Democrats enjoyed a four-point advantage. "[Even in] traditionally Republican areas," journalist Jonathan Cohn wrote in 2000, "the Republican themes that worked so well in the 1970s and '80s—cutting taxes, shrinking spending, bashing government—are losing their appeal." In addition, the government response to the September 11, 2001, terrorist attacks further discredited anti-government sentiment. The heroic actions by firefighters, police officers, and local officials reminded Americans why they needed government. Polls after the attacks showed that antigovernment sentiment among the public reached its lowest level since the mid-1960s.

The GOP's Southern Strategy also seemed somewhat outmoded by the late 1990s. Voters increasingly viewed as intolerant, if not bigoted, Republicans' angry, polarizing stances on wedge issues. "The overwhelming majority hold values more closely associated with the Republican party: the work ethic, individual responsibility and respect for the family," insisted a GOP strategist. "What can kill us is just one other value, tolerance." Indeed, tolerance of cultural differences had become a mainstream American virtue. "[T]he backlash against the civil rights and feminist movements of the 1960s has gradually petered out," Judis wrote in 2000. "Over the past 20 years, what was once a pro-life advantage has turned into a decided edge for pro-choice candidates . . . outside of the deep South and the rural Midwest." Homosexuality remained the only wedge issue in which illiberal attitudes predominated, and tolerance was growing there, too. From 1977 to 1997, for example, the proportion of Americans agreeing that "homosexuals should have equal rights in terms of job opportunities" rose from 56 to 80 percent. For many observers, including New Right leader Paul Weyrich, the public's failure to support Clinton's impeachment for his sexual transgressions confirmed the triumph in America of liberal values of tolerance.

Most important, the GOP's Southern Strategy of exploiting white hostility toward racial and ethnic minorities appeared less politically potent. The strong economy of the 1990s reduced racial competition over jobs and education while easing anti-immigrant sentiment. Additionally, conservative courts curtailed the most unpopular liberal racial programs: forced school busing and racial quotas. The racially tinged issue of crime also became less polarizing, because Clinton and other New Democrats espoused conservative views on crime prevention and the death penalty. During Clinton's presidency, moreover, the crime rate dropped for eight consecutive years, plummeting 40 percent overall, and incarcerations and executions skyrocketed. By 2000, the United States was enjoying its lowest crime rate in three decades, and only 12 percent of Americans considered crime the nation's most serious problem, down from 42 percent in 1994. As a result, fewer voters supported conservatives' harsh anti-crime measures, and even some right-wing Republicans began to question the use of the death penalty.

The lessening political appeal of the GOP's racial and cultural conservatism proved especially significant in suburban areas outside the South. "Republicans like George W. Bush are adopting a radically different tone, and those who aren't are getting creamed," observed journalist Jonathan Cohn. "The reason lies in the campaign issue conspicuous in 2000 for its absence: race. This election has turned into a referendum on what happens to Northern white hostility when you de-link it from racial resentments with which it has been enmeshed for 30 years. The answer is that it collapses." The bellwether state of California provided an important example of the trend. During the 1980s, conservative Republicans dominated California, the birthplace of Reaganism. By 2000, however, Democrats held every statewide office, and Gore trounced Bush in California by 1.3 million votes in the presidential contest.

Ironically, the GOP's Southern Strategy worked too well, reducing its chances of generating a permanent nationwide majority. By the 1990s, Deep South conservatives such as House leaders Newt Gingrich, Tom DeLay, and Dick Armey and Senate Majority Leader Trent Lott of Mississippi controlled the GOP, and George W. Bush was the first southern Republican presidential candidate ever. "[Y]ou look at our leaders, and it looks like we have lost the Civil War," complained former GOP congressman Scott Klug of Wisconsin. The party's Deep South leadership "embody a worldview that disturbs many voters outside the South, particularly women," wrote Judis. "It is as alien to Catholics in south suburban Detroit or Manchester, New Hampshire, as it is to the heathens of Silicon Valley or Manhattan." John Weaver, a top adviser to John McCain, agreed: "Our national party is a stigma in many parts of the country." Electoral results in 2000 bore this out. Outside the South, Gore won 71 percent of the electoral votes, and Democrats held an eighteen-seat advantage in the House and eight-seat margin in the Senate. "[T]he adoption of a 'Southern Strategy' by President Richard Nixon may have led to permanent minority status for the [Republican] party," concluded historian Stanley Young.

During the 2000 campaign, several conservative strategists admitted that the GOP's Southern Strategy could no longer secure a nationwide majority. It was "an old paradigm," conceded Karl Rove, Bush's chief tactician. "People are more attracted today by a positive agenda than by wedge issues." Republican consultant Ralph Reed claimed that the GOP realized that the Southern Strategy was obsolete: "This is a very different party than the one that sits down on Labor Day and cedes the black vote and cedes the Hispanic vote and tries to drive its percentage of the white vote over 70 percent to win an election." Other Republicans expressed more concern about the legacy of the Southern Strategy. "If we can't make inroads with minorities—especially with Hispanics—there will definitely be an electoral lock," warned Mike Murphy, John McCain's top strategist. "And we'll be locked out."

Heeding this advice, George W. Bush tried to distance his candidacy from the polarizing Southern Strategy by claiming to be a "compassionate conservative" and a "uniter, not a divider." He shunned the GOP's militant congressional leadership and refused to hold fund-raisers or sign direct-mail appeals for Republican candidates. "When Bush says he is a different type of Republican—different from whom? From Newt and the other Washington Republicans," remarked Marshall Wittmann of the conservative Heritage Foundation. Bush also downplayed his staunch opposition to abortion and gun control, and he declared: "I welcome gay Americans who support me." At his request, the GOP convention featured African Americans, Hispanics, women, and gay Republicans. "The change in attitude represents a stark departure from the days of the 1994 GOP revolution," noted journalist Terry M. Neal. Bush also courted Arab American and Muslim voters, making a point to condemn law enforcement's racial profiling of them. After the September 11, 2001, attacks by Islamic terrorists, President Bush rushed to meet with American Muslim leaders who condemned the attacks.

Despite his efforts at moderation, Bush made few inroads with traditional Democratic constituencies. In the 2000 election, Gore won every Democratic region, beating Bush by 45 percentage points in large cities and garnering all the electoral votes in the Northeast, the industrial Midwest, and the Pacific West (except for New Hampshire and Ohio). Exit polls revealed that Gore had also carried traditional Democratic social groups. Most strikingly, African Americans voted for him by a margin of 90 percent to 9 percent; Bush, despite disavowing the Southern Strategy, received the second lowest black vote in history. Gore also defeated his opponent among Hispanics by 36 percentage points, Jews by 60 points, women by 11 points, single people by 19 points, prochoice advocates by 45 points, gun-control supporters by 28 points, and whites who did not attend church by 26 points. And Gore's 22-point margin among union households and 20-point margin among those earning under $15,000 a year reaffirmed the Democrats' historical strength among economic liberals.

Bush thus owed his electoral-college victory to the Republicans' traditional conservative base. He won historically GOP regions, beating Gore in rural America by 22 percentage points and sweeping the electoral votes of the South, the Border states, the Plains, the Rocky Mountain states, and the Southwest (except for Maryland and New Mexico). Bush also won in traditional Republican social groups, defeating Gore among whites by 14 percentage points, men by 11 points, married people by 9 points, pro-life advocates by 52 points, gun-control opponents by 51 points, and the religious right by 60 points. Finally, his economic conservatism helped him beat Gore by 15 points among whites with more than $75,000 in annual household income and by 28 points among the male half of this affluent group.

Hence, Bush failed to extend his coalition beyond the conservative Republican base. He lost to Gore by a margin of 80 to 13 percent among self-described liberals while winning conservatives by an 81-17 margin. Conservatives backed Bush not for his moderate pretenses but for his identification with the Nixon-Reagan-Gingrich legacy of the Southern Strategy, economic conservatism, and assertive nationalism. Rather than launching a new era of moderate Republicanism, then, he continued to draw strength from the old conservative one.

A Permanent Republican (or Democratic) Majority in the Twenty-First Century?

Did Bush's victory in 2000 inaugurate a generation-long era of conservative Republican command? Only time will tell, but it appears unlikely. First of all, Bush's slim, controversial win provided him no popular mandate. Second, Republican majorities seemed too small to be able to force through conservative laws on controversial issues for a lengthy period of time. Finally, the GOP coalition could splinter under the pressures of governance: conservatives seemed bent on purging moderates from the party, and the right itself remained split between economically conservative libertarians and culturally conservative traditionalists.

Conservatives disagreed primarily over the proper role of government. Libertarians wanted it to "leave us alone," as antitax activist

Grover Norquist declared. They spurned government solutions to social questions, advocating instead such market-driven policies as school vouchers, privatization of Social Security, and empowerment zones. Libertarians also insisted that government should be uninvolved with cultural issues. By contrast, traditionalists expected the state to inculcate conservative values. "Today, it's not so clear that the American people, left to their own devices, will behave in a way that a conservative would consider 'virtuous,'" cautioned journalist David Frum. "Wishing to be left alone isn't a governing strategy," added journalists William Kristol and David Brooks. During the 1990s, libertarians and traditionalists clashed over such issues as abortion rights, tobacco regulation, Internet pornography, and biblical creationism. Divisions between libertarians and traditionalists could widen without the unifying specters of a communist threat abroad and a Democratic president at home.

Securing a permanent Republican majority would require strengthening the libertarian-traditionalist alliance while also attracting centrists and independents. To accomplish this, some GOP strategists championed a new paradigm called "National Greatness," based on revitalized American patriotism. William Kristol and other National Greatness Republicans "yearned for a past of great statesmen in the mold of Winston Churchill, a time when citizens believed in something more noble than themselves—family, country, community—an era when traditional morality was compatible, not at odds, with rigorous intellectualism," wrote Kristol's biographer Nina J. Easton. During the 2000 primaries, National Greatness Republicans united behind Senator John McCain, a Vietnam War hero. "It is John McCain," Kristol declared, "who now ha[s] a chance that occurs once a generation—to articulate a new governing agenda for a potential new political majority."

The charismatic McCain, espousing National Greatness themes, proved capable of rousing mainstream Americans. He presented a principled, maverick image and co-opted rather than denigrated popular culture. The news media and many liberals adored him despite his conservative record, and his 51 percent favorable rating among the public dwarfed his 8 percent unfavorable rating. Embracing a nonpartisan stance, he drew substantial support from independents and moderates, defeating Bush in primaries in Michigan and throughout the Northeast. "In John's mind . . . this was about going beyond the narrowest of interests, doing something fine, noble, enduring," said one of his advisers.

In effect, McCain's National Greatness strategy revived the governing formula utilized by Presidents Eisenhower and Nixon. It emphasized an assertive, unifying foreign policy and downplayed domestic issues by pragmatically granting concessions to liberals and moderates. In the 1990s, this brand of charismatic, patriotic centrism had also elevated third-party candidates Ross Perot and Governor Jesse Ventura of Minnesota. Former General Colin Powell, George W. Bush's secretary of state, was another potential National Greatness candidate.

To succeed, however, National Greatness Republicans had to overcome several formidable obstacles. First of all, the religious right, whose activism remained crucial for GOP success, attacked both McCain and Powell. The ill feelings were mutual. McCain called conservative televangelists Pat Roberston and Jerry Falwell "an evil force," and his chief strategist, Mike Murphy, declared: "I'm sick of shady theocrats." Second, the main message of religious conservatives—that America was an increasingly immoral country—clashed head on with the notion of American national greatness. Third, the end of the Cold War turned Americans' sense of priorities toward domestic policy and away from the patriotic international crusades needed to foster the National Greatness brand of politics. It remained to be determined whether the great outpouring of patriotism following the September 11, 2001, terrorist attacks could be sustained. Fourth, no consensus exists on what defined "National Greatness," either domestically or internationally, and what it specifically entailed. Finally, National Greatness was really more of a political style than a governing philosophy. For example, McCain's vague agenda of "responsible tax cuts, paying down the debt, confronting the nation's health crisis, and passing campaign finance reform" differed little from that of Clinton, Gore, and other New Democrats.

Recognizing the Republican dilemmas, many commentators during the 2000 campaign predicted that Democrats would dominate the next generation. They noted that such traditionally Democratic issues as education, Social Security, and health care predominated in 2000, and that voters preferred Democratic proposals on each of these issues. Consequently, journalist John B. Judis dismissed the GOP sweep of 2000 as a fleeting "Indian summer" masking the party's impending downfall. He compared Republicans to the Carter Democrats of the 1970s, who controlled large but tenuous majorities at all levels of government. Democrats also envisioned a new majority coalition. Political scientist Ruy Teixeira concluded that this coalition would center around three main blocs: first, the traditional base of minorities and union households; second, socially liberal, upper-middle-class white women; and third, economically liberal, lower-middle-class white women. Teixiera also argued that the party could make inroads among men in the third category. As of 2001, however, Democratic dreams of establishing a permanent majority seemed as unlikely as Republican ones.

On policy matters, the next generation will probably see neither liberals promoting ambitious social programs nor conservatives slashing government. Instead, "progressives will dominate the next political era," predicted journalist E. J. Dionne, Jr. By "progressive," Dionne meant an official who pragmatically adapts government services to solve social problems generated by the new global economy, just as Progressive Era reformers of the early 1900s addressed the social dislocations caused by industrialization in the Gilded Age. Indeed, Clinton, Gore, and other "Third Way" Democrats have explicitly adopted this philosophy. But a new progressive era does not require Democratic supremacy; pragmatic Republicans could follow in the footsteps of GOP Progressives Theodore Roosevelt and Robert La Follette. In fact, many Republican state leaders already governed in this manner.

In partisan terms, the Republican-Democrat stalemate appeared likely to persist. In 2000, Bush and Gore virtually tied in the presidential vote, the Senate tied exactly at 50-50, and Republicans won only a slim 221-212 majority in the House. The tenuous balance within the GOP and between Democrats and Republicans was apparent in June 2001 when Senator Jim Jeffords of Vermont switched from the GOP to independent status, restoring control of the Senate to the Democrats. At the state level, the GOP held a 29-19 gubernatorial majority, but each party controlled both legislative chambers in sixteen states, with the other eighteen states split or tied. "There is no majority in this country," concluded political scientist Morris Fiorina. "There are two deeply divided blocs and there is a big center up for grabs, and neither party has figured out how to capture it yet." And a potent third-party challenge seemed doubtful. Dismal showings by Reform and Green candidates in 2000 reaffirmed the U.S. tradition of two-party politics.

Stalemate persisted because divisions between Republicans and Democrats endured. "[W]e probably should have expected that the first presidential election between two baby boomers would result in gridlock," remarked journalist David S. Broder. "The generation that came of age in the 1960s was divided by so many forces," including civil rights, Vietnam, and feminism. "Every one of those experiences polarized Americans." Succeeding generations arranged themselves along these same fault lines of race, nationalism, and gender. Consequently, by the year 2000, voter loyalty to the major parties had soared. "Partisan loyalties in the American public have rebounded significantly since the mid-1970s," political scientist Larry M. Bartels concluded in 2000. "Meanwhile, the impact of partisanship has increased markedly in recent years, both at the presidential level . . . and at the congressional level." In short, the polarizing clashes that Richard Nixon exploited in 1968 still divided Americans three decades later.

BIBLIOGRAPHICAL ESSAY

For a survey of U.S. history covering the years since 1968, see Michael Schaller, Virginia Scharff, and Robert D. Schulzinger, *Present Tense: The United States since 1945* (2d ed., 1996). See also William H. Chafe, *The Unfinished Journey: America since World War II* (4th ed., 1999). Overviews of American politics since 1968 include Michael Barone, *Our Country: The Shaping of America from Roosevelt to Reagan* (1990); William C. Berman, *America's Right Turn: From Nixon to Clinton* (2d ed., 1998); E. J. Dionne, Jr., *Why Americans Hate Politics* (1991); Thomas Byrne Edsall with Mary D. Edsall, *Chain Reaction: The Impact of Race, Rights, and Taxes on American Politics* (1991); and Theodore J. Lowi, *The End of the Republican Era* (1995). The Republican party after 1968 is examined by John Calvin Batchelor, *Ain't You Glad You Joined the Republicans? A Short History of the GOP* (1996); Douglas L. Koopman, *Hostile Takeover: The House Republican Party, 1980–1995* (1996); Nicol C. Rae, *The Decline and Fall of the Liberal Republicans from 1952 to the Present* (1989); David W. Reinhard, *The Republican Right since 1945* (1983); and Robert Allen Rutland, *The Republi-*

cans: From Lincoln to Bush (1996). On conservative movements since 1968, see in addition to the works listed above, Jerome L. Himmelstein, *To the Right: The Transformation of American Conservatism* (1990); William B. Hixson, Jr., *Search for the American Right Wing: An Analysis of the Social Science Literature, 1955–1987* (1992); and Godfrey Hodgson, *The World Turned Right Side Up: A History of the Conservative Ascendancy in America* (1996).

Chapter One: Republicans in a Democratic Age, 1932–1968

For political ideas in general, a good place to start is Andrew Heywood, *Political Ideologies: An Introduction* (2d ed., 1998). Graham K. Wilson, *Only in America? The Politics of the United States in Comparative Perspective* (1998), provides a helpful introduction to U.S. political culture and ideology. On voting behavior, a useful starting point is William H. Flanigan and Nancy H. Zingale, *Political Behavior of the American Electorate* (9th ed., 1998). Paul Allen Beck, *Party Politics in America* (8th ed., 1996), offers an excellent introduction to political parties. For the history of U.S. political parties, see the essays in Paul L. Murphy, ed., *Political Parties in American History* (3 vols., 1974); and the essays in Arthur M. Schlesinger, Jr., ed., *History of U.S. Political Parties* (4 vols., 1973).

An older but still useful history of the Republican party is George H. Mayer, *The Republican Party, 1854–1966* (2d ed., 1967). Other works surveying the GOP before 1968 include Batchelor, *Ain't You Glad You Joined the Republicans?*; Charles O. Jones, *The Republican Party in American Politics* (1965); Malcolm Moos, *The Republicans: A History of Their Party* (1956); and Rutland, *The Republicans.* On the continuities and changes in the respective ideologies of the Republican and Democratic parties, see John Gerring, *Party Ideologies in America, 1828–1996* (1998). The GOP's birth is examined in William E. Gienapp, *The Origins of the Republican Party, 1852–1856* (1987). On U.S. politics during the 1860–1896 period, see Paul Kleppner, *The Third Electoral System, 1853–92: Parties, Voters, and Political Cultures* (1979); Richard L. McCormick, *The Party Period and Public Policy: American Politics from the Age of Jackson to the*

Progressive Era (1986); and Joel H. Silbey, *The American Political Nation, 1838–1893* (1991). On sectional identity and voter preference, see Richard H. Abbott, *The Republican Party and the South, 1855–1877* (1986); Richard Franklin Bensel, *Sectionalism and American Political Development, 1880–1980* (1984); David Hackett Fischer, *Albion's Seed: Four British Folkways in America* (1989); Paul Kleppner, *The Cross of Culture: A Social Analysis of Midwestern Politics, 1850–1900* (1970); and Michael McGeer, *The Decline of Popular Politics: The American North, 1865–1928* (1986). The works just listed are also useful for students of ethnic-religious identity and party loyalty; but see also Steven P. Erie, *Rainbow's End: Irish Americans and the Dilemma of Urban Political Machines, 1840–1985* (1988); and Milton Viorst, *Fall from Grace: The Republican Party and the Puritan Ethic* (1968). Works examining socioeconomic class and voter preference include Richard Hamilton, *Class and Politics in the United States* (1972); and Gwendolyn Mink, *Old Labor and New Immigrants in American Political Development: Union, Party, and State, 1875–1920* (1986). On GOP ideology before 1932, see Eric Foner, *Free Soil, Free Labor, Free Men: The Ideology of the Republican Party before the Civil War* (1970) and *Politics and Ideology in the Age of the Civil War* (1980); and Gerring, *Party Ideologies in America.*

The essays in Paul Kleppner, ed., *Continuity and Change in Electoral Politics, 1893–1928* (1987) analyze politics during the 1896–1932 era. On the Republican party during this same period, see John D. Hicks, *Republican Ascendancy, 1921–1933* (1960); and Horace Samuel Merrill, *The Republican Command, 1897–1913* (1971). On Herbert Hoover and his presidency, see David Burner, *Herbert Hoover: A Public Life* (1979); and Joan Hoff Wilson, *Herbert Hoover: Forgotten Progressive* (1975). John Kenneth Galbraith, *The Great Crash, 1929* (3d ed., 1979), analyzes the stock-market crash and the onset of the Great Depression. The social catastrophe of the Depression is covered in Studs Terkel, *Hard Times: An Oral History of the Depression* (1970).

The best recent synthesis of the Roosevelt era is David Kennedy, *Freedom from Fear: America in Depression and War, 1929–1945* (1999). New Deal policies are investigated in Anthony J. Badger, *The*

New Deal: The Depression Years, 1933–1940 (1989); William E. Leuchtenburg, *Franklin D. Roosevelt and the New Deal* (1963); George McJimsey, *The Presidency of Franklin D. Roosevelt* (2000); and Arthur M. Schlesinger, Jr., *The Age of Roosevelt* (3 vols., 1957–60). For Republican and conservative critics of the New Deal, see George H. Mayer, "The Republican Party, 1932–1952," in Schlesinger, ed., *History of U.S. Political Parties*; Leo Ribuffo, *The Old Christian Right: The Protestant Far Right from the Great Depression to the Cold War* (1983); James T. Patterson, *Congressional Conservatism and the New Deal: The Growth of the Conservative Coalition in Congress, 1933–1939* (1967); and Clyde P. Weed, *The Nemesis of Reform: The Republican Party during the New Deal* (1994). On the Democratic coalition and New Deal party system of 1932–68, see the essays in Steve Fraser and Gary Gerstle, eds., *The Rise and Fall of the New Deal Order, 1930–1980* (1989); Theodore J. Lowi, *The End of Liberalism: The Second Republic of the United States* (2d ed., 1979); and David Plotke, *Building a Democratic Political Order: Reshaping American Liberalism in the 1930s and 1940s* (1996). The decline of New Deal initiatives after 1938 is discussed in Alan Brinkley, *The End of Reform: New Deal Liberalism in Recession and War* (1995). On the Republican party in the 1940s, see Justus D. Doenecke, *Not to the Swift: The Old Isolationists in the Cold War Era* (1979); James T. Patterson, *Mr. Republican: A Biography of Robert A. Taft* (1972); and Richard Norton Smith, *Thomas E. Dewey and His Times* (1992). On the domestic impact of World War II, see Doris Kearns Goodwin, *No Ordinary Time: Franklin and Eleanor Roosevelt: The Home Front in World War II* (1994); Nelson Lichtenstein, *Labor's War at Home: The CIO in World War II* (1982); and Gerald D. Nash, *The American West Transformed: The Impact of the Second World War* (1985).

Works examining Harry S. Truman and his presidency include Alonzo S. Hamby, *Man of the People: A Life of Harry S. Truman* (1995); David McCullough, *Truman* (1992); and Gary W. Reichard, *Politics as Usual: The Age of Truman and Eisenhower* (1988). On the origins of the Cold War, see John Lewis Gaddis, *The United States and the Origins of the Cold War, 1941–1947* (1972); Melvyn P. Leffler, *A Preponderance of Power: National Security, the Truman Administration, and the Cold War* (1991); and Michael Schaller, *The*

American Occupation of Japan: The Origins of the Cold War in Asia (1985). On liberal Democrats' turn toward Keynesian economic-growth policies, see Brinkley, *The End of Reform*; and Robert M. Collins, *More: The Politics of Economic Growth in Postwar America* (2000). On Truman's second administration, see Robert J. Donovan, *Tumultuous Years: The Presidency of Harry S. Truman, 1949–1953* (1982). On the "red scare" and McCarthyism, see John Earl Haynes and Harvey Klehr, *Venona: Decoding Soviet Espionage in America* (1999); David Caute, *The Great Fear: The Anti-Communist Purge under Truman and Eisenhower* (1978); and Richard Fried, *Nightmare in Red: The McCarthy Era in Perspective* (1990). The Korean War and its effects on U.S. politics and foreign policy are examined in Burton I. Kaufman, *The Korean War: Challenges in Crisis, Credibility, and Command* (1986); and Paul G. Pierpaoli, Jr., T*ruman and Korea: The Political Culture of the Early Cold War* (1999).

Works discussing American society and culture during the 1950s include David Halberstam, *The Fifties* (1993); Kenneth Jackson, *The Crabgrass Frontier: The Suburbanization of the United States* (1985); Elaine Tyler May, *Homeward Bound: American Families in the Cold War Era* (1988); the essays in Lary May, ed., *Recasting America: Culture and Politics in the Age of the Cold War* (1989); J. Ronald Oakley, *God's Country: America in the Fifties* (1986); and Allan Winkler, *Life under a Cloud: American Anxiety about the Atom* (1993). On Dwight D. Eisenhower and his presidency, see Stephen E. Ambrose, *Eisenhower: The President* (1984); Fred T. Greenstein, *The Hidden-Hand Presidency: Eisenhower as Leader* (1982); and the essays in Shirley Anne Warshaw, ed., *Reexamining the Eisenhower Presidency* (1993). On Eisenhower and the GOP, see Charles C. Alexander, *Holding the Line: The Eisenhower Era, 1952–1961* (1975); Lee W. Huebner, "The Republican Party, 1952–1972," in Schlesinger, ed., *History of U.S. Political Parties*; and Gary W. Reichard, *The Reaffirmation of Republicanism: Eisenhower and the Eighty-Third Congress* (1975). On Eisenhower's foreign policies, see Jeff Broadwater, *Eisenhower and the Anti-Communist Crusade* (1993); and Robert A. Divine, *Eisenhower and the Cold War* (1981).

General histories of the civil rights movement include Henry Hampton and Steve Fayer, eds., *Voices of Freedom: An Oral History of the Civil Rights Movement* (1987); Manning Marable, *Race, Reform, and Rebellion: The Second Reconstruction in Black America, 1945–1990* (1991); Harvard Sitkoff, *The Struggle for Black Equality, 1954–1992* (1993); and Robert Weisbrot, *Freedom Bound: A History of America's Civil Rights Movement* (1990). On Martin Luther King, Jr., see Taylor Branch, *Parting the Waters: America in the King Years, 1954–1963* (1986) and *Pillar of Fire: America in the King Years, 1963–1965* (1998); and David J. Garrow, *Bearing the Cross: Martin Luther King, Jr., and the Southern Leadership Conference* (1986). White Southern resistance to the civil rights movement is examined in Numan Bartley, *The Rise of Massive Resistance: Race and Politics in the South during the 1950s* (1969); and David Goldfield, *Black, White, and Southern: Race Relations and Southern Culture, 1940 to the Present* (1990). On Richard M. Nixon and the 1960 presidential campaign, see Stephen E. Ambrose, *Nixon: The Education of a Politician, 1913–1962* (1987); and Theodore H. White, *The Making of the President, 1960* (1961).

The seminal work on American conservative thought after World War II is George H. Nash, *The Conservative Intellectual Movement in America since 1945* (1976). See also John B. Judis, *William F. Buckley, Jr.: Patron Saint of the Conservatives* (1988); Michael W. Miles, *The Odyssey of the American Right* (1980); Brad Miner, *The Concise Conservative Encyclopedia* (1996); Clinton Rossiter, *Conservatism in America: The Thankless Profession* (1962); and Melvin J. Thorne, *American Conservative Thought since World War II: The Core Ideas* (1990). Two useful collections of essays by postwar conservatives are William F. Buckley, Jr., ed., *Did You Ever See a Dream Walking? American Conservative Thought in the Twentieth Century* (1970); and Frank S. Meyer, ed., *What Is Conservatism?* (1964). James D. Hornfischer, ed., *Right Thinking: Conservative Common Sense through the Ages* (1996), is a convenient source for quotes by conservatives. On conservatives versus moderates in the Republican party, see Mary C. Brennan, *Turning Right in the Sixties: The Conservative Capture of the GOP* (1995); Huebner, "The Republican Party, 1952–1972"; Arthur Larson, *A Republican Looks at His Party* (1956); Rae, *Decline and Fall of the Liberal Republicans*; and Reinhard, *The Republican Right since 1945*. On Barry M. Goldwater, see Robert A. Goldberg, *Barry Goldwater* (1995); and Barry M. Goldwater, *The Conscience of a Conservative* (1960).

For an overview of American history in the 1960s, see David Chalmers, *And the Crooked Places Made Straight: The Struggle for Social Change in the 1960s* (1991); David Farber, *The Age of Great Dreams: America in the 1960s* (1994); the essays in David Farber, ed., *The Sixties: From Memory to History* (1994); Maurice Isserman and Michael Kazin, *America Divided: The Civil War of the 1960s* (2000); and Allen J. Matusow, *The Unraveling of America: A History of Liberalism in the 1960s* (1984). On John F. Kennedy and his presidency, see James N. Giglio, *The Presidency of John F. Kennedy* (1991); and Arthur M. Schlesinger, Jr., *A Thousand Days: John F. Kennedy in the White House* (1965). On Kennedy's foreign policy, see the essays in Thomas Paterson, ed., *Kennedy's Quest for Victory: American Foreign Policy, 1961–1963* (1989). Works discussing Lyndon B. Johnson and his presidency include Paul Conkin, *Big Daddy from Pedernales: Lyndon Baines Johnson* (1986); the essays in Robert A. Divine, ed., *Exploring the Johnson Years* (1981); Doris Kearns, *Lyndon Johnson and the American Dream* (1976); and Robert Dallek, *Flawed Giant: Lyndon Johnson and His Times, 1961–1973* (1998). On the identification of the Democratic party with African American advancement after 1964, see Edward G. Carmines and James A. Stimson, *Issue Evolution: Race and the Transformation of American Politics* (1989). For the 1964 presidential campaign, see Theodore H. White, *The Making of the President, 1964* (1965); and F. Clifton White, *Suite 3505: The Story of the Draft Goldwater Movement* (1967). Johnson's Great Society programs are analyzed in Gareth Davies, *From Opportunity to Entitlement: The Transformation and Decline of Great Society Liberalism* (1998); and John E. Schwarz, *America's Hidden Success: A Reassessment of Public Policy from Kennedy to Reagan* (1988). On the Warren Court, see Earl Graham, *The Due Process Revolution: The Warren Court's Impact on Criminal Law* (1977); Lucas A. Powe, Jr., *The Warren Court and American Politics* (2000); and Melvin Urofsky, *The Continuity of Change: The Supreme Court and Civil Liberties, 1953–1986* (1991). On the backlash against liberalism, see Matthew Dallek, *The Right*

Moment: Ronald Reagan's First Victory and the Decisive Turning Point in American Politics (2000); and Lisa McGirr, *Suburban Warriors: The Origin of the New American Right* (2000).

The literature on the Vietnam War is huge and growing. Good surveys include George C. Herring, *America's Longest War: The United States and Vietnam, 1950–1975* (3d ed., 1996); Robert D. Schulzinger, *A Time for War: The United States and Vietnam, 1941–1975* (1997); and Marilyn B. Young, *The Vietnam Wars* (1990). On the antiwar movement, see Terry Anderson, *The Movement and the Sixties* (1995); and Charles DeBenedetti with Charles Chatfield, *An American Ordeal: The Antiwar Movement of the Vietnam Era* (1990). On the New Left, see Todd Gitlin, *The Sixties: Years of Hope, Days of Rage* (1987); and James Miller, *Democracy Is in the Streets: From Port Huron to the Siege of Chicago* (1987). On the counterculture, see Charles Perry, *The Haight-Ashbury: A History* (1984); and Jay Stevens, *Storming Heaven: LSD and the American Dream* (1987). Feminism in the 1960s is covered in Flora Davis, *Moving the Mountain: The Women's Movement in America since 1960* (1991); Alice Echols, *Daring to Be Bad: Radical Feminism in America, 1967–1975* (1989); Sara Evans, *Personal Politics: The Roots of Women's Liberation in the Civil Rights Movement and the New Left* (1979); Betty Friedan, *The Feminine Mystique* (1963); and Ruth Rosen, *The World Split Open: How the Women's Movement Changed America* (2000). On the 1968 presidential campaign, see Lewis Chester et al., *An American Melodrama: The Presidential Campaign of 1968* (1969); and George Rising, *Clean for Gene: Eugene McCarthy's 1968 Presidential Campaign* (1997). Dan T. Carter, *George Wallace, the Origins of the New Conservatism, and the Transformation of American Politics* (1995), looks at George C. Wallace. Terry Dietz, *Republicans and Vietnam, 1961–1968* (1986), investigates the GOP's support for the Vietnam War. On electoral dealignment after 1968, see the essays in Byron Shafer, ed., *The End of Realignment? Interpreting American Electoral Eras* (1991); and Martin P. Wattenberg, *The Decline of American Political Parties, 1952–1988* (1990). On the decline of the Democratic coalition, see the essays in Fraser and Gerstle, eds., *Rise and Fall of the New Deal Order*; John R. Petrocik, *Party Coalitions:*

Realignment and the Decline of the New Deal Party System (1981); and Kevin P. Phillips, *The Emerging Republican Majority* (1969).

Chapter Two: Richard Nixon and the Paradox of the "New Republican Majority," 1969–1974

For a discussion of the conservative drift in American politics during the period 1969–74, see Berman, *America's Right Turn*; Dionne, *Why Americans Hate Politics*; and Edsall with Edsall, *Chain Reaction*. On the Nixon presidency, see the unreliable memoir by Richard Nixon, *RN* (1978), and Henry Kissinger's detailed but self-serving two-volume record, *The White House Years* (1979) and *Years of Upheaval* (1982). For an entertaining and insightful study of the 1968 GOP campaign, see Joe McGinniss, *The Selling of the President, 1968* (1969). See also Theodore White, *The Making of the President, 1968* (1969) and *The Making of the President, 1972* (1973). Among the most useful accounts of the Nixon administration are Stephen E. Ambrose, *Nixon* (3 vols., 1986–91); Joan Hoff, *Nixon Reconsidered* (1994); Melvin Small, *The Presidency of Richard Nixon* (1999); Herbert Parmet, *Richard Nixon and His America* (1991); Allen J. Matusow, *Nixon's Economy: Booms, Busts, Dollars, and Votes* (1998); H. R. Haldeman, *The Haldeman Diaries: Inside the Nixon White House* (1994); and Richard Reeves, *President Nixon Alone in the White House* (2001).

For a discussion of the "Southern Strategy," see Kevin Phillips, *The Emerging Republican Majority* (1969); Robert Scammon and Ben Wattenberg, *The Real Majority* (1970); Dan Carter, *The Politics of Race: George Wallace and the Origin of the New Conservatism and the Transformation of American Politics* (1995) and *From George Wallace to Newt Gingrich: Race in the Conservative Counter-Revolution, 1963–94* (1996); James Reichley, *Conservatives in an Age of Change* (1981); and John W. Dean, *The Rehnquist Choice: The Untold Story of the Nixon Appointment that Redefined the Supreme Court* (2001).

Books that deal with Nixon-era foreign policy and Vietnam include, in addition to Kissinger's memoir, Robert Schulzinger, *Henry Kissinger: The Doctor of Diplomacy* (1989); Seymour Hersh, *The Price of Power:*

Kissinger in the Nixon White House (1983); Melvin Small, *Johnson, Nixon, and the Doves* (1988); Jeffery Kimball, *Nixon's Vietnam War* (1998); and Jim Mann, *About Face: A History of the Curious American Relationship with China from Nixon to Clinton* (1999).

Among the best studies of the Watergate scandal are Stanley Kutler, *The Wars of Watergate: The Last Crisis of Richard Nixon* (1990) and *Abuse of Power: The New Nixon Tapes* (1997); Jonathan Schell, *The Time of Illusion* (1976); Theodore White, *Breach of Faith: The Fall of Richard Nixon* (1975); and John Dean, *Blind Ambition* (1976).

Chapter Three: Stagnation, Malaise, and Conservative Revival, 1974–1980

On American society, culture, and politics during the 1974–80 period, see Peter N. Carroll, *It Seemed Like Nothing Happened: America in the 1970s* (2000); Bruce J. Shulman, *The Seventies: The Great Shift in American Culture, Society, and Politics* (2001); and Schaller, Scharff, and Schulzinger, *Present Tense*. See also Berman, *America's Right Turn;* Chafe, *The Unfinished Journey;* Dionne, *Why Americans Hate Politics;* and Edsall with Edsall, *Chain Reaction*.

On Watergate's legacy, see Michael Schudson, *Watergate in American Memory: How We Remember, Forget, and Reconstruct the Past* (1992). See also the essays in Donald W. Harward, ed., *Crisis in Confidence: The Impact of Watergate* (1974); and Kathryn Olmsted, *Challenging the Secret Government: The Post-Watergate Investigations of the CIA and the FBI* (1996). On the imperial presidency in foreign policy, see Arthur M. Schlesinger, Jr., *The Imperial Presidency* (1973). See also Theodore J. Lowi, *The Personal President: Power Invested, Promise Unfulfilled* (1985); and James L. Sundquist, *The Decline and Resurgence of Congress* (1981).

On economic stagnation after 1973 and its effects, see Richard J. Barnet, *The Lean Years: Politics in the Age of Scarcity* (1980); Barbara Ehrenreich, *Fear of Falling: The Insecure Life of the Middle Class* (1985); Bennett Harrison and Barry Bluestone, *The Great U-Turn: Corporate Restructuring and the Polarizing of America* (1988); William Greider, *Secrets of the Temple: How the Federal Reserve Runs the Country* (1987); Samuel P. Hays, *Beauty, Health, and Permanence: Environmental Politics in the United States, 1955–1985* (1987); Donald Hibbs, *The American Political Economy: Macroeconomics and Electoral Politics* (1987); Frank Levy, *Dollars and Dreams: The Changing American Income Distribution* (1987); K. Newman, *Falling from Grace: The Experience of Downward Mobility in the American Middle Class* (1988); Lester C. Thurow, *The Zero Sum Society* (1980); Richard H. K. Vietor, *Energy Policy in America since 1945: A Study of Business-Government Relations* (1984); William Julius Wilson, *The Truly Disadvantaged: The Inner City, the Underclass, and Public Policy* (1987); Alan Wolfe, *America's Impasse: The Rise and Fall of the Politics of Growth* (1981); and Robert Zieger, *American Workers, American Unions* (2d ed., 1994).

On the conservative movement of the late 1970s, see the works listed at the beginning of the Bibliographical Essay; see also Martin Anderson, *Revolution* (1988); and Paul Gottfried, *The Conservative Movement* (1993). On the New Right and the New Religious Right, see Steve Bruce, *The Rise and Fall of the New Christian Right* (1988); Alan Crawford, *Thunder on the Right: The New Right and the Politics of Resentment* (1980); the essays in Michael Cromartie, ed., *No Longer Exiles* (1993); M. P. Federici, *The Challenge of Populism: The Rise of Right-Wing Populism in Post-War America* (1991); Christopher Lasch, *The True and Only Heaven: Progress and Its Critics* (1990); Matthew Moens, *The Christian Right and Congress* (1989); Gillian Peele, *Revival and Reaction: The Right in Contemporary America* (1984); and Richard Viguerie, *The New Right: We're Ready to Lead* (1980). David Vogel, *Fluctuating Fortunes: The Political Power of Business in America* (1989), investigates corporate America's increasing political influence. Conservative intellectuals, the conservative counterestablishment, and supply-side economics are examined in Sidney Blumenthal, *The Rise of the Conservative Counter-Establishment: From Conservative Ideology to Political Power* (1986); David Burner and Thomas R. West, *Column Right: Conservative Journalists in the Service of Nationalism* (1988); David Hoeveler, Jr., *Watch on the Right: Conservative Intellectuals in the Reagan Era* (1991); Robert Kuttner, *Revolt of the Haves* (1980); and Jean Stefanic et al., *No Mercy: How Conservative Think Tanks and*

Foundations Changed America's Social Agenda (1997). On neoconservatives, see Gary Dorian, *The Neoconservative Mind: Politics, Culture, and the War of Ideology* (1993); and Peter Steinfelds, *The Neoconservatives: The Men Who Are Changing America's Politics* (1979).

The Democratic party's decay and the backlash against liberalism during the 1974–80 period are covered in the general works listed above for Chapter Three. See also Susan Faludi, *Backlash: The Undeclared War against American Women* (1991); Thomas Ferguson and Joel Rogers, *Right Turn: The Decline of the Democrats and the Future of American Politics* (1986); Nicholas Mills, *The Triumph of Meanness: America's War against Its Better Self* (1997); Nelson W. Polsby, *The Consequences of Party Reform* (1983); Ronald Radosh, *Divided They Fell: The Demise of the Democratic Party, 1964–1996* (1996); Byron E. Schafer, *Quiet Revolution: The Struggle for the Democratic Party and the Shaping of Post-Reform Politics* (1983); and Alan Ware, *The Breakdown of the Democratic Party Organization, 1940–1980* (1985). On Jimmy Carter, see Burton I. Kaufman, *The Presidency of James Earl Carter, Jr.* (1993). Gaddis Smith, *Morality, Reason, and Power: American Diplomacy in the Carter Years* (1987), scrutinizes Carter's foreign policy. On Ronald Reagan, his life, and his presidency, see the works listed below for Chapter Four. The events surrounding the 1980 campaign are examined in the general works listed above for Chapter Three.

Chapter Four: Ronald Reagan, George H. W. Bush, and Republican Ascendancy, 1981–1992

Unfortunately, neither Ronald Reagan's ghostwritten memoir, *An American Life* (1990), nor his "authorized," partly fictional biography, *Dutch: A Memoir of Ronald Reagan* (1999) by Edmund Morris, sheds much light on the president and his policies during the 1980s. Among the most interesting Reagan biographies are Garry Wills, *Reagan's America* (1985); Lou Cannon, *President Reagan: The Role of a Lifetime* (1991); Haynes Johnson, *Sleepwalking through History: America in the Reagan Years* (1991); Michael Rogin, *Ronald Reagan, the Movie, and Other Episodes in Political Demonology*

(1987); and Robert Dallek, *Ronald Reagan: The Politics of Symbolism* (1984). The overall policies of the Reagan administration are discussed in Michael Schaller, *Reckoning with Reagan: America and its President in the 1980s* (1992); William Pemberton, *Exit with Honor: The Life and Presidency of Ronald Reagan* (1997); Sidney Blumenthal, *Our Long National Daydream* (1988); Rob Schaffer and Gary Paul Gates, *The Acting President* (1989); Barbara Ehrenreich, *The Worst Years of Our Lives: Irreverent Notes from a Decade of Greed* (1990); and John A. Farrell, *Tip O'Neill and the Democratic Century* (2001).

Many members of the Reagan administration produced "kiss-and-tell" memoirs. Among the most interesting are David Stockman, *The Triumph of Politics: How the Reagan Revolution Failed* (1986); Peggy Noonan, *What I Saw at the Revolution: A Political Life in the Reagan Administration* (1990); Michael K. Deaver, with Mickey Hershkowitz, *Behind the Scenes* (1987); George Shultz, *Turmoil and Triumph: My Years as Secretary of State* (1993); and Donald T. Regan, *For the Record: From Wall Street to Washington* (1988).

For an evaluation of Republican economic and social policies during the 1980s, see Kevin Phillips, *The Politics of Rich and Poor: Wealth and the American Electorate in the Reagan Aftermath* (1990); Michael Katz, *The Undeserving Poor: From the War on Poverty to the War on Welfare* (1989); Ehrenreich, *Fear of Falling;* Benjamin Friedman, *Day of Reckoning: The Consequences of American Economic Policy Under Reagan and After* (1988); and Martin Mayer, *The Greatest Ever Bank Robbery: The Collapse of the Savings and Loan Industry* (1990). On social and cultural policies during the 1980s and early 1990s, see Faludi, *Backlash;* Randy Shilts, *And the Band Played On: Politics, People, and the AIDS Epidemic* (1987); Jeffrey K. Hadden and Anson Shupe, *Televangelism: Power and Politics on God's Frontier* (1988); and James D. Hunter, *Culture Wars: The Struggle to Define America* (1988).

For discussions of legal affairs in the Reagan-Bush era, see Herman Schwartz, *Packing the Courts: The Conservative Campaign to Re-write the Constitution* (1988); Jane Mayer and Jill Abramson, *Strange Justice: The Selling of Clarence Thomas* (1994); and Dan

Baum, *Smoke and Mirrors: The War on Drugs and the Politics of Failure* (1996).

Reagan's foreign policies—including covert operations, the arms buildup, and the Iran-Contra scandal—are discussed in Frances Fitzgerald, *Way Out There in the Blue: Reagan, Star Wars, and the End of the Cold War* (2000); Doyle McManus and Jane Mayer, *Landslide: The Unmaking of the President, 1984–1988* (1988); Theodore Draper, *A Very Thin Line: The Iran-Contra Scandals* (1991); Steve Emerson, *Secret Warriors: Inside the Covert Military Operations of the Reagan Administration* (1988); Bob Woodward, *Veil: The Secret Wars of the CIA, 1981–1987* (1987); and Roy Gutman, *Banana Diplomacy: The Making of American Policy in Nicaragua* (1987).

Excellent treatments of the elections of 1984 and 1988 are found in Jack Germond and Jules Witcover, *Wake Us When It's Over: Presidential Politics of 1984* (1985); Jack Germond, *Whose Broad Stripes and Bright Stars: The Trivial Pursuit of the Presidency* (1988); and Sidney Blumenthal, *Pledging Allegiance: The Last Campaign of the Cold War* (1990).

The best overall study of the George H. W. Bush administration is John R. Greene's *The Presidency of George Bush* (2000). For discussions of the end of the Cold War, see George Bush and Brent Scowcroft, *A World Transformed* (1998); James Baker, *The Politics of Diplomacy: Revolution, War, and Peace, 1989–1992* (1995); Michael Beschloss and Strobe Talbott, *At the Highest Levels: The Inside Story of the End of the Cold War* (1993); and Don Oberdorfer, *The Turn: From the Cold War to a New Era: The U.S. and the Soviet Union, 1983–1990* (1991).

Chapter Five: New Democrats and Republican Revolutionaries, 1993–2000

For overviews of American politics during the 1993–2000 period, see James MacGregor Burns and Georgia J. Sorenson, *Dead Center: Clinton-Gore Leadership and the Perils of Moderation* (1999); Haynes Johnson, *The Best of Times: America in the Clinton Years* (2001); and the essays in Colin Campbell and Bert A. Rockman, eds.,

The Clinton Legacy (2000). Kathleen Hall Jamieson, *Everything You Think You Know about Politics . . . And Why You're Wrong* (2000), contains useful information on the politics of the 1990s. In addition to these works and those listed below, the authors consulted the following magazines and newspapers: the *American Prospect,* the *Nation,* the *New Republic,* the *New York Times, Newsweek, Time,* the *Wall Street Journal,* and the *Washington Post National Weekly Edition.*

Politics during the Clinton administration's first two years are examined in Elizabeth Drew, *On the Edge: The Clinton Presidency* (1994); Haynes Johnson, *Divided We Fall: Gambling with History in the Nineties* (1995); Haynes Johnson and David S. Broder, *The System: The American Way of Politics at the Breaking Point* (1996); Theodore J. Lowi and Benjamin Ginsburg, *Embattled Democracy: Politics and Policy in the Clinton Era* (1997); Stanley A. Renshon, *High Hopes: The Clinton Presidency and the Politics of Ambition* (1996); and Bob Woodward, *The Agenda: Inside the Clinton White House* (1994). Whitewater, other Clinton scandals, and the news media's investigations of them are examined in Joe Conason and Gene Lyons, *The Hunting of the President: The Ten-Year Campaign to Destroy Bill and Hillary Clinton* (2000); Howard Kurtz, *Spin Cycle: How the White House and the Media Manipulate the News* (1998); James B. Stewart, *Blood Sport: The President and His Adversaries* (1996); and Jeffrey Toobin, *A Vast Conspiracy: The Real Story of the Sex Scandal That Nearly Brought Down a President* (1999). On the Clinton health-care plan, see Jacob S. Hacker, *The Road to Nowhere: The Genesis of President Clinton's Plan for Health Care* (1997); and Theda Skocpol, *Boomerang: Clinton's Health Security Effort and the Turn against Government in U.S. Politics* (1996).

The conservative movement of the 1990s, the Republican transformation of American politics (especially in the South), and the pivotal 1994 elections are discussed in Dan Balz and Ronald Brownstein, *Storming the Gates: Protest Politics and the Republican Revival* (1996); the essays in David Brooks, ed., *Backward and Upward: The New Conservative Writing* (1996); E. J. Dionne, Jr., *They Only Look Dead: Why Progressives Will Dominate the Next Political*

Era (1996); Nina J. Easton, *Gang of Five: Leaders at the Center of the Conservative Crusade* (2000); the essays in Philip A. Klinker, ed., *Midterm: The Elections of 1994 in Context* (1996); Terrel L. Rhodes, *Republicans in the South: Voting for the State House, Voting for the White House* (2000); and Richard K. Scher, *Politics in the New South: Republicanism, Race and Leadership in the Twentieth Century* (1997).

On Newt Gingrich's Republican Revolution of 1995 and how President Clinton stymied it, see Elizabeth Drew, *Showdown: The Struggle between the Gingrich Congress and the Clinton White House* (1997); James G. Gimpel, *Legislating the Revolution: The Contract with America in Its First 100 Days* (1996); Newt Gingrich, *Lessons Learned the Hard Way* (1998); Lynda Killian, *The Freshmen: What Happened to the Republican Revolution?* (1998); David Maraniss and Michael Weisskopf, *Tell Newt to Shut Up!* (1996); Nicol C. Rae, *Conservative Reformers: The Republican Freshmen and the Lessons of the 104th Congress* (1998); and the essays in Nicole C. Rae and Colton C. Campbell, eds., *New Majority or Old Minority: The Impact of the Republican Congress* (1999). On Clinton's "triangulation" strategy, see Dick Morris, *Behind the Oval Office: Winning the Presidency in the Nineties* (1997); and Christopher Hitchens, *No One Left to Lie To: The Triangulations of William Jefferson Clinton* (1999). On welfare reform, see Gary C. Bryner, *Politics and Public Morality: The Great American Welfare Reform Debate* (1998); and Gwendolyn Mink, *Welfare's End* (1998). On the 1996 election campaign, see Paul R. Abramson, *Change and Continuity in the 1996 Elections* (1998); the essays in Gerald M. Pomper et al., eds., *The Election of 1996: Reports and Interpretations* (1997); and Bob Woodward, *The Choice* (1996). Race relations in the 1990s are analyzed in Andrew Hacker, *Two Nations: Black and White, Separate, Hostile, Unequal* (1995); and Cornel West, *Race Matters* (1995).

On the events leading to President Clinton's impeachment, the best work is Toobin, *A Vast Conspiracy*. See also Peter Baker, *The Breach: Inside the Impeachment and Trial of William Jefferson Clinton* (2000); Benjamin Ginsburg and Martin Shefter, *Politics by Other Means* (2d ed., 1999); Michael Isikoff, *Uncovering Clinton: A Reporter's Story* (1999); and Richard A. Posner, *An Affair of State: The Investigation, Impeachment, and Trial of President Clinton* (1999).

On U.S. foreign relations during the Clinton era, see William G. Hyland, *Clinton's World: Remaking American Foreign Policy* (1999); and David Halberstrom, *War in a Time of Peace: Bush, Clinton, and the Generals* (2001). See also Larry Berman and Emily O. Goldman, "Clinton's Foreign Policy at Midterm," in Campbell and Rockman, eds., *The Clinton Presidency: First Appraisals* (1995) and "Engaging the World: First Impressions of the Clinton Foreign Policy Legacy," in Campbell and Rockman, *The Clinton Legacy;* Burns and Sorenson, *Dead Center;* Jonathan Clarke and James Chad, *After the Crusade: American Foreign Policy for the Post-Superpower Age* (1995); Drew, *On the Edge;* John Spanier and Stephen W. Hook, *American Foreign Policy since World War II* (1998); and the essays in Peter Trubowitz et al., eds., *The Politics of Strategic Adjustments: Ideas, Institutions, and Interests* (1999). See also the journals *Foreign Affairs* and *Foreign Policy,* as well as the magazines and newspapers listed at the beginning of the bibliography for this chapter. On U.S. relations with particular countries, see Michael Schaller, *The United States and China into the Twenty First Century* (2001); Stephen F. Cohen, *Failed Crusade: America and the Tragedy of Post-Communist Russia* (2000); and Thomas H. Henriksen, *Clinton's Foreign Policy in Somalia, Bosnia, Haiti, and North Korea* (1996). On the former Yugoslavia, see Richard Holbrooke's memoir, *To End a War* (1998); on Northern Ireland, see Tim Pat Coogan, *The Troubles: Ireland's Ordeal, 1966–1995, and the Search for Peace* (1995).

On George W. Bush, Al Gore, and the 2000 election, see Jeffrey Toobin, *Too Close to Call: The Thirty-Six Day Battle to Decide the White House* (2001); E. J. Dionne, Jr., and William Kristol, eds., *Bush v. Gore: The Court Cases and the Commentary* (2001); Richard Posner, *Breaking the Deadlock: The 2000 Election, the Constitution, and the Courts* (2001); Alan M. Dershowitz, *Supreme Injustice: How the High Court Hijacked Election 2000* (2001); and Vincent Bugliosi, *The Betrayal of America: How the Supreme Court Undermined the Constitution and Chose Our President* (2001). See also the newspapers and magazines listed at the beginning of the bibliography for this chapter and relevent articles cited below.

Conclusion: The Rise and Fall of Republicans: Conservative Strategies, 1968–2001

The political science literature on party systems, critical elections, and electoral realignment is immense. Important works include Walter Dean Burnham, *Critical Elections and the Mainsprings of American Politics* (1970); the essays in William N. Chambers and Walter Dean Burnham, eds., *The American Party Systems: Stages of Political Development* (1975); the essays in Jerome M. Clubb et al., *Partisan Realignment: Voters, Parties, and Government in American History* (1990); Everett Carll Ladd, Jr., with Charles D. Hadley, *Transformations of the American Party System* (1978); Giovanni Satori, *Parties and Party Systems: A Framework for Analysis* (1976); and the essays in Arthur M. Schlesinger, Jr., ed., *The History of American Presidential Elections, 1789–1968* (3 vols., 1971).

The decline of Republicans' conservative strategies during the 1990s and in the 2000 campaign is examined in Eric Alterman, "Your Show of Shows," *Nation,* August 21–28, 2000, 13; Dan Balz, "A Page from the Opposition's Playbook," *Washington Post National Weekly Edition,* June 19, 2000, 10; Charles Babington, "Bush Keeps House GOP at Arm's Length," <http://www.washingtonpost.com>, October 30, 2000; Jonathan Cohn, "Fade to Black: Why Republicans Can't Win without the Race Card," *New Republic,* November 13, 2000, 21–24; Robert Dreyfuss, "The Double-Edge Wedge," *American Prospect,* August 28, 2000, 24–26; Thomas B. Edsall, "No More 'Southern Strategy,'" *Washington Post National Weekly Edition,* August 14, 2000, 12, "Conservatives Eroding Hard Line," *ibid,* July 3, 2000, 12–13, "Gore May Be Picking Up a Double-Edged Sword," *ibid,* August 28, 2000, 14, and "A Thumbs Down from Black Voters," *ibid,* December 18, 2000, 11; John B. Judis, "The New Politics of Abortion," *American Prospect,* July 31, 2000, 12–13, and "Sex Appeal: Why Feminism Wins Elections," *New Republic,* December 18, 2000, 15; Lawrence F. Kaplan, "Trading Places: How the Democrats Became Hawks," *New Republic,* October 23, 2000, 23–27; Stephen

Moore, "Who's the Party of Big Government Now?" *Washington Post National Weekly Edition*, July 24, 2000, 22; Terry M. Neal, "The GOP Follows Bush to the Middle," *Washington Post National Weekly Edition*, June 5, 2000, 11; Peter Slevin, "A New Low for Violent Crime," *Washington Post National Weekly Edition*, September 4, 2000, and "The GOP's Lost Its Bite on Crime," *ibid.*, 10.

For discussions on the possibility of either a permanent Republican or Democratic majority, see Larry M. Bartels, "Partisanship and Voting Behavior, 1952–1996," *American Journal of Political Science* 44 (January 2000): 35–50; David S. Broder, "Is the Party Over? Despite George W's Popularity, a Poll Shows That the GOP Is Divided and in Decline," *Washington Post National Weekly Edition*, December 6, 1999, 14, and "Polarized Baby Boomers," *ibid.*, November 20, 2000, 4; Jonathan Cohn, "Fort Lauderdale Diarist: Dixieland," *New Republic*, December 25, 2000, 42; Nicholas Confessore, "The Winner: Clintonism: George W. Bush and the Decline of Movement Conservatism," *American Prospect*, December 4, 2000, 12–14; E. J. Dionne, *They Only Look Dead;* John B. Judis, "The Hunted: Moderate Republicans: Suicide or Murder?" *New Republic*, April 17 and 24, 2000, 32–36; "Indian Summer: Why the GOP Is Weaker than It Looks," <http://www.tnr.archive>, October 22, 1998, "The Spirit of '76: Why W Won't Stop an Emerging Democratic Majority," *New Republic*, November 6, 2000, 27–29, and "Two More Years," *American Prospect*, December 4, 2000, 10–11; Robert G. Kaiser, "Deeply Divided And That's No Surprise," *Washington Post National Weekly Edition,* November 20, 2000, 22; William Kristol, "The New Hampshire Upheaval," *Washington Post National Weekly Edition*, February 7, 2000, 27; Robert Kuttner, "The McCain Temptation," *American Prospect*, March 13, 2000, 4–5; William E. Leuchtenburg, "The Election of 2000," *OAH Newsletter*, February 2001: 1, 22; Joshua Micah Marshall, "The Other Republican," *American Prospect*, December 18, 2000, 10–11; Richard Morin, "The Narrowing Generation Gap," *Washington Post National Weekly Edition*, December 18, 2000, 34; Ruy Teixeira, "Lessons for Next Time," *American Prospect,* December 18, 2000, 12–14; Sean Wilentz, "Third Out: Why the Reform Party's Best Days Are Behind It," *New Republic*, November 22, 1999, 23–25; and Stanley Young, "The GOP Minority," *Washington Post National Weekly Edition*, December 18, 2000, 26.

INDEX

The Republican Ascendancy: American Politics, 1968–2001
Developmental editor: Andrew J. Davidson
Copyeditor: Nancy Trotic
Production editor: Lucy Herz
Proofreader: Claudia Siler
Indexer: Pat Rimmer
Printer: Versa Press